From Homeland to New Land

The Iroquoians and Their World

EDITORS

José António Brandão

William A. Starna

WILLIAM A. STARNA

From Homeland to New Land: A History of the Mahican Indians, 1600–1830

UNIVERSITY OF NEBRASKA PRESS LINCOLN & LONDON

An earlier version of chapter 6 was originally published as "From the
Mohawk-Mahican War to the Beaver Wars," in *Ethnohistory* 51, no. 4 (2004):
725–50. © 2004 by The American Society of Ethnohistory.
All rights reserved. Reprinted by permission of the publisher,
Duke University Press.

Library of Congress Cataloging-in-Publication Data
Starna, William A.
From homeland to new land: a history of the Mahican Indians, 1600–1830 /
William A. Starna.
pages cm. — (The Iroquoians and their world)
Includes bibliographical references and index.
ISBN 978-0-8032-4495-5 (hardback)
1. Mahican Indians—History. 2. Ethnohistory—New York (State) I. Title.
E99.M12S83 2013
974.7004'97—dc23   2012045812

Set in IowanOldSt by Laura Wellington.

For Eileen

CONTENTS

ILLUSTRATIONS

Figures

Maps

ACKNOWLEDGMENTS

I would like to thank James Bradley, José António Brandão, Colin Calloway, Jack Campisi, Jaap Jacobs, Daniel Mandell, Eileen McClafferty, Ruth Piwonka, Martha Dickinson Shattuck, and David Silverman, who read drafts of various chapters, and in Eileen's case, the completed manuscript. Nosey, my furry muse, was a constant companion throughout, usually stretched out next to my keyboard.

Charles Gehring shared with me his knowledge of seventeenth-century Dutch and the history of New Netherland. On Mahican and other Eastern Algonquian languages, I received expert advice and instruction from Ives Goddard. The Moravian mission diaries and allied German-language manuscripts referenced here were translated by Corinna Dally-Starna. Christopher Vecsey kindly guided me through the complexities of American Indian religions. I am grateful for the generosity shown me by these scholars, colleagues, and friends.

George Hamell, Paul Huey, James Folts, and Kevin McBride answered my questions on, respectively, Iroquois, Dutch, Munsee, and Connecticut Valley history and ethnology. The staff at Milne Library, State University of New York, College at Oneonta, as always, was of welcome assistance. Heather Beach, Special Collections, provided scans of period maps, while Terrisa Rowe, Interlibrary Loan, tracked down numerous sources for me. The remaining maps were drawn and produced by Kristen Cella. Kate Simeon assisted in preparing the illustrations. I thank one and all.

The manuscript received critical and helpful readings from two reviewers selected by the University of Nebraska Press, one of whom, Dean Snow, graciously identified himself. Thank you.

This book is dedicated to Eileen Mary McClafferty, whose presence in my life, strength of spirit, warm heart, and affection are valued more than words can express.

The manuscript leading to this book was written under cooperative agreement H1950080001, administered by the National Park Service, with the assistance of the Research Foundation, State University of New York.

INTRODUCTION

This is a story, one of the many that has been or could be told about the Mahicans, an Indian people who lived along the tidal waters they called Muhheakunnuk, today's Hudson River. It spans the years between 1600 and 1830, beginning just before the accepted first contact with European interlopers and ending with the removal of these Natives from New York State, their numbers having been augmented by Indians of Munsee and later other Delaware heritage.

No thought was given to writing a definitive history of the Mahicans, an impossible task no matter the intention. As Francis Jennings has put it, the goal for historians should be to open the field rather than attempt to close it.[1] The focus here is instead on the related themes of space—in the now common idiom, cultural landscapes—and movements through time, both of which are firmly rooted in historical context. Thus, the first objective is to situate the Mahicans in their homeland when it is most reasonably and securely possible, from about the middle decades of the seventeenth century into the eighteenth. The second is to trace the activities of Mahican communities as they sought to address their own needs and interests—economic, political, and otherwise; engage with Native friends and foes; and equally important, deal with the ever-encroaching and soon dominant European presence.

Arguably the most disruptive, tangled, yet transformative period of Mahican history took place in the years between 1630 and 1730. Then, two decades before the violence and disruptions of the mid-eighteenth-century French and Indian War, came a general coalescence of the Mahicans at Stockbridge, Massachusetts, and at the end of the American Revolution, a move to New Stockbridge, in the heart of Oneida country. Denied any possibility of returning to their homeland, the final destination of these Natives, reached by about 1830, was Wisconsin.

It is no surprise that most of what is known of the Mahicans is derived from the records of colonizers. Absent any other mention, the first to approach their country was Henry Hudson and his crew aboard the *Halve Maen* in early fall 1609. Within a few short years the Dutch colony of New Netherland took shape, its farmsteads and homes centered chiefly around Manhattan in the south and the upper reaches of the Hudson River in the north. Fort Orange, at present-day Albany, was built in 1624, several years after Fort Nassau, a fur trading post on the river, had fallen into disrepair, the result of spring floods. Six years later the patroonship of Rennselaerswijck was created, the vast holdings of which would eventually encompass much of the heart of Mahican territory. In 1652 the growing settlement around Fort Orange became the Dutch village of Beverwijck. Until the English takeover in 1664, it is primarily Dutch administrative records, a handful of historical accounts, and the sundry correspondence and reports of the colony's citizens that provide glimpses of Mahican culture. These materials are only somewhat supplemented by scattered English and French sources. The rest, at least on the basis of what appears in some of the histories written over the past century or so, is mostly guesswork.

The takeover in 1664 extended England's claims of territorial and governmental jurisdiction from western New England to beyond Albany, placing its mostly Dutch settlers under the Crown's authority. It also signaled an escalation of the economic and political competition between England and New France and its Indian allies. Along with most other Indians in the region, the Mahicans were drawn into the struggle — maintaining or shifting their loyalties to the Europeans as they saw fit — which was played out alongside age-old, and then newly engendered, Native conflicts that were invariably tied to their involvement in the fur trade. The documentary record over this period of time also grew, reflecting the actions of an imperialistic power having superceded the Dutch, who, unlike the English, showed little inclination to enlarge their colony of New Netherland or to command the Native people with whom they interacted. Nonetheless, while these materials allow for a moderately thorough tracking of Mahicans in their entanglements, near and far, with the Natives and Europeans who surrounded them, they offer little in the way of ethnological insight into their communities.

The multiple effects of land loss, wars, disease, and the inexorable intrusion of Europeans took their toll on the Mahicans. In the third decade of the eighteenth century they would form the Native population at the lately established "praying town" of Stockbridge and, moreover, carry the name Stockbridge Indians. With their move to central New York after the Revolution, they became known, more often than not, as the New Stockbridge Indians. But as before, there is little to be learned about their communities in terms of society and the routine of everyday life anytime in the eighteenth century. Instead, the story turns decidedly to the avarice and duplicity of the governments of colonial Massachusetts and then the state of New York, attended by missionary zeal and interference, land loss, and relocation, all amid the occasional internal dispute.

The documentary record that remains from just prior to and then through the turn of the nineteenth century until removal is one that reflects mainly the administrative, legislative, and land concerns of New York and the United States. To this can be added ecclesiastical matters that were often inseparable from government interests, usually with the consent, and at times the complicity, of a significant portion of the Native population. Still, the New Stockbridge Indians endeavored mightily to determine and control their own destiny by employing alternating strategies of accommodation, resistance, and self-generated political initiatives. Nevertheless, they found themselves ensnared, along with many other Native communities, by the federal government's determination to remove Indians west of the advancing frontier, a design that dated from the earliest days of the Republic. The Indian Removal Act of May 28, 1830, by and large codified and served to fully enforce what had long been unofficial policy.

A brief discussion on terms used in this history. It has become fashion for many historians to use the term *Mohican* rather than *Mahican*—the earliest attested form being *Mahicans* (1614)—when referring to these Native people. The most frequently given reasons are that until 2002 the federally recognized tribe—Stockbridge-Munsee Community—was officially known as the Stockbridge-Munsee Community of Mohican Indians of Wisconsin, and furthermore, that Mohican is the more familiar term, although to whom remains unexamined.[2] There usually is added some form of the following caveat: that Mohican should not be confused with Mohegan, the name of the Indian people of eastern Connecticut, or with James Fenimore Cooper's fictional Mohicans. As for Cooper, it is doubtful that anyone would take his fictional composites of Native people seriously enough to believe that they might reflect historical reality. Even so, these often stated yet hardly demonstrated mix-ups would end if the linguistic designation *Mahican*, representing the Mahican language, was used in the same manner as Munsee or Unami. These latter two terms correspond to language groups formerly present in the lower Hudson Valley, western Long Island, New Jersey, eastern Pennsylvania, and northern Delaware. Contained within these language groups were numerous named groups of Indians speaking dialects of either Munsee or Unami.

None of the speakers of Munsee or Unami—while residing in their homelands—formed single sociopolitical entities, *tribes*, for want of a better designation. This was also the case with the Mahicans.[3] During the early to mid-eighteenth century, for example, there were a number of autonomous Mahican communities in and around the Hudson and upper Housatonic Valleys, undoubtedly related through kinship and often through alliances. They included Kaunaumeek, Freehold, Wechquadnach, Stockbridge, the mixed community at Shekomeko, a few others along the Hudson in Dutchess County, that at Westenhoek (Westenhook), and forming part of the Native population at Schaghticoke (N Y). Indeed, there is nothing in the record to suggest that multiple, self-governing communities were other than the norm at contact. There is, however, evidence of longstanding dialectical differences within Mahican, a factor that has something to say about settlement history.

By the time of the American Revolution and thereafter, *Mohican* (with Stockbridge and New Stockbridge) had become the preferred name of these Indians. This change basically reflects the Anglicizing of *Mahican*, *Mahikander*, and *Maikens*, names that seem to have resulted from the early Dutch use of Munsee-speaking interpreters who pronounced the name *mà·hí·kan, mà·hí·kani·w*, Mahíkanɑk.[4] Given this background, and in the interests of consistency and ethnological integrity, *Mahican* rather than *Mohican* is used throughout this work.

In terms of a general methodology, I have followed the lead of historian Daniel Richter, where phrases such as *"the* Mahicans," *"the* Munsees," or *"the* Mohawks," in addition to others, should be understood as references to the activities of a particular leader or groups of leaders. They should not be interpreted as a single voice or as a representation of the decision-making process of a unitary sociopolitical entity. The same holds in instances where *"the* Dutch," *"the* English," or *"the* French" are used. Additionally, this history of the Mahicans is structured to present to readers what can be learned about these Native people employing the full range of primary sources, as well as a selected number of authoritative secondary works. In all cases, the attempt has been made to verify historical evidence by comparing accounts found in multiple sources, based on the premise that this will reduce errors that might result from placing reliance on a single source.[5]

Insofar as descriptions of Mahican culture are concerned, and where the documentary record is especially sparse, the drawing of analogies to surrounding groups, whether to other Algonquians or to the Iroquoians, has largely been avoided. An analogy can be useful only if there is a link between elements of Mahican culture found in the surviving record and the elements of a better-known culture or cultures to which the analogy is made. For example, it cannot be assumed that a ritual or a political process recorded for a nearby Native group was identical or even similar to that found among the Mahicans absent any mention in the record on the Mahicans of such matters or the attendant behaviors.

Other than several relatively brief commentaries, no detailed analysis or description of missions or missionaries among the Mahicans, nor of the practice or affect of Christianity on these people, has been undertaken. Rather, these tasks have been left to other historians, several of whose works on these themes are found in the endnotes. Even so, the most recent study on Stockbridge points to how very little is known about the religious lives of the Indians there.[6] Moreover, Christianity cannot be said to have played an assignable part in the relocation of these Indians to New York—it was external forces, the most destructive being the theft of their lands in Massachusetts by predatory colonials. And as will be seen, the later removal of these Indians to Wisconsin is linked directly to the cupidity of New York State and its citizens, aided and abetted by the federal government.

Eschewing any semblance of the "Great Man" theme, this story is neither driven nor shaped by references to the few identified leaders who left a mark on the historical record, either through the pens of European chroniclers and record keepers or by their own hands. It is, by design, about a people writ large—the Mahicans.

Prologue

All I know of my ancestors commences with the first emigrant from Holland who came over in 1633 [*sic*], and settled in what is now Rensselaer County in the State of New York.

—President MARTIN VAN BUREN, *Autobiography*

In May 1631 one Cornelis Maesen van Buijrmaelsen sailed for New Netherland aboard the ship *Eendracht*. He had been engaged by the patroon, Kiliaen van Rensselaer, to serve as a farm laborer for a period of three years. At the end of his contract he returned to Holland and in 1636, accompanied by his wife Catelijntje Martens and a servant, sailed once again to the colony. For the next decade he and Catelijntje, their family over time growing to include five children, worked a farm for the patroon on or close by Papscanee Island, a short distance below Fort Orange (Albany). Some time prior to early April 1648, Cornelis and Catelijntje died together, apparently in a flood of the Hudson River.[1] The children survived. It is noteworthy that the lands at Papscanee where Cornelis and Catelijntje settled and made their home had been purchased of certain Mahican "chiefs and owners" by Jacob Planck, the then agent for the colony, on April 23, 1637.[2] In May 1665 Wattawit, a Mahican Indian, sold a parcel of land "behind Kinderhook" to Volckert Janse (Douw) and Evert Luycasse (Backer), in part to satisfy unspecified debts. Three years later Governor Nicolls granted a patent to the same Evert Luycasse (Luykasse), along with John Hendrickse Bruyn, Dirk Wesselse, and Pieter van Alen, for a tract of land south of and adjacent to the 1665 conveyance, one-fourth of which was held by Wesselse (also Wessels). According to the deed of record, "Wessels" had sometime earlier sold his parcel to "Martin Cornelisse van Buren," a resident of "the Manor of Rensselaerswyck."[3]

Martin Cornelisse van Buren (1638–1703) was a son of Cornelis Maesen (also Maas, Maes, Maersz, Maertsz, Martsen, Maessen) and great-great-grandfather to President Van Buren. Upon Martin's death, the lands "lying at the Kinderhoeck with house, barn, ricks and all that appertains thereto, acquired by me from Dirk Wessellse," were offered to a son, Pieter, and a daughter, Cornelia.[4] It was this conveyance that permanently established the Van Buren family in Kinderhook, the president's birthplace.

Pieter Martense van Buren (1670–1755) married Ariaantje (Ariaanje) Barents (Barentse) in Albany in 1693. One of their four sons, Marten Pieterse van Buren (b. 1701), married to Dirkje (Dirckje) van Alstyne, was the president's grandfather. Martin van Buren's father, Abraham Martense van Buren (1737–1817), who would marry Maria Hoes (1747–1817) about 1776, was one of Pieter and Ariaanje's surviving children, three of whom had died young.[5]

With the birth of Martin van Buren in 1782, six generations of his family had lived and prospered on lands where once resided the Native inhabitants of the Hudson Valley — the Mahican Indians. But this fact is more than simply a sidebar — a moment of historical curiosity — to the larger story of the Mahicans. It was Martin van Buren, after all, following in the footsteps of the politics of the day, who would play a central role in putting these Indians on a path that would take them from their homeland to a new land.

One

Landscape and Environment

In life and lore the Hudson Valley has long fascinated the multitudes that have contemplated its expanse, sailed its waters, or lived and labored among its forested hills, meadows, and tributary streams. Narratives about the valley are legion, whether they appear as sketches of the early exploits of adventurers and entrepreneurs from the United Provinces of the Netherlands; recount the enchanting tales of Rip van Winkle and Sleepy Hollow; or speak to the creation and administration of first the colony and then the state of New York. And assuredly, there is all of what took place before and after these selected few, though familiar, benchmarks.

Other depictions of the Hudson Valley can be found on canvas, most notably those created in the middle decades of the nineteenth century by the Hudson River painters, whose collected works are widely considered to represent the first wholly American school of art. The landscapes produced by the likes of Thomas Cole, Asher B. Durand, Frederic Edwin Church, and others framed vistas of the valley in dramatic and reverential luminescence. These naturalistic, if romantic, images extolled the beauty and majesty of the American "wilderness," presaging perhaps present-day environmentalist ideas of nature. In other ways, however, these paintings suggest what have been fundamental themes in American history, namely, "exploration" and "settlement," accompanied by the cant of colonialism.[1]

Missing entirely from this picture is any recognition or immediate knowledge of the views that American Indians—obviously the original inhabitants of the Hudson Valley—may have held of its sweep and grandeur. If anyone thought to ask, whatever may have been heard was not recorded. Nor is there any evidence that Indians came forward to see to it that their words would be put down for posterity. All that is known to exist of a Native voice is a short history and sketch of Mahican culture written in 1791 by Hendrick Aupaumut (1757–1830), which offers little description of the lands on which he had been born and raised.[2] It is certain, however, that Indians saw and experienced of their valley all of what Europeans did for themselves—and, without doubt, even more—but little remains of the substance of what it was they had to say.

The Hudson River flows over three hundred miles from its source in the serene, deep forest setting of Lake Tear of the Clouds, high in the Adirondack Mountains, south to the bustle and clamor of New York Harbor. Drawing water from countless rivulets and streams crisscrossing an expanse of several thousand square miles, the river descends four thousand feet over its 160-mile-long upper reach to a mean water elevation of just two feet above sea level at Albany. Several miles above Albany the Mohawk River, the Hudson's largest tributary, joins from the west to complete the remaining 150-mile, straight-line journey south to the surroundings of Manhattan Island, adding another nine thousand square miles of watershed. From its mouth north to Troy, the Hudson is a tidal river that undergoes a reversal in flow four times a day, the average tidal range being about four feet.[3] Under normal fresh water flow conditions, salt water intrusion reaches Highland Falls, fifty miles north of lower Manhattan Island, information useful in assessing the quality of the fishery available to Native people—the Mahicans in particular—as described by Europeans.

In addition to the Mohawk River, the upper and middle valley contains numerous other tributaries that lend relief to the surrounding landscape and provide historical context for both Na-

Landscape and Environment

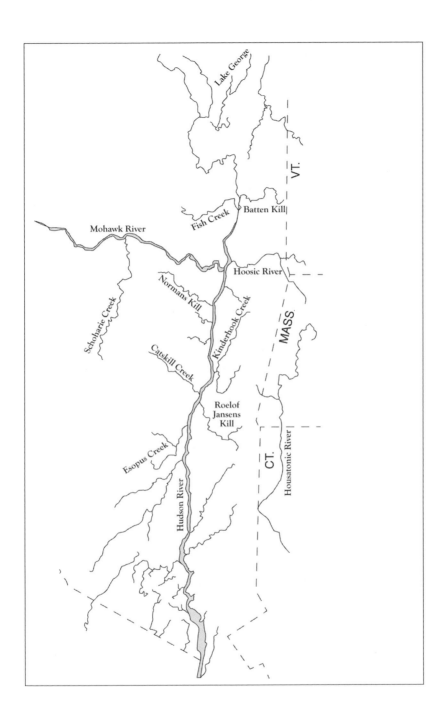

MAP 1. The Hudson Valley and Environs.

tive people and colonists (maps 1 and 2). On the east side, from north to south, are the Batten Kill at about Schuylerville, east of Saratoga Springs; the Hoosic River at Stillwater; the Poesten Kill and the Wynants Kill at Troy; the Kinderhook and Claverack Creeks, which later merge to form Stockport Creek at Columbiaville; and the Roelof Jansens Kill, opposite and south of Catskill. For reasons to be explored later, the Roelof Jansens Kill and its environs are routinely regarded as the linguistic and cultural boundaries between Mahican and Munsee speakers in the valley.

On the west side of the Hudson, below the confluence of the Mohawk River, and also on a north-to-south line, flows the Normans Kill, a stream that was of critical importance during the first decades of the fur trade and the establishment of the colony of New Netherland. Farther downriver are the Vloman Kill, Coeymans Creek, Coxsackie Creek, Catskill Creek, and finally, the Esopus and Rondout Creeks at Kingston.

The main reach of the Hudson is geologically less a river than it is an estuary of the Atlantic Ocean, its shallow-graded bed permanently inundated by tidal flow.[4] The river's channel, from midvalley north to Albany, is something of a hydrological chameleon, underlain as it is by gravels and silts derived from deposits of glacial drift carried as part of the stream load from the northern, nontidal reach of the river. The resulting and constantly shifting shoals have been hazards to navigation dating to the early seventeenth century. Adding to the channel's ongoing transformation are the islands that have come and gone, their existence predicated on the directions and strengths of the river's currents and the seasonal changes in water levels, linked primarily to the amount of snow melt in the watershed but also to spring and fall rains. While sailing from New York to Albany in 1769, surveyor Richard Smith reported that a short distance above the mouth of Coeymans Creek on the west side of the river there was "an Island of about Two Acres covered with

Landscape and Environment

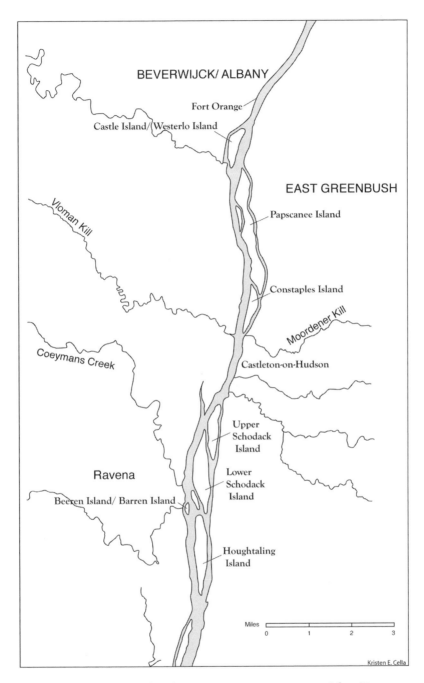

BEVERWIJCK/ ALBANY

Fort Orange

Castle Island/ Westerlo Island

EAST GREENBUSH

Vloman Kill

Papscanee Island

Constaples Island

Moordener Kill

Coeymans Creek

Castleton-on-Hudson

Upper
Schodack
Island

Ravena

Lower
Schodack
Island

Beeren Island/ Barren Island

Houghtaling
Island

Miles

0   1   2   3

Kristen E. Cella

MAP 2. The Core of Mahican Country, 1600–1700. After Huey,
"Mahicans, the Dutch, and the Schodack Islands."

young Button wood [sycamore] Trees which Island, our Skipper says, has arisen there to his Knowledge within 16 years and since he has navigated the River."[5]

The lower one-third of the Hudson Valley, beginning above Manhattan, is characterized by impressive promontories or bluffs, most of which are on the west side. These soon coalesce into a virtually unbroken line of precipitous, scrub- and tree-covered rock faces in the direction of West Point and Storm King Mountain, with intervals of steep elevations on the east bank. Above Beacon, high slopes of varying heights predominate, broken by stream mouths; hollows; low, relatively narrow terraces; ravines; points of land extending into the river; and rocky islands. At Coxsackie, however, the river narrows considerably, making flooding from spring freshets an annual event. Over many centuries this has allowed for the formation and then continual replenishment above this point of deep, expansive, and fertile alluvial flats — bottom lands — that attracted and were of great value to first Native and then colonial farmers. Added to this are wetlands of swamps, marshes, and bogs, which are most extensive in the upper third of the valley. Possessing significant biodiversity, these were areas from which Natives could draw critical plant, animal, and raw material resources.

There exist from the seventeenth and eighteenth centuries several descriptions of the Hudson — both river and valley — in particular the stretch beginning a short distance above Kingston and extending to above Troy, roughly the area within which lived the Mahicans. The first of these is from the brief report of Robert Juet (1610), an officer serving on Henry Hudson's ship the *Halve Maen*. His concerns, understandably, were with the river's channel, especially the depth of its waters and the presence of shoals. Both were measures of the possible hazards to his ship, which, nonetheless, did not prevent its grounding on occasion when it sailed too close to a "banke of Oze in the middle of the river" or the river's edge. As the ship neared present-day Albany, crewmen went ashore and "gathered good store of Chest-nuts."

Then, walking along the west side, they found "good ground for Corne and other Garden herbs, with great store of goodly Oakes, and Wal-nut trees, and Chest-nut trees, Ewe trees [Canadian or American yew], and trees of sweet wood in great abundance, and great store of Slate for houses, and other good stones."[6]

Johannes de Laet's chronicle (1625), while not firsthand, does contain the valuable extracts from Hudson's journal suggesting that he may also have had access to a ship's log or accounts kept by sea captains who sailed the river after the *Halve Maen*. This supposition is strengthened by the plain fact that throughout De Laet provides the names that the Dutch had assigned to reaches, hooks, islands, and other points of land, all important navigational markers for anyone on the river. Beginning about midvalley, he mentions Playsier's Reach and Vasterack, where the latter's most northern point was at about Nutten Hook on the east bank opposite Coxsackie. The river along these reaches was "dotted with sands and shallow, both on the east side, and in the middle of the river." From "Kinderhoeck [Kinderhook]" and beyond, "the river at its greatest depth has but five fathoms of water, and generally only two or three." Above Kinderhook "there are several small islands in the river, one of which is called Beeren [today Barren] Island." Several others in this part of the river, notably, Houghtaling, Lower Schodack, and Upper Schodack Islands, figure importantly in Mahican history.[7] "The land," De Laet wrote, "is excellent and agreeable, full of noble forest trees and grape vines, and nothing is wanting but the labor and industry of man to render it one of the finest and most fruitful lands in that part of the world."[8]

In a 1644 narrative describing the Mohawk Indians, Johannes Megapolensis, a minister whose home was on the east side of the Hudson opposite Fort Orange, thought to include information on the Hudson River. In this river, he wrote, "are very beautiful islands, containing ten, twenty, thirty, fifty and seventy morgens of land."[9] The soils in the area were exceptionally good, he explained, "but the worst of it is, that by the melting of the snow, or heavy rains, the river readily overflows and covers that low land."[10] Flooding such as this was a constant source of frustration, not to mention danger, for farmers who worked the islands and the adjacent low-lying floodplains. Yet as mentioned before, these waters acted to annually replenish soils so that Megapolensis could report that "in this ground there appears to be a singular strength and capacity for bearing crops, for a farmer here told me that he had raised fine wheat on one and the same piece of land eleven years successively without ever breaking it up or letting it lie fallow."[11]

Jasper Danckaerts (1680), a Labadist agent in America to find land for a religious colony, traveled the length of the Hudson River, about which he nevertheless wrote very sparingly. Sailing north above what is today Kingston, he gave what was becoming a familiar description of this stretch as "difficult to navigate, and beset with shoals and passages" and that it was impossible to proceed "without continual danger of running aground."[12]

In 1749 the intrepid Pehr (Peter) Kalm, a student of the great botanist Linnaeus, made his way up the Hudson River on one leg of a tour that would take him through the colonies of New York, New Jersey, and Pennsylvania, and also to southern Canada. Leaving the vicinity of present-day Newburgh, his sloop sailed past stony and forested lowlands on both sides of the river, "there being no spot of ground fit for cultivation," and tellingly, not seeing a single settlement there. Beginning at about the midway point between New York and Albany, he saw to his west the distant Catskill Mountains, and close-by there were well-cultivated lands, "especially on the eastern shore, and full of great plowed fields; yet the soil seemed sandy." Farther on, now beyond Rhinebeck, "the country on the eastern side was high, and consisted of well cultivated soil. We had fine plowed fields, well-built farms and good orchards in view." The west bank, while high as well, was "still covered with woods, and we now and then, though seldom, saw one or two little settlements." Then, nine miles below Albany, Kalm reported that "the coun-

Landscape and Environment

try on both sides of the river was low and covered with woods, only here and there were a few scattered settlements. On the banks of the river were wet meadows, covered with sword grass (*Carex*), and they formed several little islands." These were likely the Schodack, Houghtailing, and Barren Islands. Approaching Albany he saw broad alluvial flats and "more carefully cultivated" fields. Here the river "was seldom above a musketshot broad, and in several parts were sandbars which required great skill in navigating the boats."[13]

The final related description of the river and the surrounding landscape of the mid- to upper Hudson Valley is that of Richard Smith in 1769, mentioned before. Smith had set out from Burlington, New Jersey, "with a View to survey a large Tract of Land then lately purchased from the Indians."[14] He was to supervise a party of surveyors sent to map the boundaries of the Otego patent, located in the present-day towns of Oneonta and Otego on the upper Susquehanna River, some ninety miles southwest of Albany. Booking passage on a sloop, skippered, fittingly, by a Dutchman, one Richard Scoonhoven, Smith and his men sailed upriver. Picking up his observations from a point above Kingston, Smith observed that the "Kaatskill Mountains" were to the northwest and appeared to be "very near tho they are at a considerable Distance. The Country on both Sides continues still hilly and rugged." Sixty miles from Albany "the Aspect of the Farms rough and hilly like all the rest and the soil a stiff clay." The hills sloping toward the river were covered with wheat. On the west side, near the mouth of Catskill Creek, was "A Quantity of low cripple Land," and farther up, "good low Bottom fit for Meadow." This was at the location of "Bears" or "Bearen" Island," that is, Barren Island, "said to be the Beginning of the Manor of Renslaerwic[k] which extends on both Sides of the River." Here Smith describes one of the Schodack Islands, the upper end of which "is a fine cleared Bottom not in Grass but partly in Wheat & partly in Tilth." Further attesting to the changes in island forms in this part of the river, Smith's editor added the following footnote: "This island by the action of the water has since been divided into two, which are known as Upper and Lower Schodack Islands."[15]

Taking into account the now four centuries of dairy, market, and truck farming; the emergence and proliferation of rural villages and towns; industrialization; and large-scale urbanization, all of which have been accompanied by the development of transportation networks and an elaborate infrastructure, the Hudson River Valley nonetheless retains its natural beauty and form. Yet today there exist factors that have done much to diminish the ability of its residents to share in the region's bounty. This is true, in particular, for the river itself.

Seventeenth-century observers left detailed descriptions of a pristine waterway rich in marine and freshwater fish and shellfish. The most lengthy list of species is found in Adriaen van der Donck's *Description of New Netherland* (1655). "According to season and locality," Van der Donck wrote, the Hudson was home to sturgeon, salmon, striped bass, shad, pike, trout, minnow silverfish, sucker, eel, lamprey, sunfish, tomcod, herring, mackerel, plaice, and sheepshead, among others. He also reported lobster, crab, conch, clams, oysters, and mussel.[16] Several of these fish and shellfish are restricted to the more saline stretches of the river nearer its mouth and also to Long Island Sound. In his earlier report Juet noted that "the River is full of fish" and that his crewmen had taken numbers of "Mullets, Breames, Bases [bass], and Barbils."[17]

The most valuable and readily available fish for Native people would have been the anadromous herrings, shad, striped bass, and lamprey, which ascended the river and its tributaries in the spring in huge numbers, and would have been taken with little difficulty and in equally large numbers with nets and spears. Such runs of fish occur today, although for a variety of reasons, most tied to environmental degradation, they are noticeably reduced in size. Because of the presence of chemical pollutants in the river, which have found their way into the bodies of fish, the state has been forced to place severe restrictions on eating even these. At present, from Troy north to Hudson Falls there is a "don't eat" warning in effect for any and all fish. South of Troy to the bridge at Catskill, formerly a part of Mahican territory, there is a "don't eat" advisory for women of childbearing years and children under fifteen. For all others there are just four species that can be eaten once a month, shad once a week. All other fish are off-limits.[18] This is in stark contrast to a time when fish were a dietary mainstay for both Indian and Dutch residents of the valley, including the more distant Mohawks, who along with later arriving European populations fished its waters.[19]

The composition of the Hudson Valley woodlands today corresponds to the chestnut, oak, and yellow poplar zone of the Southern Hardwood Forest. The surrounding region, including the Catskills to the west and the Taconic Mountains to the east, is representative of the Northeastern Hardwood Forest of birch, beech, maple, and hemlock.[20] Natives of the Hudson Valley and southern New England made extensive use of the yellow poplar (aka tulip tree), the white pine, the chestnut, and the eastern cottonwood to manufacture dugout canoes, often of considerable size. Other woods provided materials from which weapons, utensils, tools, and houses were fashioned. Moreover, trees such as the hickories, walnuts, and beeches provided Indian and colonial alike with nuts, an important supplement to other foodstuffs. A potentially more significant source of food would have been wild, primarily vascular plants. Nonetheless, as in other areas of New York and the northeast in general, there is little direct evidence for their exploitation or use by Indian people save for the scattered mentions by European observers and the remains of seeds that are often recovered from archaeological contexts. One approach to addressing this question is to acknowledge the broad availability of edible wild plants, understanding, nonetheless, that virtually nothing is known regarding either their value or their palatability to Natives of the Hudson Valley prior to or into the seventeenth century and beyond. There are, however, useful comparative data available from the Catskills and the Upper Susquehanna Valley to the west, in addition to descriptions of the use of plants and plant foods in nineteenth- and twentieth-century Iroquois communities.[21] Also to be counted are non-edible plants such as hemp, rushes, gourds, and others, raw materials from which woven bags, baskets, cordage, mats, and containers were manufactured.[22]

Within these forests there existed, and in most instances still exist, a great range and variety of mammalian, avian, and other fauna.[23] Many of these were noticed, remarked upon, and listed by early European observers.[24] Those animals that first and foremost drew the attention of the Dutch were, for them, and very quickly for Native people, the economically important fur-bearers; namely, the beaver, then otters, martens, foxes, minks, but also bears and "wild cats."[25] Of special interest is that the earliest, most comprehensive, if at times quaint discussion on the natural history of the beaver in the Americas is found in Van der Donck's *Description*.[26]

There were, of course, many other creatures that were of critical significance to the Indians, providing food and also hides and pelts to be used as clothing and footwear. Of these, the ubiquitous white-tailed deer is ranked first among the mammals that Indians hunted. In rough order, deer are followed by raccoons, squirrels, muskrats, black bears, and woodchucks. In addition there were elk, river otters, porcupines, fishers, hares, and rabbits. Also present in the forests and open meadows of the Hudson Valley were chipmunks, wolves, turkeys, lynx, bobcats, mice, voles, and others.[27]

An assortment of avian, amphibian, and reptilian fauna were present in the Hudson Valley at contact, an unknown number of which may have been exploited by Native people as subsistence choices. Van der Donck provides an extensive listing of birds, both migrants and year-round residents, virtually all of which can be found in the region today. They include raptors, song birds, water birds, and what are now regarded as game birds.

Landscape and Environment

The chief exception is the passenger pigeon (*Ectopistes migratorius*), a migratory species that appeared in vast numbers in the spring and whose squabs were harvested by Natives throughout the eastern woodlands. These birds were also hunted by newly arrived Europeans and, certainly, their descendants. The passenger pigeon was declared extinct in 1914. Van der Donck and other observers paid much less attention to reptiles and amphibians, although these too were plentiful.[28]

For present-day residents of the Hudson Valley, the region's climate and weather patterns are no mystery. Moreover, these elements of the environment have, over the long run, remained relatively stable. The most detailed description of the valley's seasons and climate is, again, from Van der Donck, who had resided in the patroonship of Rensselaerswijck from 1641 to 1644, moving then to Manhattan, where he remained until the end of the decade when he sailed for the Netherlands. He returned to his estate on the Hudson above Manhattan several years later, meeting his death in an Indian attack in 1655.[29]

"The swift messenger and foster mother of commerce, the wind, blows in New Netherland from all points of the compass, without the regularity of monsoons and trade winds," Van der Donck wrote.[30] North winds in the winter brought cold weather, while in the summer south and southwesterly winds prevailed. Calm days were common at midwinter. Northwest winds were often "very sharp, violent, and persistent." Thunderstorms, occurring mostly in the spring, "seldom go on for more than three days." Warm air and haze, along with rainy weather, arrived on southerly winds. Rapid shifts in the winds brought equally rapid changes in temperatures. "The air in New Netherland," Van der Donck concluded, "is as dry, pure, and wholesome as could be desired, and so clear, agreeable, and delicate as would be hard to match anywhere else," a distinct advantage, he suggested, for those who were sickly or not in the best of health.

Commenting on the seasonal variations in temperature, Van der Donck offered that "the heat is bearable and in the hottest part of summer is often tempered by a sea wind, a northerly breeze, or a shower. The cold is more severe than the climate seems to suggest and, owing to the keen air, sharp and penetrating, though always dry when the wind is from the north." There was no wiser advice than "to dress so as to withstand the cold," the most extreme of which, he observed, was not long-lasting.

During the familiar-to-all dog days of summer "the humidity is seldom oppressive," Van der Donck said, "nor does it continue for long. Yet there is plenty of rain in season, more in some years than in others. It pours down freely, seeping down to the roots, and quite soon the weather is fine again and the sky clear. Thunder and lightning, which are common in warm weather, thoroughly cleanse and clear the air. For the rest the weather depends, with exceptions, on the time of year."

Spring generally made its appearance in March. "Then all of nature bursts free, fish dart forth from muddy depths, the trees bud, and the grass sprouts." By May the grass and foliage were in full green. Gardens might be planted and fields sowed in April, or a bit later "if one is not quite ready for it." Although "most of the changeable and turbulent weather occurs at this time," forests were not yet choked with grass and brushwood, but once they were cleared by intentionally set fires, "the land is now most accessible, the trees are in flower, and sweet scents pervade the forest." Then came the summer, which might begin in May, "but is reckoned from June so as not to make it too long." Although quite hot, summers were "seldom so rainy that it becomes tiresome." Dry periods, Van der Donck remarked, were mitigated by frequent and heavy dews that acted to refresh plants and herbage.[31] Still, "no one wearies of the summer, however long it may seem, before it draws to a close, for in that season man and beast alike enjoy its bounty everywhere."

Fall in the Hudson Valley today is universally viewed as the most delightful of seasons. And so it was in the seventeenth century. "The autumns in New Netherland are normally as fine, lovely, and pleasant as could be desired anywhere on earth," wrote Van der Donck, "not only because the fruits that await-ed the passing of summer now yield up their treasure and the fields their surplus, but mainly because the season is so well tempered as regards heat and cold; and the weather it brings is fine and lovely as though it were in the month of May." Many mornings began with a slight haze that would quickly vanish with the warmth of the sun. Rains were infrequent and usual-ly fell as showers. Otherwise, they seldom lasted longer than two or three days. "For the rest the weather is fine and wonder-ful day after day, with bright sunshine and moderate tempera-tures." But then would come winter.

Van der Donck expressed great surprise that New Nether-land, "situated on the same latitude as Spain and Italy and as hot in the summer, is yet so cold in winter." But the cold was drier, he believed, posing an immediate threat to plants that were not cold-resistant. On the other hand, he explained, this same cold produced the much desired animal furs that "actually surpass those of Muscovy in beauty and quality." Still, the cold was not so severe "as to be harmful and hard to bear; in many respects it is desirable and beneficial in that it clears the land of vermin and removes all pungent and injurious. It also firms up the skins of bodies and plants and improves their fitness." It is doubtful, however, that today's residents would express the same posi-tive note about winter's "benefits" as did Van der Donck.

Native people of the valley, Van der Donck volunteered, ap-parently bore up well under winter's cold and harsh conditions. "Even the Indians," he said, "who do not wear the thick clothes we do and go about half naked, withstand the cold well and have no fear of it, nor are they ever overcome or noticeably harmed by it. On bitterly cold days, perhaps, they will not disport them-selves in the open so much. Then it is mainly the women and children who do, as the men are not so keen on it, except in summer or on warm days." One might hazard the guess that, from the Indians' point of view of winter, the devil was in the details.

TWO

Natives on the Land

The Arrival of Europeans: First Impressions

The meetings of Indians and Europeans—Dutch, French, and English, but earlier Basques, Portuguese, and Italians—on the coast and soon thereafter in the interior of northeastern North America, began a long period of a mutual stocktaking. Where appropriate, it is the rare history that does not provide something of these encounters, however clouded by time and inclination the tales might be. Because of the scattered, cursory, and often adumbrated nature of the accounts left by sailors, soldiers, and other enterprising first arrivals, assessments have been broadly regional in scope rather than being directed at a specific locality. At the same time, they tend to incorporate the experiences of many Native peoples rather than a single group, while others have been topical in approach. Until relatively recently most efforts centered on the views Europeans held of Indians, with little attention paid to what Indians might have volunteered about events taking place around them.

Beginning in the mid-1970s, however, there began a countervailing move to create an "Indian perspective" in writing histories, which some believed might be found in contemporary Native voices. Whatever promise adopting such a point of view has offered, it can easily be argued that no modern-era non-Native or, for that matter, Native has the wherewithal to call up from a past some four centuries deep anything resembling an "Indian perspective." This is not to say that comparative, carefully parsed, and culturally sensitive readings of the accounts left by Europeans do not lead to a deeper understanding of Native people, especially for the early years of contact.[1] Arguably the most effective methodology to accomplish this task — ethnohistory — is today practiced routinely by many anthropologists and historians.[2] Briefly stated, and for present purposes, ethnohistory marries firsthand descriptions that flowed from the pens of early European explorers and colonists with similarly recorded Native oral traditions; for example, stories of the earliest encounters told by Indians to these same Europeans, or sometimes decades later to those who had followed in their footsteps. Information drawn from these sources is then measured and tested against what can be found in the ethnological literature, all of which is fixed firmly in historical context.

There exist just a few recorded descriptions of the initial meeting of Europeans — widely assumed to have been Henry Hudson and his mixed Dutch and English crew — and Mahicans that contain within them impressions, if only tenuous, of these Native people. The first two are from Emanuel van Meteren and Robert Juet, the latter, in all probability, the navigator on the *Halve Maen*.[3] Van Meteren, a historian, served for many years as Dutch consul in London. His general history of the Netherlands, published in 1610, contains a short section on Hudson's third voyage to the "New World," from April to November 1609, with the *Halve Maen* entering Sandy Hook Bay on September 2. It is likely that Van Meteren's information was drawn from Juet's journal, which lends credibility to his rather brief remarks: "In the lower part of the river they [Hudson's crew] found strong and warlike people; but in the upper part they found friendly and polite people, who had an abundance of provisions, skins, and furs . . . and many other commodities . . . [that] they traded amicably with the people."[4]

It has been suggested that this perceived line of demarcation between the Indians living in the lower and upper valley, which may have been in the vicinity of Germantown and Catskill, corresponded roughly to the geographical, cultural, and linguistic boundaries that separated the Mahicans from the Munsees.[5] As Juet reported, it was on upper New York Bay that one of Hudson's crew was killed by an arrow shot to the throat. This followed from a favorable appraisal during the time the ship was at anchor in Sandy Hook. There, Juet wrote, "the people of the Countrey came aboard of us, seeming very glad of our comming, and brought greene Tabacco, and gave us of it for Knives and Beads. . . . They desire Clothes, and are very civill." The next day the Indians again boarded the ship. At nightfall "they went on Land againe, so wee rode very quiet," adding, with some foreboding, "but durst not trust them."[6] But the question arises as to just who was most or least trustworthy. Suspicious of the Indians they had chanced upon some weeks earlier while the *Halve Maen* was in Penobscot Bay to replace a shattered foremast, the crew had made a preemptive move: "Then we manned our Boat & Scute with twelve men and Muskets, and two stone Pieces or Murderers, and drave the Salvages from their Houses, and tooke the spoyle of them, as they would have done of us."[7]

On the *Halve Maen's* return downriver, at about Stony Point in the Hudson's lower reach, the Indians there took an even more bellicose stance, but lost close to a dozen men to Dutch swords, muskets, and small ordinance in what were clearly one-sided skirmishes. What appears obvious from the Indians' hostility, and interestingly, their lack of fear, is that they seem to have previously weathered unhappy meetings with Europeans probing New York Bay and the river's entrance in their search for a passage to Asia, experiences that perhaps were contributing factors to their and the seamens' deadly clashes.[8]

This supposition is bolstered by events upriver, where Juet described the Indians, assuredly Mahican-speakers, as being noticeably different from those previously happened upon. Sailing past where the Catskill Mountains lay to their west, and a short distance below present-day Hudson and Athens, the ship's crew "found very loving peeple, and very old men: where wee were well used." Nearing Albany, "our Masters Mate went

Natives on the Land

on land with an old Savage, a Governour of the Countrey; who carried him to his house, and made him good cheere." Indians soon "came flocking aboord, and brought us Grapes and Pompions, which wee bought for trifles." Then, in what suggests that either word of Hudson's arrival had traveled quickly upriver to their communities or that the Mahicans themselves had the occasion to see Europeans before this, they carried to the ship "Bevers skinnes, and Otters skinnes, which wee bought for Beades, Knives, and Hatchets."[9] If the Mahicans had not previously hosted European intruders, there is the likelihood they had learned something of or had paid visits to French fur traders active on the St. Lawrence and near the mouth of the Richelieu River sometime before 1609.

Although it may have been an oversight, Juet does not mention those Munsees encountered near the river's entrance having furs with them to trade for Dutch tools and "trifles." Instead, they first offered the ship's crew tobacco, and at later meetings "Hempe," in addition to foods such as currants, corn, beans, and oysters.[10] But food was also what the Mahicans first carried to the ship. Moreover, that Indians would exchange furs for European goods was something clearly understood by Hudson and his crew before leaving Amsterdam, and a practice of which they had gained direct knowledge while in Penobscot Bay. In his journal Juet recorded that the Indians there had brought "many Beaver skinnes, and other fine Furres, which they would have changed for redde Gownes. For the French trade with them for red Cassockes, Knives, Hatchets, Copper, Kettles, Trevits, Beades, and other trifles."[11]

The *Halve Maen* did not sail blind to the "New World." It obviously had among its ship's stores an appreciable supply of just the kind of trade goods that Indians both valued and desired. Hatchets and knives, of course, had recognized and immediate utility for the Indians, who often "dismembered" such items, converting pieces into other traditional tool forms.[12] Glass beads, however, which Juet had referred to as "glasse Buttons" while the *Halve Maen* lay off Cape Cod, in addition to the red coats mentioned before, required more intimate cultural knowledge of their appeal.[13] This could only mean that Hudson had done his homework before setting out from Amsterdam, reading about previous voyages and transactions with the Natives of North America or conferring with ships' captains and others who had sailed there. A principal informant on such matters may have been none other than the already famous John Smith, who, according to Van Meteren, had corresponded with Hudson, sending him maps and, perhaps in his letters, details on the Indian people with whom he was dealing in and around Jamestown. But there are strong suggestions that Hudson also had access to and consulted other maps and navigational charts much before he undertook his third voyage.[14]

Other critical information about Indian preferences for European goods almost certainly was gathered from fur traders who had been operating on the St. Lawrence since the late sixteenth century. They sailed from home ports in Brittany and Flanders, most notably from Rouen, whose merchants had been granted a series of monopolies over the trade on that great river.[15] One would expect that along with what ships' captains and traders learned about the goods that Indians most coveted, stories were also swapped about their behavior and what might be expected of them. This, combined with the prevalent strains of European cultural and religious chauvinism, added to which were the political, social, and economic agendas and the wariness of Native people, may help explain the shapes and outcomes of these early contacts.

Although the central character on the European side of the presumed first encounter with Mahicans was Henry Hudson, little of what he saw and recorded has been preserved. The journal that Hudson kept is believed lost. All that survives are the excerpts that Johannes de Laet—who at some point had read the actual journal, or possibly a copy—incorporated into chapter ten of his "New World," published in Dutch in 1625. This explains why Hudson's English appears modern. The entire text of "New World," including the excerpts from Hudson's journal, had been written in Dutch by De Laet and, much later, in 1841, was translated into English and published by the New York Historical Society.[16]

About half of what De Laet reproduced from the journal describes events in New York Harbor. Once upriver, however, Hudson met with a headman of the Mahicans and was taken to a small village. "On our coming near the house," he wrote, "two mats were spread out to sit upon, and immediately some food was served in well made red wooden bowls." Hunters sent out promptly returned with a pair of pigeons. "They likewise killed at once a fat dog, and skinned it in great haste, with shells which they get out of the water." These most hospitable Indians, Hudson tells us, "supposed that I would remain with them for the night," but he chose instead to return to his ship. "The natives are a very good people," he marveled, "for, when they saw that I would not remain, they supposed that I was afraid of their bows, and taking the arrows, they broke them in pieces, and threw them into the fire, etc."[17]

De Laet, who never traveled to the Americas, although he corresponded with or was given access to the reports and journals of those who had, offered further impressions of the Indians who lived in the Hudson Valley, however indeterminate their identity. "They are revengeful and very suspicious," he observed, and because they apparently held fast to these inclinations they "often engaged in wars among themselves, they are very fearful and timid." Still, he argued, his words framed by the received wisdom of the day, "with mild and proper treatment, and especially by intercourse with Christians, this people might be civilized and brought under better regulation," concluding, "they are, besides, very serviceable, and allow themselves to be employed in many things for a small compensation; even to performing a long day's journey, in which they discover greater fidelity than could be expected of such a people."[18] Evidently unsatisfied with limiting his remarks to just this one occasion, De Laet later rephrases his characterizations: "They are like most barbarians suspicious and fearful, although greedy of revenge; they are fickle, but if humanely treated, hospitable and ready to perform a service; they ask only a small remuneration for what they do."[19]

Isaack de Rasière, secretary to the Dutch West India Company in New Netherland from 1624 to 1628, saw things differently on the question of the Indians' aptitude for employment. The men, he said, were "very inveterate against those whom they hate; cruel by nature, and so inclined to freedom that they cannot by any means be brought to work." But there were other more intemperate voices, in particular that of one Reverend Jonas Michaëlius (1628), recently arrived in Manhattan. "As to the natives of this country," he groused, "I find them entirely savage and wild, strangers to all decency, yea, uncivil and stupid as garden poles, proficient in all wickedness and godlessness." For good measure, and applying a curious anatomical standard, he added that "they are as thievish and treacherous as they are tall; and in cruelty they are altogether inhuman, more barbarous, far exceeding the Africans." All this and more after having spent just four months in the colony.[20]

A somewhat less reliable narrative, that of news gatherer and pamphleteer Nicolaes van Wassenaer, is nonetheless of use, as it covers a period of time — 1621 to 1631 — about which little is known of conditions in the colony. Like his countryman De Laet, Van Wassenaer never set foot in New Netherland. It must be conceded, however, that although his sources are unnamed, and moreover, that the subjects of his descriptions are not identified, many of the details of Indian life he reported ring true when compared with contemporary firsthand accounts. But Van Wassenaer said very little about Indian character, other than his mentions that they were, as a general condition, "very cunning in trade" and were not, "by nature, the most gentle." On this latter note he suggested that if the colonists were not as well

Natives on the Land

armed as they were, they would be more frequent targets of Native people. The Indians in the Hudson Valley, he concluded, although "very well disposed so long as no injury is done them," were, in the final analysis, "a wicked, bad people."[21]

Adriaen van der Donck, in his brief comments on Native people who also are not identified by name or place, provides a more nuanced portrayal: "Although generally speaking, nature has not endowed them with surpassing wisdom, and they must develop their best judgment without formal training, yet one finds no fools." Beyond this, Van der Donck believed Indians to be "notably melancholy, unaffected, calm, and of few words. . . . While not given to gross lies, they are not very careful with the truth or in keeping their word either." Their intelligence, he thought, reflected "merely a reasonable knowledge based on experience." As had others, Van der Donck saw Indians as "vengeful and headstrong" people who, when "entrusted with too much . . . tend to become thievish."[22]

It is impossible to know the thoughts of those Indians who watched the *Halve Maen* sail first up and then back down the Hudson River. The same holds true for the years that followed, when Dutch ships brought fur traders and soldiers, and then administrators, farmers, merchants, artisans, and others, into the valley. Juet tells us that, in New York Harbor, the first Indians the ship's crew spotted "came aboord of us, seeming very glad of our comming." But Juet had also described the Indians who came to the ship in their canoes while it lay off Penobscot Bay to be "seeming glad of our comming."[23] Was the Indians' behavior in either instance typical of when strangers were approached, or did the manner of their welcome stem from having previously encountered Europeans and was meant to signal their interest to trade? Whatever the case, two days later the Indians assumed a very different posture, attacking a small boat returning to the *Halve Maen* as it lay at anchor south of the Narrows, the reasons for which Juet left unspoken. Obviously, something or someone seems to have provoked these Indians, either then or perhaps at an earlier time, transforming what had been, for the briefest of moments, a friendly relationship into one of mutual suspicion and fraught with tension. Reaching the upper valley, neither Juet nor Hudson offers anything that survives of their thoughts of the Mahicans, although both leave the impression that, having been cordially received, the Indians must have been pleased to see them.[24] Then, for the next century and a half, with but a single exception, Indian voices are silent, or at least unrecorded, on whatever views they may have entertained about these or other European intruders.

Van der Donck is that exception. "When some of them first saw our ship [*Halve Maen*] approaching in the distance, they knew not what to make of it and dreaded that it be a ghostly or similar apparition from heaven or from hell; others wondered whether it might be a rare fish or a sea monster, and those on board devils or humans, and so on, each according to his inclination. Strange reports of the event were current in the country at the time," he added, causing "great despondency among the Indians, as several of them have declared to me more than once." What then follows in the story is noteworthy: "This we take as certain proof that the Dutch were the first finders and possessors of New Netherland. Because there are Indians whose memories go back more than a hundred years and who, if others had been there before us, [they] would have made mention of it, and if they had not seen these themselves, would at least have heard of it from their ancestors."[25]

The source of the tale that Van der Donck recounted was "the many Indians, or natives, still living there and old enough to remember." The same can be said for the handful of other tales, of a vintage actually associated with the first European arrivals, that have been reported from elsewhere in the Northeast. They are, however, different in their composition and detail from Van der Donck, whose mentions of "heaven," "hell," and "devils" do not reflect anything of Indian cosmological leanings and thus, must be labeled suspect. From William Wood (1634) of Massachusetts Bay Colony it is learned that the Indians "tooke the first Ship they saw for a walking Iland, the Mast to be a Tree, the Saile white Clouds, and the discharging of Ordinance for Lightning and Thunder, which did much trouble them." A year earlier, a Montagnais told the Jesuits of his grandmother's recollections of the first French ship her people had seen on the St. Lawrence. "They thought it was a moving Island; they did not know what to say of the great sails which made it go."[26] Yet the remainder of the story that Van der Donck insists some Indians gave him was, without doubt, of his own creation. Incorporating such "information" into his treatise was meant to establish a firm historical, and thus legal, footing for Dutch claims of discovery to New Netherland, which the English had unrelentingly challenged from virtually the time of Hudson's voyage.[27]

The next known rendition of the first arrival of Europeans is from summer 1754, when the commissioners of several colonies and Iroquois headmen gathered for what was to be the most important meeting of the era, the Albany Congress. Also present, although in a minor role, was a contingent of Indians from Schaghticoke (New York), accompanied by so-called River Indians, many of whom had traveled from Stockbridge. Together these were a mix of Mahicans and refugees from New England's Indian wars.[28] At one point in the proceedings, a nameless River Indian recounted this story of the first "White people": "Our Forefathers had a Castle [village] on this River [the Hudson], as one of them walked out he saw something on the River, but was at a loss to know what it was, he took it at first for a great fish, he ran into the Castle and gave notice to the other Indians, two of our Forefathers went to see what it was and found it a Vessel with Men in it, they immediately joyned hands with the people in the Vessel and became friends."[29]

As with Van der Donck's story, this too takes an interesting turn, revealing the Indians' most pressing concerns: the loss of their lands, their precarious economic situation, and, although unstated, their anxiety over the fast-approaching war. "We will give you a place to build a Town," the Indians, presumably Mahicans, had said to the "White people" who arrived shortly after Hudson. "Our Forefathers," they continued, "told them they were now a small people," and taking note of the Europeans' apparent vulnerability, they "took and sheltered them under their arms." The Mahicans saw at once that the interlopers in their country were few, but since these Indians "were very numerous and strong, we defended them in that low state." And then, with the business of the congress before them, the Indians laid out their case to the commissioners. Now the situation was reversed, they began, "you are numerous and strong, we are few and weak, therefore we expect that you will act by us in these circumstances, as we did by you in those we have just now related." The Indians' spokesman went on to raise their chief complaint: that [white] people were "living about the Hills and woods, although they have not purchased the lands — when we enquire of the people who live on the[se] lands, what right they have to them, they reply to us that we are not to be regarded, and that these lands belong to the King." The encroachments on what they claimed were their lands, the Indians added, had driven off the game, "and we are not like to get our livings that way; therefore we hope our Fathers will take care that we are paid for our lands, that we may live."[30] Their plea, however, fell on deaf ears. The commissioners had more important matters to attend to. At the close of the congress, the Schaghticoke and River Indians left empty-handed. They had, nonetheless, reaffirmed their allegiance to the Crown.

The last recorded, thoroughly Mahican narrative to address the arrival of Europeans is from John Quinney in 1854. Quinney (1797–1855), born in central New York, was a descendent of a Mahican headman and became an important leader of the Stockbridge community in Wisconsin. In a speech presented at a Fourth of July gathering in Reidsville, New York, southwest of Albany, Quinney offered his take on the encounter. "At a remote period, before the advent of the Europeans," he told his

Natives on the Land

audience, "their [the Mahicans'] wise men foretold the coming of a strange race, from the sunrise, as numerous as the leaves on the trees." The prophecy was realized, and for the very first time the Mahicans "beheld the 'pale face.'" Although few in number, "their canoes were big." The visitors' white skin suggested illness, and asking for "rest and kindness," they were given both. "They were strangers and we took them in—naked, and we clothed them." At first the Mahicans were astonished yet filled with pity for these strangers, views, according to Quinney, that soon were "succeeded by awe and admiration of superior art, intelligence and address. A passion for information and improvement possessed the Indian—a residence was freely offered—and covenants of friendship exchanged."[31]

Quinney's brief account makes no mention of the one element common to the previous two, namely, a "rare" or "great" fish. It does, however, repeat the description of the arriving Europeans as being few in number and in need of aid and shelter. But Quinney was no ordinary person. He not only was a leader of his people but also acted as their principal representative in dealings with the United States and New York governments. He dominated the political scene for over two decades.[32] In doing so, Quinney may have had occasion to read or otherwise familiarize himself with some of the historical and administrative records concerning his ancestors in the colony and state of New York, including that of the 1754 Albany Congress and the petition of the Schaghticoke and River Indians, which tells the story of that first meeting between Hudson and the Mahicans. And as that story laid out the disadvantaged condition of these Indians amid land loss, poverty, and an impending war, Quinney's followed a similar, although wider path. "My friends," he began the familiar yet entirely accurate refrain, "I am getting old, and have witnessed, for many years, your increase in wealth and power, while the steady consuming decline of my tribe, admonishes me, that their extinction is inevitable—they know it themselves, and the reflection teaches them humility and resignation, directing their attention to the existence of those happy hunting-grounds, which the Great Father has prepared, for all his red children."[33]

Where were his people who had once numbered 25,000, and could field 4,000 warriors, Quinney asked? "They have been victims of vice and disease, which the white man imported." The intruders were also the source of the factionalism and feuding that tore at the fabric of Mahican communities, he explained, rendering them a disorganized and defeated people. Finally, Quinney revisited the central complaint that had been made at the 1754 Albany Congress — of lands lost — one that would be repeated over time not only by Indians in New York but also by those living throughout the East. "Nothing that deserved the name of purchase was ever made," he maintained. Deeds were often given without payment or for lands other than those stipulated. The titles to lands allegedly abandoned were extinguished, with laws made only after the fact to confirm questionable takings. "Oh! what a mockery!! to confound justice with law," Quinney lamented. Then he issued this challenge to his audience: "Will you look steadily at the intrigues, bargains, corruption and log-rolling of your present Legislatures, and see any trace of the divinity of justice?"[34]

There is a final tradition that, while purportedly Delaware or Lenape in origin, is at the same time linked to the Mahicans. It was first published in Moravian John Heckewelder's 1819 *History, Manners, and Customs of the Indian Nations*, regarded by many — for better or worse — as a standard source on period Indian ethnology. The tale that Heckewelder had taken down "many years since from the mouth of an intelligent Delaware Indian," being a "correct account of the tradition existing among them," describes in some detail the first arrival of Europeans. Although its immediate source was the Delaware Indian, Heckewelder allowed that the Mahicans "concurred in the hospitable act" of welcoming the Europeans.[35] This was not, however, Heckewelder's first telling of the story, nor did it originate with the same author. Two decades earlier, in 1801, a nearly identical version had surfaced, one that Heckewelder said had been related "verbatim" to him forty years earlier "by aged and respected Delawares, Momeys [Munsees], and Mahicanni (otherwise called Mohigans, Mahicanders)." Further, "It is copied from notes and manuscripts taken on the spot," a task, one must presume, Heckewelder handled himself.[36]

The picture of Heckewelder sitting down at an unspecified location, and by his reckoning at a time before he had begun work as a missionary, to record what is a composite oral tradition from Indians of several different nations, stretches the imagination. That he disagrees with himself as to the source of the tradition does not improve things. Yet he does, in part, save himself with this qualification: "As I receive my information from Indians, in their language and style, I return it in the same way. *Facts* are all I aim at, and from my knowledge of the Indians, I do not believe everyone's story. The enclosed account is, I believe, as authentic as anything of the kind can be obtained."[37] This or similar expressions of wariness surrounding Native veracity do not mean, however, that the individual threads that had been woven together to produce the tale are not of value or import. But they must be understood in context and by their purpose as intended by the Indians who told their stories and in the manner that they were recorded.

The geographical location of the first encounter as Heckewelder has it — at the mouth of the Hudson River — makes it difficult to link it to the Mahicans or to what little is known of their first encounter traditions. There are, nonetheless, several elements in the story that exist in the earliest accounts. One that fits with what the Indians imparted to Van der Donck is that the *Halve Maen* was initially believed to be a large fish (or perhaps another kind of animal). However, in short order it becomes a multicolored house filled with living creatures. The creatures were men, one of whom was dressed in red. He offered the Indians drink, which when consumed by one of them, caused him to stagger about and fall to the ground. Others join in the drinking and become intoxicated. The man in red then hands out to the Indians beads, axes, hoes, and stockings.[38] The red clothing, this time put on the backs of Indians, was reported by Juet as the *Halve Maen* passed through Munsee country, as was the drunkenness while among the Mahicans. But neither mentions of red clothing—whether coats, cassocks, or duffels—or drunkenness are unique. Both are found in any number of first accounts.[39] Then comes the self-deprecating image that Heckewelder tells us the Indians painted for him, of wearing the hoes and axes given them as ornaments around their necks.[40] As attractive as it is, the tale of a land scam, where the Dutch requested "only so much land as the hide of a bullock would cover," which, when cut into a thin, continuous strip and laid on the ground, encompassed a larger expanse of land than the Indians had imagined, was linked by Heckewelder to Dido (aka Elissa), the mythical Queen of Carthage. This admission perforce removes it from the context of a Native tradition.[41] A virtually identical rendering is said to have come from the Micmacs, along with a variation collected from the "Lenapees," where chair lacing or caning was employed.[42]

The narratives of what are assumed to be "first contact" or "first encounter" events between Indians and Europeans in the Hudson Valley, most probably and not surprisingly, may represent forms of myth built around pieces of history—real events. Myths are widely acknowledged to be a means by which people the world over explain the origins of one thing or another. Their fundamental purpose is to provide a concurrent or *post factum* justification, a frame of reference, for what goes on in a society. Yet it is difficult to construe the brief oral traditions presented, the elements of which are limited to the arrival of the *Halve Maen*, as anything more than simple literary forms, that is, interpretations of an asserted experience. Importantly, however, in the 1754 and 1854 versions they reflect attempts to inform their audience of a particular Indian concern at a particular time or, in Van der Donck's exposition, his own "national"

loyalties amid claims of discovery. Heckewelder's is an elabora-
tion on a theme. To impute any further meaning, even for Heckewelder's two more lengthy narratives, would be conjecture.[43]

Mapping the Mahicans

The earliest map to identify the Mahicans by name and location
is the "Figurative Map of 1614," attributed to or based on information supplied by Adriaen Block, the history of which is ex-
haustively discussed in Stokes's *Iconography of Manhattan Island*
(map 3).[44] Presented to the States General of the Netherlands in
October of that year, it depicts the entire coastline from northern
New England to New York Bay, in addition to the interior sections of southern New England west of Narragansett Bay and for
the length of the Hudson Valley to Albany. The map, however,
is a composite, with the coast of New England, south to about
Cape Cod, drawn from the maps of Samuel de Champlain published in 1613 and the lost maps of Jan Cornelisz May, who had
sailed the coast of New France in 1611–12. Block may also have
seen other maps, including perhaps a rough draft of Hudson's
discoveries at the mouth of the Hudson River.[45]

Adriaen Block (b. ca. 1567, d. 1627), a native of Amsterdam,
was a career seaman and enterpriser who, before 1611, when he
made his first voyage to North America, had sailed to Italy, the
East Indies, and along the Iberian coast. His second voyage in
early 1612 was aboard the *Fortuyn*. He sailed again on the *Fortuyn* late in 1612, returning to Amsterdam at the end of July 1613.
It may have been on this trip that construction of Fort Nassau,
the fortified trading house at the mouth of the Normanskill
River at about Albany, was begun. On a fourth voyage, Block's
ship, the *Tijger*, was destroyed by fire, presumably while at Manhattan Island. He is believed to have returned to *patria* on Hendrick Christiaensen's ship, also named the *Fortuyn*, that previously had been operating on the Hudson.[46]

Block's survey of the coast of southern New England, the first
made by a European, probably was completed before his fourth

MAP 3. Block Map, 1614 (detail). From I. N. Stokes, *Iconography of Manhattan*, volume 1, 1915. Reprint, New York: Arno Press, 1967.

voyage. Also, there is every indication that he had sailed up both the Connecticut River and the Hudson, in the latter case, to near Albany.[47] It is this section of the "Figurative Map" that Block is believed to have produced himself. Of immediate interest is his drawing of the Hudson Valley, which is shown from its mouth above Manhattan Island to Fort Nassau, on Castle Island just south of Albany. Block's notation at this latter location, in Dutch, translates as follows: "Fort Nassau is 58 feet wide inside the walls in a square/the moat is 18 feet wide." In the left-hand margin at this point is written: "The house is 36 feet long and 26 wide in the fort."[48] At about the midway point of the river,

Natives on the Land

MAP 4. Hendricksz Map, 1616 (detail). From I. N. Stokes, *Iconography of Manhattan*, volume 1, 1915. Reprint, New York: Arno Press, 1967.

beginning on the west side and extending across to the east, is printed "Mahicans" in large Roman script, the earliest known attestation of this name.

A second map, routinely referred to as the "Figurative Map of 1616," was produced by Cornelis Hendricksz, skipper of the *Onrust*, the first ship built by the Dutch in the Americas (map 4).[49] After spending three years in New Netherland, Hendricksz returned to *patria*, where his patrons presented a petition to the States General, requesting trading privileges for the territory he had "discovered" while there. It was submitted with a short report and his map, which together confirm that he had fully explored the Hudson River during his sojourn, perhaps completing a survey contemplated by Block or Hendrick Christiaensz.[50] On this map the word "Mahicans" is placed on the east side of the Hudson, across from Fort Nassau on Castle Island and adjacent Papscanee Island. Shown lower down are the Schodack Islands. As is discussed and established later, this section of the valley was the core settlement area of the Mahicans from contact through to about the middle of the eighteenth century.[51] Subsequently produced maps, the information for many of which was derived from those drafted earlier, place "Mahicans" or "Mahikans" at this northerly location. These include Willem Blaeu's "Nova Belgica et Anglia Nova" (1635) and Janssonisus's 1636 reprint of De Laet's 1630 "Nova Anglia Novum Belgium et Virginia," among others.[52]

Blaeu's "Nova Belgica et Anglia Nova" (1635) is of added interest as it contains two drawings in the upper right-hand corner that are identified as Mahican villages (map 5). However, there is no evidence for or firsthand descriptions of palisaded villages anywhere in the Hudson Valley or bordering western New England for the contact or postcontact period. Furthermore, one of these villages strongly resembles "The towne of Pomeioc" on North Carolina's coastal plain, done in watercolor by John White during his visit to the region in 1585.[53] Later on, both villages from the Blaeu map appear in an illustration, along with the figure of an Indian, in a 1651 Dutch-language publication. Now, however, the villages have been transformed, the caption reading, *"een Mahakuaes Indiaen met hun Steden en woningen,"* that is, "A Mohawk Indian, with their towns and dwellings."[54]

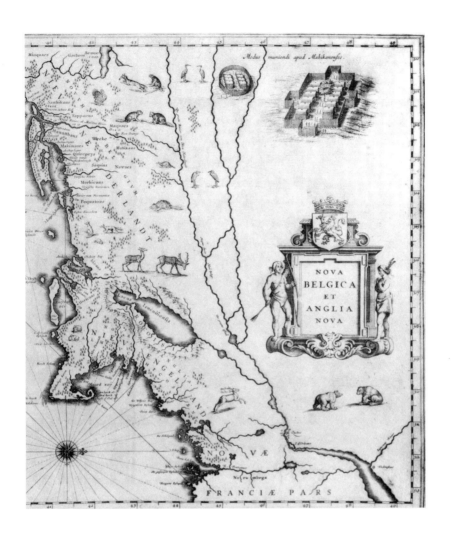

MAP 5. Blaeu Map, 1635 (detail). From I. N. Stokes, *Iconography of Manhattan*, volume 1, 1915. Reprint, New York: Arno Press, 1967.

Three

Mahican Places

Sites, Subsistence, and Settlements

Archaeological sites reflecting contact and postcontact period Native lifeways in the upper Hudson Valley, while present in some number, have been inadequately or incompletely studied. Moreover, descriptions of artifact assemblages, along with settlement and subsistence data, in the few instances where they have been examined and interpreted, remain largely unpublished. Reflecting something of this inattention is the fact that there is but a single though authoritative syntheses of the region's archaeology from 1600 forward.[1] It is also noteworthy that the association of these sites with Mahican people is based almost exclusively on their location in what is believed to have been Mahican territory, a nonetheless credible assumption given the supporting historical documentation, to which some limitations must apply.[2]

There are more than thirty reported late precontact sites in the upper Hudson Valley believed to be Mahican.[3] Most are in proximity to the Hudson River or are found along tributary streams. They form three geographical clusters, two of which are on the Hudson (map 6). Here the more northerly cluster of the two is on both sides of the river, from just above Albany, south to the Schodack Islands. The other, also on both sides, extends from Four Mile Point at the mouth of Stockport Creek south to the vicinity of the Roelof Jansens Kill below Germantown (maps 1 and 2). The six sites comprising the third cluster are to the north of the previous two, in the southern two-thirds of Saratoga County. Whether this last cluster encompasses lands

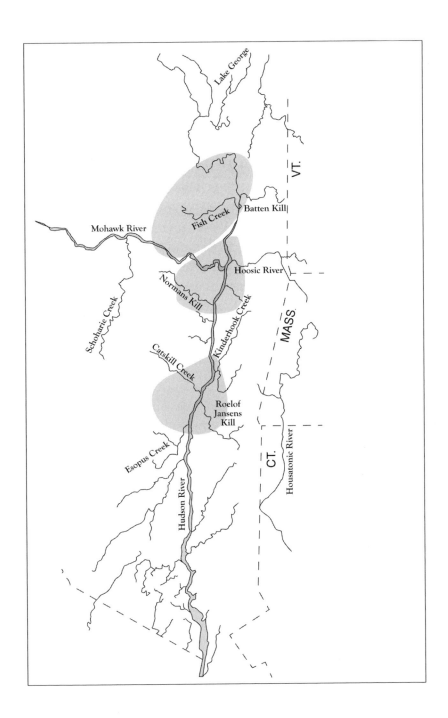

Lake George

VT.

Mohawk River

Fish Creek

Batten Kill

Hoosic River

Normans Kill

Schoharie Creek

Kinderhook Creek

MASS.

Catskill Creek

Roelof
Jansens
Kill

Housatonic River

Esopus Creek

CT.

Hudson River

MAP 6. Mahican Site Clusters, 1600. After Bradley, *Before Albany*.

that were once part of Mahican aboriginal territory is contestable. From the outset it is not possible to tie artifacts or any other evidence recovered from these sites to ethnic Mahicans or, for that matter, to other nearby, historically known Native groups.

The lack of cultural specificity of site assemblages in the region, especially along the boundary between Mahicans and Mohawks, has long been recognized.[4] That is, most archaeologists agree that the means to determine whether the occupants of a precontact or contact period site were unambiguously Mahicans or Mohawks through an analysis of artifacts — in particular, ceramics — does not presently exist, although there are other voices.[5] Moreover, historical documentation for Mahican occupancy or even nominal control of the lands within which lies the third cluster and beyond is generally lacking or, where present, has been accorded undue probative value.[6]

A consensus interpretation of Mahican settlement and subsistence patterns for the late precontact period, where sites are found near prime fishing areas and arable lands close to the river, is one reflecting the activities of foragers, fishermen, and, to a somewhat lesser extent, horticulturalists. Although corn and other crops were grown, routinely requiring a semisedentary people, these Indians appear to have been relatively mobile, their dispersed homesteads and camps suggesting seasonal occupations and adaptive flexibility and opportunism. Of the makeup of their settlements, however, little is known.

The first and, to date, only Mahican dwellings known archaeologically are from the Goldkrest site, a small riverside camp on the east bank of the Hudson near Papscanee Island, south of Albany. Discovered in 1993, site excavations uncovered the outlines of an oval structure twenty-six by thirty-six feet and another, rectangular in floor plan, thirteen by thirty-six feet.[7] The former presents a house form common to Algonquian-speakers resident throughout southern New England — the wigwam. The latter more closely resembles a typical Iroquois house, although it is much smaller.[8] Still, it is recognized that rectangular pole-framed and bark structures were common to Native groups in the mid-Hudson Valley and the adjacent Housatonic Valley, to the east, from at least the early eighteenth century and perhaps before.[9]

There are seven sites attributed to Mahican occupancy for the early postcontact period, circa 1600 to 1624.[10] As with the previous set of sites, all are located on the Hudson River or its tributaries stretching the considerable distance from Fish Creek south to the Schodack Islands (maps 1, 2, and 6). Although these sites have been subject to relatively little archaeological examination, they do not appear to differ in any significant degree from the previous settlement pattern of small, seasonal camps. In what survives of Hudson's journal is the only known description of a Mahican dwelling for the period. At the place where he had been taken ashore by a Mahican headman, he saw "a house well constructed of oak bark, and circular in shape, with the appearance of having a vaulted ceiling." A new translation of this passage reads: "a house well constructed of oak bark, and rounded as if it had been an arch." In either case Hudson is describing the dome shape of a wigwam, the ubiquitous dwelling of Algonquian-speakers whether resident in the Hudson Valley, on Long Island, or throughout much of New England.[11]

For the period 1624 to 1640, very little is known of Mahican sites. There are just four whose artifact assemblages fit the time frame, two on each side of the river. Of more than passing interest, however, are two locations that appear on the so-called map of Rensselaerswijck, drawn in 1632, one labeled "*Monemins* [Moenemins, Moenimines] *Casteel*" and the other "Unuwats [Unúwats] Casteel."[12] Dutch *Casteel* (*Kasteel*) is castle, a term routinely applied to fortified or palisaded Native settlements by seventeenth-century Dutch settlers of New Netherland. Monemin's castle may have been on Peebles Island at the confluence of the Mohawk and Hudson Rivers, while Unuwat's castle is believed to have been in north Troy. However, no evidence for either place has been discovered or has survived in the face of extensive ur-

ban development.[13] The consensus among historians and archaeologists nevertheless remains: at no time did the Mahicans erect
palisaded villages. Still, it is important to note that on the so-
called Minuit Map, dating from 1630, at what appear to be the
same locations as the above-mentioned castles, there is written
"*vasticheyt*," that is, "stronghold," which in English suggests a fortified place or a secure place of refuge (OED).[14] Whether the application of this term was to indicate a palisaded village or something else is anyone's guess. What can be said is that there are
no other mentions of anything resembling a palisaded village or
settlement in the primary documents on New Netherland or for
the Mahicans residing in the upper Hudson Valley.[15]

There are nine sites containing components reflecting Indian
occupation for the decade from 1640 to 1650, all of which are in
accepted Mahican territory. Of significance during the course
of this decade was the growth of the colony on the upper river around Fort Orange, accompanied by an increased demand
for land, which would over time be acquired from individual Mahicans. And while remaining on their traditional lands,
most Mahican settlements appear to have been situated outside of the boundaries of the patroonship of Rensselaerswijck,
although this may be an artifact of site visibility rather than oc-
currence.[16] There is little evidence of subsistence practices, although the presumption must be that there had been few substantive changes from previous times. In addition, it has been
suggested that by midcentury there were two groups of Mahicans on the river, one of which, having split off from the other,
becoming the "Katskils" or "Katskil" (Catskill) Indians. Their
land holdings were said to be on the west side of the Hudson,
below the southern boundary of Rensselaerswijck.[17] Whether
such a division of the Mahicans had in fact occurred, or rather, that the Mahican-speaking Catskill Indians had always been
in place as a separate community on the west side of the river
but before about 1650 had gone unnoticed or unreported by the
Dutch, is discussed later.[18]

Mahican Places

From midcentury to the English takeover in 1664, the Mahicans began a shift away from what had been the center of their territory, now Rensselaerswijck and beyond, while at the same time, choosing to cultivate alliances to their east. To their west, however, there continued the Mahicans' longtime antipathy to, and now and again clashes with, the Mohawks. The handful of widely scattered sites considered to be Mahican offers little other than their presence. Although it might be surmised that sites may today lie beneath developed municipalities such as Catskill and Hudson, or are yet to be discovered, this is cold comfort to researchers intent on understanding more of Mahican people through archaeology.

Demography

Estimating the aboriginal population of North America, including that of the Mahicans, is not an inconsequential undertaking.[19] The implications behind the careful appraisal of numbers of people for understanding subsistence economies, settlement types, and sociopolitical organizations, and through this, the broader questions of cultural dynamics and adaptation, are significant. Moreover, given the widely recognized devastation wrought by exogenous epidemics and the accompanying decline in populations, rigorously derived demographic data can be of considerable assistance in providing a window into the postcontact experiences of Indian people. These often appear as a number of interrelated biocultural factors that served to disrupt in-place cultural systems.

However, for all practical purposes, calculating the size of Mahican populations or attempting to evaluate previous estimates are exercises in futility. This is the case whether pre-epidemic or immediate post-epidemic populations are considered, not to mention those for the decades that followed into the colonial period. First, there is a lack of a substantive and testable archaeological record against which to measure populations. That is, archaeologists cannot, at present, provide the "addresses" for whatever number of Mahican people might have existed from 1600 through to the Revolution, although there are a few exceptions from the early eighteenth century.[20] Missing is adequate information on house types or the number and form of Mahican settlements for any time period, essential elements for generating sound population estimates.[21] Second, there are insufficient data from documentary sources, including firsthand accounts, from which numbers of people might be calculated.

An oft-cited estimate of the precontact Mahican population is derived from hypothesizing the extent of the territory occupied or controlled by these Indians (17,000 square kilometers) against an equally hypothesized population density of 31 persons per 100 square kilometers. The resulting population size is 5,300, subsequently revised to 6,400.[22] Clearly, however, these or similarly derived figures must remain at the level of conjecture due to the lack of knowledge on what may actually have been the boundaries of Mahican aboriginal territory, setting aside questions about the relative accuracy of the population density used. Recent late precontact estimates, projected from existing archaeological data, are lower, in the range of 2,000 to 3,000, although these are by admission impressionistic. Nonetheless, once the full range of the available evidence is carefully weighed, these numbers are probably the most realistic.[23]

The earliest documented figure given for a Mahican population is from Kiliaen van Rensselaer, the patroon of Rensslaerswijck, writing in 1634: that "in their time" the Mahicans had been "over 1600 strong."[24] For unknown reasons, this number has in at least three cases been reported as a count of warriors only, leading to an aggregate population estimate of 4,000 to 4,500, and a second of 8,000.[25] In the same paragraph, it is noted, Van Rensselaer gives the totals, in morgens, of cleared land ("over 1200") and "mountain and valley" land ("far more than 16,000") that he evidently believed was still held by the Mahicans, suggesting that both the population and land mass estimates may have stemmed from in-field observations, perhaps by his representative in the colony, Bastiaen Jansz Krol.[26] Four years earlier, Krol had arranged with several Mahicans to purchase the huge tract of land on the northern stretch of the Hudson River that would become Van Rensselaer's patroonship, encompassing approximately what is today Columbia and Albany Counties.[27] If these lands had, in fact, been excluded from other Native holdings, Van Rensselaer may have been referring to the islands (and environs) at Schodack, which the Mahicans initially resisted alienating. Indeed, they did not begin selling off parcels of their lands there until the 1640s.[28]

In the end, however, there is no way of knowing to whom Van Rensselaer was alluding when he furnished a population figure of "over 1600 strong." Was his count restricted to those Mahicans living in and around Rensselaerswijck? Was he aware of or did he consider Mahican communities located elsewhere in the area—for example, that in the vicinity of Catskill Creek and another in the upper Housatonic Valley—the presence of which in that region is discussed later?[29] These questions are unanswerable.

Epidemics: Impact and Aftermath

The generally untroubled first years of contact between the Dutch and Indians of the Hudson Valley were undoubtedly marked by mutual appraisals, measured speculation, and certainly, economic considerations. However, standing in the shadows were European-introduced diseases that would prove catastrophic for Native communities wherever they struck. This is not to say that Indians had no experience with illness and debilitation before the arrival of Europeans. Several lines of evidence point to the presence of viral influenza and pneumonia, along with other respiratory disorders. There were dysenteries, salmonelloses, and other forms of food poisoning, in addition to arthritides resulting from infection, trauma, and metabolic and neurogenic disturbances, among others. There also were anemias and a host of dental pathologies. Somewhat more controversial are the questions regarding whether tuberculosis and syphilis were present before contact or had been introduced by Europeans or Africans.[30]

The first reported exogenous epidemic in the Northeast struck the coastal Algonquians of New England in 1616. First diagnosed as bubonic plague, to which have been added hepatic failure due to a hepatitis virus and, most recently and convincingly, leptospirosis complicated by Weil syndrome, it does not appear to have spread into the interior.[31] Dutch sources are silent on what would have been an obvious contagion among the Indians of the Hudson Valley until the late 1620s. In a letter to merchant Samuel Blommaert, describing Manhattan Island and surroundings, along with the local Indians, Isaack de Rasière, secretary to the Dutch West India Company, wrote: "Up the river [the Hudson] the east side is high, full of trees, and in some places there is a little good land, where formerly many people have dwelt, but who for the most part have died or have been driven away by the Wappenos."[32] This statement is suggestive of a malady of unknown origin that appears to have killed a noticeable number of Munsee-speakers in the immediate vicinity of the lower valley, perhaps representing the earliest exogenous epidemic in the area. It may have been smallpox, the most deadly of the foreign diseases (followed by strains of typhus and measles). Others believed imported by Europeans included diphtheria, cholera, scarlet fever, typhoid, mumps, pertussis, pleurisy, and poliomyelitis.[33]

The earliest European-introduced contagion reported for the interior was the 1633 smallpox epidemic. Its widespread and destructive nature is confirmed by virtually every English, Dutch, and French observer of the period. Although there is no direct evidence that the Mahicans were affected, the Mohawks, less than a two-days' walk west, did not escape the disease, losing an estimated 60 percent of their people.[34] Nonetheless, given De Rasière's reporting of what to all appearances were disease-related deaths among Munsees above Manhattan, and then the 1634 report of smallpox among the Mohawks, it must be con-

Mahican Places

cluded that the Mahicans were also involved at about the same time, although precisely when and to what degree is unknown. There is but a single hint from the period of the impact of exogenous epidemics on Indians living in the Hudson Valley. Writing in 1655, Adriaen van der Donck was told by unidentified Indians that since the arrival of Europeans, "their numbers have dwindled owing to smallpox and other causes to the extent that there is now barely one for every ten."[35]

It has been claimed that by 1700 Mahican populations had decreased from several thousand to 500, however, no source for this latter figure is provided.[36] What can be documented at about this date is that the number of "River Indians," those living at Schaghticoke on the Hoosic River northeast of Albany, had been reduced over the preceding decade to 90 men from 250, suggesting a population decline from an aggregate of about 750 to under 300.[37] This Indian community, which had been established by New York's colonial governor Edmund Andros in 1677, consisted of Mahicans and refugee groups from New England—Sokokis, Pocumtucks, Nonotucks, and others—that had arrived following King Philip's War.[38] It is not possible, therefore, to extract from these or other data the total number of Mahicans in the region, ending, for all intents and purposes, further efforts to estimate their population.

The Mahicans, as did all other Native people in the Northeast, most certainly suffered untold losses from the diseases that were carried to them by Europeans and also by neighboring Indians who had become infected. But this was not a one-time event. As was the case elsewhere in the Americas, the Mahicans were visited by recurrent epidemics that exposed them to cycles of population decline. While acknowledging the absence of any firsthand descriptions of what might have occurred, such casualties, beyond question, had a profound effect on their communities. Reliance instead must be placed on drawing comparisons to groups where there is more complete information.

It is accepted, for example, that high rates of disease mortality were accompanied by steep drops in fertility, thereby restricting the ability of a population to recover its numbers. Socialization processes, along with political organizations, became disordered as high rates of death led to the loss of important leaders, not to mention knowledgeable and influential persons, the so-called culture bearers. Routine tasks associated with subsistence and the maintenance of settlements could not easily be carried out; health care practices were severely challenged; genealogical ties, obviously critical to the kin-based social fabric of all Native communities, were severed; and technological knowledge was lost. There are, moreover, indications that the toll in Indian lives aroused anxiety about the efficacy of religious beliefs or spirituality. The depiction of the aftermath of the seventeenth-century epidemics as a "new found Golgatha" is unfortunately, and tragically, fitting.[39]

Four

Native Neighbors

The Mohawks and the Upper Iroquois

Beginning some thirty-five miles west from where the Mohawk
River enters the Hudson was the homeland of the Mohawks,
an Iroquoian-speaking people (map 7). Their large, often palisaded, and densely populated villages, situated on hilltops and
low terraces adjacent to the Mohawk River, were confined to an
area that extended just under forty miles along a narrow east to
west axis. Their heavy investment in labor-intensive horticulture, evidenced by extensive fields of corn, beans, and squashes
planted on the river's fertile flats, mandated a commitment to
sedentism, while the returns from hunting, fishing, and foraging completed the subsistence cycle. Although precise boundaries cannot be known, the land area that the Mohawks exploited
away from their villages and fields, chiefly for hunting, extended
north toward the Adirondack Mountains; south to the Catskills;
west to the boundary they shared with the Oneidas, between
East and West Canada Creeks; and east to about the confluence
of Schoharie Creek and the Mohawk River.[1]

Firsthand knowledge by Europeans of the Mohawk homeland
and settlements did not come until the visit of three employees of the Dutch West India Company in 1634. Led by Harmen
Meyndertsz van den Bogaert, the party was directed by the commissary of Fort Orange to travel west into Iroquois country to
investigate the decline in the fur trade. The trio would travel as
far as Oneida country, some one hundred miles into the interior.
While among the Mohawks, Van den Bogaert reported that there

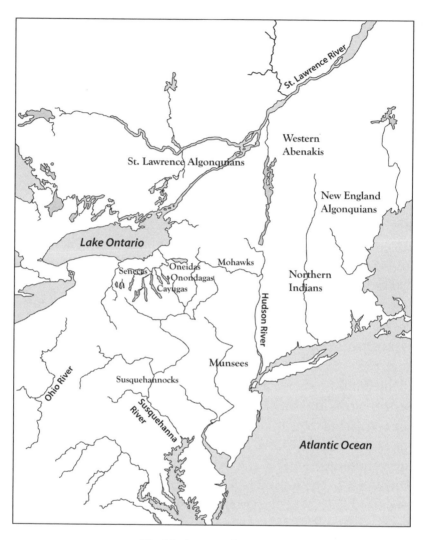

MAP 7. The Native Northeast, 1600–1675.

were eight villages, several of which were palisaded.[2] It has been proposed, however, that not all eight were fully occupied, as the Mohawks may have been in the midst of moving from older villages to those newly constructed at the time when Van den Bogaert passed through. The Mohawk population just prior to 1634

Native Neighbors

and the devastation wrought by the first exogenous epidemics in this region is estimated to have been about 7,500.[3]

To the west of the Mohawks were located four other Iroquois peoples, all of whom would, to one degree or another, eventually be participants in the economic and political activities centered around Fort Orange and then Albany. These were the Oneidas, immediately west of the Mohawks, followed in order by the Onondagas, the Cayugas, and the Senecas, closest to the Niagara frontier. Through time Oneida settlements remained concentrated around Oneida Creek in Madison and Oneida Counties. During the early 1600s there appears to have existed a single, large, strongly palisaded village. And as was true for all of the Iroquois, Oneida villages closely resembled the neighboring Mohawk farming communities. All indications are that these Indians' hunting territories extended north toward the St. Lawrence lowlands and south to the Susquehanna Valley.[4] The Dutch at first referred to the Oneidas as "Sinnekens" (var.). On occasion, however, Sinnekens was also used as a collective for any and all of the Iroquois who lived west of the Mohawks. Only later was the term applied and restricted to the westernmost group, the Senecas.[5]

West of the Oneidas were the Onondagas, whose two villages in the seventeenth century were located in the area between Cazenovia Lake and Onondaga Creek. Onondaga hunting parties roamed the region north toward Lake Ontario and south to about the fork of the Chenango and Tioughnioga Rivers above Binghamton.[6] Moving farther west were the three villages of the Cayugas, sited between Cayuga and Owasco Lakes. As with the other Iroquois, these Indians' hunting territories also lay to their north and south, stretching from Lake Ontario to the Susquehanna River.[7] Last were the Senecas, a populous Iroquois people whose historic homeland was south of Rochester, between the Genesee Valley and Canandaigua Lake, where they occupied two large principal villages. The Senecas hunted the area north to Lake Ontario and south to the headwaters of the lesser

Finger Lakes. After the mid-seventeenth century, they extended the boundaries of their hunting and fur-trapping lands to the west, eventually ranging into Ohio and southern Ontario.[8]

The Munsees: Downriver Algonquians

Munsee is an Eastern Algonquian language that was spoken by the numerous Native communities that occupied western Long Island, northern New Jersey, northeastern Pennsylvania, and the Hudson Valley, north from the river's mouth to about Catskill on the west bank and Tivoli on the east, then west to the upper Delaware Valley, and east to about the New York–Connecticut border. At no time did any of these groups form single political units. Nonetheless, given their cultural and linguistic affinities, even in the face of their wide geographic distribution and the existence of many named groups, they have been historically and collectively referred to as Munsees.

The consensus view of Munsee-speaking groups, whose names are found recorded in the earliest primary sources, in addition to their approximate locations, is as follows. South from about Catskill and the Mahican-speakers living on the west side of the Hudson to the highlands at West Point were the Esopus Indians. Just south of the Esopus were the Waoranecks and Warranawankongs. Inland from these groups, occupying the Delaware River valley proper, were the Minisinks. Adjacent to these Indians were the Opings and then the Rechgawawancks. Farther south were the Haverstraws, Tappans, and Hackensacks. The Raritans, who occupied northern New Jersey after about the mid-seventeenth century, were, in fact, Wiechquaeskecks who had removed from the east side of the Hudson. Living in the highlands south of Sandy Hook Bay were the Navasinks.[9]

On the east side of the Hudson, moving south from the Mahican-Munsee boundary at about the Roelof Jansens Kill, were the Wappingers, a name incorporating what appears to have been a separate group, the "Highland Indians." These Indians occupied much of Dutchess and Putnam Counties. Below the Wapping-

FIG. 1. *Unus Americanus ex Virginia*, by Wenceslaus Hollar (1607–1677), 1645. (Probably a Munsee Indian?) Library of Congress.

ers were the Kichtawanks, then the Sinsinks around Ossining, the Wiechquaeskecks in the southern portion of Westchester County, and last the Rechgawawanks, who resided at about Yonkers, the Bronx, and Manhattan Island. There are hints in the early records for the existence of other although poorly understood groups to the east of these. Western Long Island Indians included the Nayacks, Marechkawiecks, Canarses, Rockaways, and others.[10]

Seventeenth-century firsthand accounts describing what were clearly Munsee groups offer little about their communities, subsistence practices, or settlement patterns (fig. 1).[11] What accounts do exist depict a people practicing a mixed economy based on hunting, fishing, foraging for wild plant resources, and the planting of corn, beans, and squashes, as was the case for the Mahicans. Given the incompleteness of the archaeological record, in addition to the scarcity of documents, it is impossible to assess the importance of any of these food-producing activities relative to others, or how they may have been carried out in terms of method, scheduling of effort, or seasonal emphasis. There is a similar general lack of evidence for or descriptions of Munsee house types or the configurations of their camps or hamlets. Within the last decade, however, useful comparative archaeological modeling of subsistence economies and settlement patterns has been carried out for late precontact and postcontact period sites in the mid-Hudson Valley.[12]

Munsee pre-epidemic population estimates are many and varied, the most recent claiming 12,000. Earlier estimates range from 24,000 to 51,000. In the absence of a strong archaeological record, however, these figures must remain tentative.[13]

The Housatonic and Connecticut Valley Algonquians

Identifying, naming, and locating seventeenth-century Housatonic Valley groups, in particular those inland occupying the area beginning twenty to thirty miles north from Long Island Sound, pose some problems. This is due in large part to the upper valley's ruggedness and inaccessibility, which delayed early European exploration and settlement. Thus, there are few firsthand accounts from the early period, excepting those materials generated by colonial administrations. In addition, and related to the lack of written records, there have been difficulties in working out the complex linguistic boundaries in the valley and in adjacent eastern New York. A clearer picture, such as it is, does not emerge until about 1700 and somewhat later for the northern two-thirds of the Housatonic Valley.[14]

There is little doubt that the upper Housatonic Valley, from roughly the far northwestern corner of Connecticut into southwestern Massachusetts and then west from these locales into New York, was early on occupied by Mahican-speakers, that is, by what have been called the Westenhook or Housatonic Indians. In the first decades of the eighteenth century these Indians were reported living in two villages, Wnahktukook and Skatehook in Massachusetts colony, with possibly another just west of Stockbridge. Linguistic evidence suggests, however, that previous generations may have been in the area for a considerable period of time. Also in the early eighteenth century, and downriver from the Housatonics into Connecticut, there were at least two other small communities of Mahicans. However, the duration of their tenure in the valley is unknown.[15]

From about this point in the valley, south from the Macedonia Creek watershed, which drains into the Housatonic River at Kent, to about Derby, lived a number of named Native communities that remained poorly understood until the last third of the seventeenth century, including the Weantinocks, Potatucks, and others. Those Indians nearest Long Island Sound, referred to collectively as the Paugussetts, had been contacted by Europeans in the early 1600s.[16]

Excepting the Mohawks and the other Iroquois, all of whom practiced an intensive horticulture supplemented by hunting, fishing, and foraging, the Natives of this part of western New England lived very much like those in the adjacent Hudson Valley. A wide range of available plant and animal resources seems to have been exploited, in addition to an unquantified reliance on horticultural products, the usual corn, beans, and squashes. For this region in particular, community size and configuration at contact are difficult to determine. Mat and bark-covered wigwams are believed to have been the dwellings of choice throughout.[17]

The Lake Champlain Region

This region begins at the St. Lawrence River, running directly south the length of the Richelieu River and along the east side of Lake Champlain. It then follows the Berkshires, continuing to the Vermont-Massachusetts border. To the west it crosses the St. Francis and Connecticut Rivers, reaching the White Mountains and the Merrimack River Valley. This was the homeland of the Western Abenakis, commonly called the Abenakis, from their own name *wǫbanakii*. Component cultural groups within the Abenakis were the Sokokis of the upper Connecticut Valley, including the Cowasucks at Newbury, Vermont, and the Winnipesaukees and Penacooks of the upper Merrimack River. There is uncertainty about the affiliation of the Amoskeag, Souhegan, Nashaway, Pawtuckett, and Naamkeek farther down the Merrimack. The entire Vermont shore of Lake Champlain had been Abenaki country, documented as such since the 1670s and probably for decades earlier, with settlements positioned at the mouths of many of the major feeder rivers. However, by the eighteenth century most of the Indians in these places had withdrawn to Missisquoi, near Swanton.[18]

There is very little known ethnographically about this region or the Abenakis who resided there for much of the seventeenth century. Indeed, it is generally regarded to be terra incognita until after King Philip's War in 1676.[19] The rest is reconstruction employing late precontact assumptions and postcontact responses to European intruders and the consequent movements of Native groups throughout this part of New England, where a highly flexible, fluid, and opportunistic lifeway was most advantageous. Reflecting this adaptation, Native people appear to have organized themselves into small core communities that were then linked to dispersed family groups that hunted, fished, and foraged, following the changing seasons and resource availability in the surrounding area. There are mentions of horticulture being practiced and the existence of corn fields.[20] It has been estimated that some 10,000 Abenakis were resident in the Merrimack and upper Connecticut River drainages and east of the Richelieu River and Lake Champlain before they were struck by European-introduced diseases.[21]

The St. Lawrence Valley Algonquians

The Algonquian-speakers north of the St. Lawrence Valley, distant from and peripheral to the Mahicans, were communities of closely related peoples who inhabited the Ottawa Valley and the adjacent region to the east. Those in the Ottawa Valley were the Otaguottouemins, Kichesipirini, Matouweskarine, Weskarini, and Onontchataronon, in addition to others, all of whom were collectively referred to as the Algonquins.[22] To the east were the Montagnais. In the history of New France and in the colonies, the Algonquins and Montagnais, along with the Iroquoian-speaking Hurons, were known as the French Indians, that is, the Native allies of the French.

Evidence for reconstructing Algonquin culture for the seventeenth century is extremely limited and difficult to assign to any particular group. It is assumed, however, that the Algonquin subsistence economy was similar to that of the nearby Nipissings and Ottawas, where emphasis was placed on hunting and fishing. Because of the region's short growing season, the practice of horticulture could be only marginally successful and a risky endeavor at best. Algonquins lived in longhouses, that is, lengthy pole-and-bark structures having rectangular floor plans.[23] There are no population estimates for these Natives.

The Susquehannocks: Iroquoians of the Susquehanna Valley

The Susquehannocks were known to the Dutch, and also to the Swedes on the Delaware River, as the Minquas. Susquehannock was the seventeenth-century English name for these Indians. In the eighteenth century it became Conestoga, a corruption of a name given them by the Iroquois. The French, borrowing from the Hurons, used Andaste. By the time of Hudson's arrival, the Susquehannocks had relocated from the upper Susquehanna Valley between about Athens, Pennsylvania, and the Binghamton, New York, area, to the Lycoming Valley along the North Branch of the Susquehanna River. There these Indians, who were fully involved horticulturalists, constructed and lived in one or two large, heavily fortified towns.[24]

During much of the seventeenth century the Susquehannocks successfully resisted attempts by Europeans to settle in their lower Susquehanna Valley country. As a consequence, there are virtually no firsthand reports or descriptions of their culture, the ethnographic details of which remain essentially unknown. What does exist, however, is a relatively substantial record documenting trade relations, diplomatic meetings, and military engagements with Europeans and other Natives. None of this, however, protected these Natives from disease, unrelenting warfare, and then out-migration, which rapidly and catastrophically reduced their numbers from about eight thousand at the time of the encounter to just two or three hundred less than a century later. The Susquehannocks entirely disappear from the archaeological and documentary record by the end of the 1700s.[25]

Five

The Ethnographic Past

Assessing the Documentary and Published Record

The Native people living in the Hudson Valley at the time the Dutch arrived either had previous firsthand encounters with Europeans or were well aware of their presence in nearby regions, in particular, the St. Lawrence Valley. To what degree these experiences may have affected the form or complexion of Indian societies at this early date is unknown. In the absence of a written language, their histories were undoubtedly recalled through epic tales, complex cosmologies, or other narratives, none of which were recorded save for Hendrick Aupaumut's late eighteenth-century account.[1] There are no other detailed descriptions volunteered by the Mahicans themselves (or by neighboring Native groups) of their way of life at or following contact. What survives instead are the commentaries, reports, and correspondence of European observers, the substance and quality of which vary considerably.

Information sufficient to reconstruct, in any comprehensive manner, an early to mid-seventeenth-century ethnographic portrait of the Mahicans is lacking. Dutch sources from the period—there are few others—that remark upon the Mahican people are notable in their lack of specifics or, it must be said, their indication that there was anything more than a passing interest in these Natives, at least enough to write about.[2] Much of this is explained by the focus of the Dutch on the trade in furs, their raison d'être in New Netherland. Moreover, assuming a stance much different from the French in Canada or the English in New England, the Dutch never launched an effort to proselytize the Indians. Such activity, as it did elsewhere, would likely have produced correspondence or reports offering details on the Indians deemed useful to those who would minister among them.[3] Prior to the English takeover in 1664, just eleven ordained ministers had, at varying times over the half century of Dutch dominance, assumed posts in New Netherland, five of whom returned to *patria* after their contracts had expired.[4] Being spread as thin as they were, whether serving congregations of their countrymen in New Amsterdam or at Fort Orange (later Beverwijck) and the patroonship of Rensselaerswijck, surely forestalled any substantive interaction of a religious bent with the Indians around them.

It is also the case that the Dutch, unlike the English and French, did not establish their colony of New Netherland following the usual imperialistic European design. On the contrary, it was "the laxity of Dutch imperialism" that drove the venture. That is, the Dutch maritime empire "never developed the territorial commitment usually associated with the empires of Holland's chief rivals for imperial splendor." Rather than operating, as did other European powers, under the weight of government restrictions, it was the financial potency of private merchants that fueled successes in New Netherland and in other Dutch colonies. Moreover, New Netherland's path, from trading post to settlement colony, rendered it unique alongside its Dutch contemporaries.[5] Equally important, the existence of the colony was not widely perceived as something to fear by Native people living outside of its borders who apparently saw for themselves economic, social, political, and even military advantage to be had. This is not to say that there was no resistance from within, as the bloody and tragic wars waged between the Munsees and the ultimately victorious Dutch in the 1640s and again in the late 1650s into the 1660s attest.[6] There is little to suggest that Dutch interests in the Natives extended much beyond their perceived utility as traders in furs or persons from whom land could be

The Ethnographic Past

purchased, that is, as economic assets, or as potential threats to the colony's survival. Little else of their way of life seems to have mattered to the Dutch.

The depiction of a presumed and, regrettably, routinely accepted ethnographic past for the Mahicans resident in the Hudson Valley in the seventeenth century exists in the form of a small number of relatively recently published works, none of which are entirely reliable. The first of these, published by Ted J. Brasser in 1974, fails to systematically reference or identify the sources from which he supposedly drew his information, which renders much of what he reports about the Mahicans unverifiable. Many of the works Brasser does list are dated, anecdotal, or barely ancillary local and academic histories that do little more than repeat each other, offering no new information beyond what was known from the scattered Dutch accounts.[7] The second set of works, by Shirley W. Dunn, either uncritically restates many of Brasser's unfounded assertions or creates others through the injudicious application of comparisons to adjacent Native groups.[8] In the end what Brasser and Dunn produced contain a good number of largely unsupported, if not invented, constructions of Mahican culture, replete with astonishingly well-rounded descriptions of their settlements, seasonal activities, economy, ceremonies, social organization, ideology, kinship, and the like.[9]

Rather than acknowledging the spottiness and frustrating incompleteness of the primary sources and then applying (at minimum) the method of controlled comparison as a first effort to close the evidentiary gap, both Brasser and Dunn instead chose to borrow heavily and indiscriminately from the literature on Algonquians and Iroquoians, in particular the Mohawks. In the majority of cases the analogies drawn, done in the near total absence of suggestions in the historic or ethnological record that there might be some basis for their application to the Mahicans, are unjustified or off the mark. The result is a rather unhelpful pastiche on Mahican culture that has, unfortunately, made its way into the mainstream literature, where many of Brasser's and Dunn's misconceptions are uncritically repeated.[10]

The primary sources, which are limited in their number and scope, furnish but a bare outline of what was specifically *Mahican* culture in the seventeenth century. Complicating matters, it is often impossible to know precisely which Indians of the Hudson Valley and environs these early accounts were describing—the Mahicans, the Munsees, the Mohawks, or a mix, a composite, made up of two or all three of these Native groups. For example, in his history Van Wassenaer describes a ritual practitioner, calling him *Kitzinacka*, a name that is Munsee in origin. Later he provides words for the numbers one through ten, all of which are in the Mohawk language. Still later, he writes about Mahican beliefs of the afterlife.[11] Suggesting, perhaps accurately, a kind of region-wide cultural uniformity among the Indians, De Laet mused that the Indians of New Netherland were all "of the same general character as all the savages in the north," differing "from one another in language though very little in manners."[12] About a decade later, David de Vries compared the Indians in the vicinity of New Amsterdam to the Mahicans upriver: "their manner of living is for the most part like that of those at Fort Orange; who, however, are a stronger, and a more martial nation of Indians—especially the Maquas [Mohawks]."[13]

The most detailed descriptions by far of the Indians of the Hudson Valley are by Adriaen van der Donck, writing first in 1649 and again in 1655. Yet his portrayals contain little that point to a specific Native group, leaving readers to infer affiliations through other information. What is more, there are strong indications that in several important instances Van der Donck relied on the writings of his seventeenth-century peers, such as Champlain, who was describing St. Lawrence Valley Algonquians; Van den Bogaert, who had paid a visit to the Mohawks and Oneidas in 1634–35; Megapolensis, whose focus was the Mohawks; De Vries, writing on the Munsees; Roger Williams, who lived among the Narragansetts of southeastern New England;

and perhaps others.[14] Similarly, a decade after the English take-over, Jasper Dankaerts produced a journal of his and fellow La-badist Peter Sluyter's travels through the mid-Atlantic colonies and into Massachusetts. It includes a general account of the Indians in the region. The ethnographic detail he recorded, however, is derived chiefly from Van der Donck, along with other writers of the period. What might be considered Dankaert's original contributions focus by and large on what he believed to be the character and demeanor of Native people.[15]

Drawing comparisons to seventeenth-century Natives residing in regions immediately adjacent to Mahican country must be approached with caution. Written descriptions of the period—Dutch, English, or French—tend to present an unfavorable view of the Indians or, conversely, a sometimes idyllic one. Seldom do we see a rendering of the more rounded middle ground—a normative view of Native cultures. In most cases Europeans were barely, if at all, conversant in the languages spoken by the Indians they were observing. Neither were they afforded, nor did they usually choose to entertain, a full view of the societies they encountered. Driven by their immediate interests in trade and colonization, and constrained by their general lack of understanding and biases, Europeans tended to impose their own views and standards on Native people and their cultures.

A Way of Life: Seventeenth-Century Mahican Culture

What the Land Provided

Ethnographic information found in the primary sources specific to the *Mahicans* at contact and thereafter is limited in scope. The exceptions are the general, yet incomplete, descriptions of subsistence practices, leadership, and religion. As mentioned before, the Mahicans practiced a foraging, fishing, and farming economy that is readily inferred from the routine observations in the documents of Native foodstuffs including game, fish, and wild fruits, along with corn, beans, and squashes. Given the ecological and cultural history of the mid-Atlantic and southern New England regions, the widespread presence of these food resources among Native groups is not surprising.[16] What is not understood, however, is the degree to which the Mahicans relied on certain foods, that is, the portion of their diet that consisted of either fish, game, wild plants, or crops of corn, beans, and squashes—and as a corollary, the apportionment and management of time and labor in the practices of hunting, fishing, gathering, and farming.

Although it is impossible to know the relative contributions of food varieties to the Mahican diet, there is little doubt as to the importance of farming. Entering a house in the Mahican village that he visited, Hudson remarked on the "great quantity of maize, and beans of the last year's growth" stored there. Near the house "for the purpose of drying [was enough] to load three ships, besides what was growing in the fields."[17] Some years later, in 1634, Kiliaen van Rensselaer would report that the "territory" that the Mahicans apparently had retained after vast tracts of land had been sold off, included "over 1200 morgens [2,400 acres] of cleared land . . . the 1200 cleared morgens being not only fat, clayey soil of itself but yearly enriched by the overflow of high water there when the ice breaks and jams. The same lies ordinarily from three to five feet above water, according as the tide runs high or low (and yet it is fresh water)."[18]

Translated by Van Laer as "cleared land," the original Dutch in this passage is *suyver lant* 'clean land', that is, tillable or arable land that had been made ready by human agency.[19] On such lands the Indians grew corn, the stalks of which supported varieties of pole beans. Squashes or pumpkins grew in the spaces between corn hills. Van der Donck remarked that the Indians in the lower valley were "unacquainted with plowing and spadework, and do not keep their lands tidy." Yet "they raise so much corn and green beans that we purchase these from them in fully laden yachts and sloops."[20] Van Rensselaer's further mention of soils being "fat" or fertile, also clayey, and that they were amended through the actions of spring floods, in addition to their elevation above the Hudson River, point to their forming the river flats probably in the vicinity of Papscanee or the Schodack Islands. That the Mahicans had prepared portions of this acreage on which to farm is a reflection of their considerable investment in horticulture. This, in turn, suggests that the labor-intensive nature of a farming economy would have required the Mahicans to have been more sedentary than previously thought.[21] Nonetheless, due regard must be given to the possibility that, in the intervening quarter of a century between Hudson's voyage and Van Rensselaer's report, the Mahicans had increased their reliance on farming. If so, this may have been a response to their involvement in the fur trade, forcing a shift in emphasis in their economy; or to the sale of their lands, thus limiting their access to the full range of otherwise available game and wild plant resources; or to a combination of these and undoubtedly other factors.[22]

Leaders and Governing

The interest that the Dutch expressed in leadership among the Natives they encountered is not surprising given their own notions of government and the need to identify and then transact whatever business there was with those presumed to be persons of authority. This was especially the case for the purpose of purchasing Indian land, a process that began in Mahican country in 1630. In his instructions to Bastiaen Jansz Krol, at the time the commissary at Fort Orange, Van Rensselaer directed that lands be acquired from the Mahicans, the neighboring Mohawks, or "such other nations as have any claim to them." However, in the event that Krol could "not purchase the said lands from one or two nations, that he purchase the same from all who pretend any right to them."[23] The implication is that a purchase from a nation, rather than from any other entity, would perforce be accomplished through an arrangement between Krol and those who ostensibly represented that nation, that is, its leaders. Even so, there is only limited evidence to suggest that land purchased in the upper Hudson Valley by Van Rensselaer, or subsequently by any other Dutch official or private person, was done with the participation of identifiable Mahican leaders. This circumstance reveals more about the reality of such transactions when compared to the stated, perceived, or imagined ideal of how they should have proceeded.[24]

Shedding further light on the overall business of Native leadership was the promulgation of the provisional regulations for the colonists of New Netherland by the West India Company in 1624, by which officials there were authorized "to make alliances and treaties with foreign princes and potentates in that country residing near their colonies."[25] The titles for those holding positions of power or authority found in the regulations follow European usage. Even so, it is evident that any such engagements with the Natives, including the Mahicans, would have required the involvement of their headmen. As historian Oliver Rink explains it: "In the early years of New Netherland's settlement, the Dutch were very careful to appease the Indians of the region and to avoid conflict," although "the [West India] Company's assumption of the power to make alliances and treaties with the Indians would cause the colony much grief in the future."[26]

The Dutch early on recognized that there were leaders among the Indians in the Hudson Valley, at the time of Hudson's voyage characterizing an elderly Mahican man a "Governour of the Countrey," and others as "chiefe men."[27] De Laet, writing in a context that included excerpts from Hudson's journal, observed that Natives "much less have they any political government, except that they have their chiefs, whom they call Sackmos, or Sagimos." He later expanded his description, noting *"sackmos"* and *"sagamos"* are "not much more than heads of families, for they rarely exceed the limits of one family connection."[28] In like fashion Van Wassenaer reported that "there is little authority known among these nations. They live almost all equally free. In each village, indeed, is found a person who is somewhat above the others and commands absolutely when there is war and when they are gathered from all the villages to go to war. But the fight once ended, his authority ceases." This chief, he continued, is named "a *Sacjama*, but above him is a greater *Sacjama* (pointing to Heaven) who rules the sun and moon."[29] Michaëlius provided "*Sackiema*, by which name they — living without a king — call him who has the command over several hundred of them."[30] All of these terms are phonetic variations of Proto-Eastern Algonquian *sa·ki·ma·w* 'leader' or 'chief', rendered by the English as "sachem" or "sagamore" and by the Dutch as "*sakemaas*" or "*sackamacker*." *Sackamacher*, as used by the Dutch, was derived from Unami *sa·k·i·ma* 'chief' via pidgin Delaware.[31]

Isaack de Rasière, a West India Company official writing from Manhattan, saw Indian governments as "democratic." "They have a chief Sackima whom they choose through election, who generally is he who is richest in sewan [wampum], though of less consideration in other respects."[32] When an opinion voiced by the Sackima is agreed to by the community, "they give all together a sigh — 'He!' — and if they do not approve, they keep silence, and all come close to the Sackima, and each sets forth his opinion till they agree."[33] In much the same way, Van der Donck observed that "government is of the popular kind, so much so that it is in many respects defective and lame. It consists of the chiefs, the nobles, and the tribal and family elders. Only when military matters are being considered are the war chiefs consulted as well. These together constitute all there is of council, governance, and rule." Still, these comments by Van der Donck must be weighed carefully for there are signs that at least one detail of his knowledge of political process was drawn from writings on New England Indians.[34] There are additional examples of such borrowings to be found in the primary documents.

From all indications, much of the decision-making process took place in councils of one sort or another. There, the Indians

consider everything at great length and spare no time when the matter is of any importance. . . . When a matter has been decided in the aforesaid manner, the populace is summoned to the chief's house or wherever the council has met. A person gifted in eloquence and a strong, penetrating voice is called upon to speak. He recounts in the fullest detail, in a formal address and as agreeably as he can, what was deliberated, decided, and resolved.[35]

David de Vries, a participant in what he described as a peace council with some "two or three hundred" Munsees, found the lengthy, ritual-laden process, not at all to his liking. "There was one among them who had a small bundle of sticks, and was the best speaker, who began his oration in Indian." Used as mnemonic devices, the sticks were laid down one at a time to mark or emphasize points of the speaker's presentation. "Then he [the speaker] laid down one of the sticks, which was one point," De Vries wrote. "He then laid down another stick. This laying down of sticks began to be tedious to me, as I saw he still had many in his hand." Finally, though, "the speaking now ceased and they gave to each of us ten fathoms of *zeewan* [wampum]—which is their money. . . . Then they all rose up and said that they would go with us to the fort [Fort Orange] and speak with our governor."[36]

How Mahicans assumed leadership or emerged as leaders is unknown, nor are their duties or responsibilities described. The same is true about decision making. However, as with similarly organized small-scale, egalitarian societies in the region—which would on most levels exclude the Iroquoians—headmen held their positions through merit or achievement and decisions were reached through consensus.[37] De Laet's observation, just cited, that Native leaders in the Hudson Valley were "not much more than heads of families" is undoubtedly as accurate as any statement to be found in the primary literature. This is especially the case given that there is no evidence that during the seventeenth century the Mahicans formed a single political or social unity.

Religious Expression

Most early European observers referred to Indian, sometimes Mahican, religious phenomena and their often presumed shortcomings. Nonetheless, it is difficult to know, on the basis of the surviving primary record, how much early Dutch chroniclers actually experienced or understood of what they thought to be religious behaviors, if this is what they saw at all. The earliest known comments on religion among Hudson Valley Indians, who are left nameless, are the most instructive. In 1624 Van Wassenaer observed: "We as yet cannot learn that they have any knowledge of God, but there is something that is in repute among them. What they have is transmitted to them by tradition, from ancestor to ancestor. They say that mention was made to their forefathers many thousand moons ago, of good and evil spirits, to whose honor, it is supposed, they burn fires or sacrifices. They wish to stand well with the good spirits; they like exhortations about them."[38]

Van Wassenaer went on to conclude that the Indians cared "nothing for the spiritual, they direct their study to the physical, closely observing the seasons," yet his account nonetheless provides a number of characteristics commonly associated with religion.[39] Included are the Indians' "tradition" of knowledge regarding "good and evil spirits"; the "sacrifices" offered them; their "exhortations" about "good spirits"; their wishes to "stand well" in their regard, all of which are unquestionably aspects of religious behavior.[40]

Although divination is usually regarded as part and parcel of religious practices, it was Van Wassenaer's view that "the science of foretelling or interpreting of events is altogether undeveloped and unknown to [the Indians in the Hudson Valley]; delivering no oracles or revelations of the one or the other sort, as they have very little knowledge of future or past things."[41] In an example of religion put to work for the benefit of the community, he described the role or responsibilities of the *Kitzinacka* (Munsee), who, Van Wassenaer supposed, was a "priest," remarking: "When any one among them is sick, he [the *Kitzinacka*] visits him; sits by him and bawls, roars and cries like one possessed. . . . When a child arrives at the age of twelve, then they can determine whether he shall be a *Kitzinacka* or not. If he says so, then he is brought up to such office. Becoming of age, he undertakes the exercise of it."[42]

One of the most frequently cited, if disparaging, portrayals of Native religion is that by a firsthand observer of Hudson Valley Indians—the Reverend Jonas Michaëlius. Writing in 1628, he found Native people to be "proficient in all wickedness and godlessness; devilish men, who serve nobody but the Devil, that is, the spirit which in their language they call Menetto; under which title they comprehend everything that is subtle and crafty and beyond human skill and power. They have so much witchcraft, divination, sorcery and wicked arts, that they can hardly be held in by any bands or locks."[43] For all of his fulminations, Michaëlius nonetheless hints at a possible relationship between "Menetto" and daily Indian concerns.

In the Latin edition of his *Nieuwe Wereldt* (1633), De Laet elaborated on the subjects of Native religion and the important concept of "Menetto": "They have no sense of religion, no worship of God; they indeed pay homage to the Devil, but not so solemnly nor with such precise ceremonies as the Africans do. They call him in their language *Menutto* or *Menetto*, and whatever is wonderful and seems to exceed human capacity, they also call *Menetto*; evidently in the same manner in which, as we have mentioned above, the Canadians use the word *Oqui*."[44]

Manétto (var.), under French-language influence written as the familiar *Manitou*, is an Algonquian word used to express power—natural and supernatural, positive or negative—or the cultivation of power. More broadly, it suggests tutelary spirits that embody such power. Expressions of *Manitou* were to be found among Algonquian-speakers throughout the Northeast.[45]

Van der Donck's midcentury comments on Indian religion followed the tone set by his countrymen: "They are all heathens, have no particular religion or devotion, and no known idols or images they venerate, let alone worship. . . . They do know something of God . . . and are in great fear of the devil, for he harms and torments them. When they have been out fishing or hunting, they customarily throw a portion of the catch into the fire without ceremony and say, 'There, devil, you eat that.'" Echoing Van Wassenaer, Van der Donck continued: "They live without religion and inner or outward devotion; even superstition and idolatry are unknown to them, and they follow the dictates of nature alone."[46]

These descriptions aside, there is no way to know the religious preferences or practices of the Indians of the Hudson Valley at or before contact, save for falling back on ill-conceived ethnographic analogies and generalizations written centuries later and found primarily in the secondary literature. What can prudently be said is that these Indians, including the Mahicans, most probably structured their way of life in a manner similar to other northeastern Natives—that is, around locally configured modes of diverse, uncompartmented, and, importantly, dynamic relationships to persons and powers in their environment, both naturals and supernaturals.

Lacking in the record of the 1600s are mentions of planting or harvest ceremonies, rites of passage, or other similar expressions of religion.[47] There are, however, three instances of Mahican ritual behavior that were recorded at Stockbridge in 1734 and 1735, all of which are appropriately contextualized temporally and described in detail later.[48] For now, in one of these a deer taken in a hunt is butchered and, following an invocation by a ritual functionary, is boiled and eaten. A few modern historians have, with some license, referred to this event as a "Deer Sacrifice ritual."[49] Beyond this, there are one or two other references to what were likely religious activities. Described, for example, is a divination ritual that took place in one of the upper Housatonic villages in February 1735, which observer Timothy Woodbridge saw as a form of "devotion" and "a Method of Worship," an interesting counter to Michaëlius's jaundiced views.[50]

The general nonappearance of "religious" elements in firsthand accounts from New Netherland or elsewhere in the Northeast, which usually result from their being unrecognized or simply denied to exist by early observers, raises the provocative question of the possibility of Indian nonbelief, or perhaps more accurately, a religious indifference on the part of Native people. Infrequently confronted in the literature, any resolution of this matter is made difficult by the scarcity of or an inability to interpret the evidence, but also by the absence of literacy in traditional Native societies and thus written doctrine or other commentary from which an assessment might be made.[51] Yet the idea that religion, in whatever form, may have been of small concern to some Native minds cannot be dismissed as a possible explanation for what is lacking in the record.[52]

Society

Although the details surrounding Mahican social organization for the seventeenth century are unknown, a number of general, comparative statements are found in the primary documents. Van Wassenaer, De Rasière, and De Vries all describe a system of bridewealth operating among Indians of the Hudson Valley. Bridewealth — the payment of valued goods by the social unit of the intended husband to the intended wife's social unit to validate their union — was a practice common to Native groups throughout the Northeast and elsewhere.[53] Bridewealth is not, however, a predictor of other elements of social organization, such as the form of descent groups or postnuptial residence. Suggestive of descent is an observation by Van Wassenaer, who may have been the source for a nearly identical comment by De Rasière: "It excites little attention if any one [of the Indians] abandon his wife; in case she have children, they usually follow her."[54] In addition Van der Donck, who may have read Van Wassenaer and De Rasière, also linked the disposition of children after a marriage was dissolved to descent, writing: "In a divorce the children follow the mother; many nations reckon descent accordingly."[55] A child staying with its mother or her family after a marriage ended is usually characteristic of matrilineal descent, and thus, the presence of a matrilineage. That is, the child's birthright lies with its mother, her family, and her lineage. It remains, nonetheless, that there is insufficient evidence in the primary sources to determine, with any confidence, the forms of social organization and kinship present among the Natives of the Hudson Valley at contact or thereafter.

Polygyny, a man having more than one wife, is reported for a number of northeastern Native peoples. Ted Brasser overinterprets as evidence for this practice Van Wassenaer's comment that "it is very common among them for one man to buy and to have many wives, but not in one place; when he journeys five or six leagues he finds another wife who also takes care of him." This behavior most likely reflects a form of what has been labeled "wife lending," an expression of hospitality reported chiefly in societies where there are polygynous marriages. De Vries's observation, which follows Van Wassenaer in time, that among the Munsees "the men are not jealous, and even lend their wives to a friend," appears as confirmation.[56]

The question of whether the Mahicans were organized into clans—actual or often fictive descent groups composed of several lineages—during the seventeenth century cannot be answered. Their existence among these Native people is not mentioned or described until Hendrick Aupaumut's history written about 1790. And then his assertions must be carefully considered. "Our Nation was divided into three clans or tribes, as Bear Tribe, Wolf Tribe, Turtle Tribe," said Aupaumut. "Our ancestors had particular opinion for each tribe to which they belonged. The Bear Tribe formerly considered as the head of the other tribes, and claims the title of hereditary title of Sachem. Yet they ever united as one family."[57]

In surrounding Eastern Algonquian groups early on the clan system was either absent or only weakly developed.[58] Indians in the region, at contact and for decades thereafter, resided in lineage-based communities. Moreover, the lack of clans is not unusual given the small, dispersed, and relatively mobile nature of these communities. Of interest, however, is that the clans Aup-aumut named—Turtle, Bear, and Wolf—were (and are) found among the Mohawks, just across the Hudson from the Mahican homeland, and, importantly, also among the Oneidas, next to whom the Stockbridge Indians lived beginning about 1785.[59] At minimum, then, what Aupaumut offered about Mohawk and Oneida clans, as compared to those he identified among his own people, is striking. There is also Aupaumut's description of the process to replace a deceased leader, a "sachem" in his words, which is strongly reminiscent of what was reported for the Iroquois at about the same time.

Language

Mahican, a now-extinct Eastern Algonquian language, consisted of at least two major dialects.[60] Western Mahican was spoken in the interior of the upper Hudson Valley. By the early to mid-eighteenth century, it was the dialect of the Indians at Shekomeko, located in northeastern Dutchess County, as recorded by Moravians who founded a mission there in 1740.[61] Eastern Mahican, also known as Stockbridge Mahican, was spoken by communities whose homeland was in the upper Housatonic Valley of southwestern Massachusetts and far northwestern Connecticut. It was the dialect of the Indians living at the Stockbridge mission in southwestern Massachusetts, and later at New Stockbridge in central New York, surviving until the 1930s following their move to Wisconsin a century before. Another Algonquian language, Loup B, contains demonstrated lexical and phonological affinities with Eastern Mahican. It was the original language spoken in the Westfield River area, between the Housatonic and Connecticut Rivers.[62]

The historical and sociopolitical relationships between Mahican speakers in the Hudson Valley and those on the Housatonic are poorly understood. Brasser, for example, considered Wampano-speakers resident at Weantinock, who later moved to Pachgatgoch (aka Scaticook, Schaghticoke, and various oth-

The Ethnographic Past

er versions) in the mid-Housatonic Valley of Connecticut, along with the Wappingers of the mid-Hudson Valley, to be Mahican components. Dunn has surprisingly claimed that Mahican and Mohegan, the latter language spoken in eastern Connecticut, were "very similar" languages, thus indicative of the "closeness of the Mohicans [Mahicans] to [Indian] nations in New England."[63] The Mahicans, however, were linguistically and ethnically distinct from these groups. Wampano (also Wompona) was a divergent, eastern dialect of Munsee, while the Wappingers spoke another Munsee dialect.[64] Situated between Eastern Mahican and Mohegan (Mohegan-Pequot) were a number of diverse dialects (or languages) now lumped under the term Quiripi. The Mahicans and Mohegans were not neighbors and, of course, were not related.[65]

The existence of the two dialects, one on the upper Hudson and the other on the upper Housatonic, appears to settle the question of the length of time Mahican Indians had occupied the upper Housatonic Valley, in addition to the degree of interaction between Western and Eastern Mahican dialect speakers. As a general principle, dialects develop where communication between two or more communities of speakers of the same language is limited, a reflection of historical or sociopolitical factors operating through time. Insofar as the Mahican speakers are concerned, it is likely that those living in the upper Hudson Valley had less interaction with their brethren in the upper Housatonic Valley, who, on the basis of linguistic evidence, were to some degree in communication with Indians to their east.[66] Later, the appearance of Dutch and English intruders, along with the resultant political disruptions and demographic shifts, changed the nature of the relationships among Indian communities situated between the Connecticut and Hudson Rivers, bringing them into closer contact.

Until now, a degree of uncertainty has existed about whether the geographically separated Mahican groups were identical, related, or distinct populations. Patrick Frazier speculates that the Housatonic Mahicans "once lived closer to the Hudson, but moved east to the Housatonic, where among other things it was less crowded and where game was probably more plentiful." Elsewhere, statements on their affiliation and origins are somewhat more equivocal, with questions raised about Mahican occupancy of the upper Housatonic Valley in the early and mid-seventeenth century. Dunn maintains that it was "very likely, although not documented, that some of the Mohicans [Mahicans] were attracted from the Housatonic Valley to the Hudson Valley when the Dutch first came, in order to trade furs and obtain products, and possibly to strengthen the nation in its fight with the Mohawks." Brasser, on the other hand, and also lacking evidence, has this movement reversing by 1700, when "many Mahican families removed to the territory of the related Housatonok [sic] Indians, after the latter were all but exterminated by the smallpox."[67]

What may be the first reference to the Housatonic Mahicans is from 1663 and the Esopus wars: "This *Mohawk* had also said that five Indian Nations had assembled together; namely the *Mahicanders*, the *Catskills*, the *Wappingers*, those of *Esopus* besides another tribe of Indians that dwell half way between *Fort Orange* and *Hartford* [Housatonic Mahicans?]"[68] Soon thereafter, in 1666, fur trader John Pynchon (1626–1703) mentioned the "Indians at Ausatinoag [Housatonic]" firmly anchoring these Indians to the area.[69]

The Ethnographic Past

Six

The Mahicans and the Dutch

The Trade in Furs

Dutch ships began appearing on the Hudson River soon after Henry Hudson's explorations in September and early October 1609. Although the record is meager, the first vessel known to be dispatched to engage in the fur trade in what would be called New Netherland was the *St. Pieter* out of Amsterdam in 1611. Its voyage had been commissioned by a group of investors calling itself the Van Tweenhuysen Company. Others quickly followed. In 1613–14 the company sent out the *Fortuyn*, whose crew would build a small fortified trading house on an island in the Hudson River behind which flowed the Normans Kill, a large tributary that today marks the southern limit of the city of Albany. The trading house was named Fort Nassau. The island became best known as Castle Island.[1]

There is no reason to doubt that the Mahicans were the first to bring their furs to the handful of Dutch traders manning Fort Nassau, very quickly to be joined by Mohawks, Munsees, and western New England Algonquians. None of these Native people, however, was unmindful of the appearance of Europeans in the region much before the arrival of the Dutch, especially those who had made their way into the Ottawa and St. Lawrence Valleys by the early decades of the sixteenth century.[2] Even so, little is known of the first years of the fur trade in the Hudson Valley, which was overseen between 1614 and 1618 by the New Netherland Company. Once its letters patent expired, with no renewal forthcoming, the trade fell into the hands of independent traders, some of whom were nonetheless connected to merchants formerly with the company. Their dealings with the Indians on the upper river are, for the most part, unreported, except for two violent episodes, one involving the Mohawks and the other involving unidentified Indians.[3] Nothing is known of Mahican-Dutch interactions for this early period.

In 1621 the Dutch West India Company was chartered to carry on the war with Spain after the expiration of the Twelve Years' Truce (1609–1621). In New Netherland, however, the company's charge was confined to manage, and to reap profits from, fur trade operations in the colony. In the meantime, Fort Nassau, whose builders had not taken into sufficient consideration its low elevation on the Hudson River, was abandoned about 1618 due to floods. It was replaced in 1624 by a small redoubt situated on the west bank a short distance north, christened Fort Orange, erected to house a handful of Walloons from the thirty families that had sailed aboard the *Nieu Nederlandt* to begin the colonizing effort in the upper valley.[4]

For a period of time shortly before and following the building of Fort Orange, the fur trade and the future of New Netherland were in doubt. Authorities there faced a cascade of difficulties, among which were Indian complaints of mistreatment by West India Company employees; Indian-Indian conflicts that would escalate into the Mohawk-Mahican war; the grumblings of get-rich-quick colonists unhappy with the less than auspicious circumstances in which they instead found themselves; and the overall bad management, alleged malfeasance, and high-handedness on the part of director Willem Verhulst. In early 1626 Verhulst was arrested and deported. He was replaced by his assistant, Pieter Minuit.[5]

The documents surrounding the establishment of Fort Orange and the fur trade in the upper Hudson Valley offer little in the way of information on the Mahicans. What did catch the attention of the Dutch and, subsequently, historians of the period was the war that embroiled the Mahicans, the Mohawks, and also the Dutch, beginning about 1626.

The Mohawk-Mahican War

Circumstances surrounding the often written about Mohawk-Mahican war are presented in some detail and for several reasons: to provide the full geographic and cultural context of Indian-Indian conflict present at the time that the United Provinces, France, and England had first established their colonies in the Americas, information useful in understanding subsequent violent encounters; to offer the necessary comparative framework for Dutch/French/English-Indian and, importantly, Indian-Indian economic endeavors and the competition that followed; and, finally, to permit a more comprehensive assessment of changing Native strategies and adaptations in the face of the European presence.[6]

For many years, historians considered the Mohawk-Mahican war of the mid-1620s to be the first and defining example of a conflict fought in direct response to the European-introduced fur trade. The Mohawks are said to have attacked the Mahicans to force open a desperately needed corridor to the Dutch trading post at Fort Orange, having had no direct access to European goods before about 1610 and only limited access until the Mahicans were defeated about 1628; to control and restrict, when necessary, the ability of surrounding Indians to trade at Fort Orange; and to put themselves in the best possible position to pirate furs that other Indians carried to the French on the St. Lawrence River. Furthermore, it has been argued, the diplomatic, military, and economic strategies employed by the Mohawks in this war presaged or established the pattern for Iroquois involvement in the destructive Beaver Wars of the mid-seventeenth century. Notwithstanding any of these claims, it is demonstrated here that the actions of both the Mahicans and Mohawks were but a continuation of the enmity that characterized Indian relationships throughout the region and were only loosely tied to any of the economic concerns of the fur trade.[7]

A number of questionable assumptions that underlie the claims just listed bear examination. The first concerns the timing of Mohawk access to European trade goods. Recent archaeological studies demonstrate that such goods first surface on Iroquois sites after 1525, with copper pots and iron axes predominating. By about 1580 the variety of trade goods was expanding, with items appearing in larger but nonetheless modest amounts. Donald Lenig concluded that these goods had been obtained from French traders at Tadoussac and from elsewhere in the St. Lawrence Valley. In his *Native and Newcomers*, Bruce G. Trigger modifies the position he had taken in his 1971 article on the Mohawk-Mahican war, suggesting that the Indians may have traded with Frenchmen who traveled beyond Tadoussac after 1580. A contemporary Dutch source confirms that the French were indeed trading farther up the St. Lawrence River and probably had been doing so for a few years. On the face of a 1614 map of New Netherland and its environs, attributed to Adriaen Block, the Dutch sea captain and trader, is the hand-written comment: "As well as can be understood from the reports and explanations of the Maquaas [Mohawks], the French come with sloops to the upper part of their country to trade with them."[8]

As just mentioned, the Dutch had actively been trading on the Hudson River since about 1610 or 1611. And again it was not until 1614 that the first permanent Dutch trading post, Fort Nassau, was erected near present-day Albany. It was accessible and open to the Mohawks, who, along with the Mahicans, were reported to be trading with the Dutch sometime before 1616.[9] Thus, although looting may have been one means by which the Mohawks acquired trade goods, it certainly was not the only means, nor necessarily the most common.

The second assumption, which in great part is refuted by the above discussion, is that the Mohawks were landlocked, or oth-

The Mahicans and the Dutch

erwise cut off from the Dutch, and that this circumstance acted to limit their participation in the fur trade. In contrast to this view, Francis Jennings observes that, from their villages stretching westward on a line from the Mohawk Valley to the Finger Lakes region, "the Iroquois were able to travel with relative ease and swiftness in almost any direction. . . . For several decades in the seventeenth century, the Iroquois Mohawks, who were closest to Albany, exploited their location even at the expense of other Iroquois nations." Trigger adds a qualification, noting that the Mahicans did not monopolize the trade at Fort Orange and that the Mohawks were able to travel freely to trade there—and so were many others. Writing in 1624, Van Wassenaer described where some of the Indians arriving at Fort Orange had come from: "In the interior are also many, as the Maquas [Mohawks]. Full fifty leagues higher are found likewise many villages, all of which come to this river [the Hudson] to trade from the interior." Although other historians contend that the Mahicans had forced the Mohawks to "pay tribute in return for the privilege of access to the trading post," and that trade at Fort Orange "depended on the willingness of Mahicans to allow Mohawks to pass through their country (and the willingness of Mohawks to extend the same courtesy to members of the four more westerly nations of the League)," no supporting evidence is provided.[10] Accordingly, there is only one conclusion to be drawn: not unlike other Indians in the region, the Mohawks traded wherever their feet, and sometimes their canoes, could carry them.

A third assumption is that the Dutch considered the Mohawks marginal to their economic interests and instead were looking to the north and the supply of finer furs to be had there to realize greater profits. That furs from New France, and especially beaver furs, were superior in quality to those obtained farther south is an assertion most readily attributed to Harold Innis, one that has routinely been repeated by historians writing on the period.[11] This belief has actually grown in significance as the attempts to define precisely what constituted the economic motives behind the Beaver Wars have continued. For many years scholars have argued whether and at what point in time the beaver was exterminated in Iroquoia. "But the whole debate is somewhat beside the point," writes Daniel Richter, "because the most marketable pelts came from cold regions far to the north of Iroquoia, by the 1640s the Five Nations simply could not obtain enough beavers of the right kind on their own lands."[12]

Early on, Lenig brushed aside any such claim, noting that there was neither archaeological nor historical evidence to support it.[13] Notwithstanding, there do exist several early French accounts that mention the superiority of furs from the "north" when compared to those available from what is an unspecified, yet clearly distant, southern locale.[14] However, efforts to find anything in the record that would suggest that the Dutch or the Iroquois recognized a difference in furs linked to geographical or environmental region were unsuccessful.[15] More to the point, there is nothing in the scientific literature that demonstrates any significant qualitative differences between beaver pelts obtained from eastern Ontario/Quebec and the adjacent American states.[16] The question of the quantity of furs available from one region to another in the seventeenth century cannot be reached empirically, and no mention of it is found in the primary documents.

A fourth assumption, in part related to that discussed above, is that the Dutch were actively pursuing the northern fur trade, a move that potentially would be detrimental to the Mohawks, and one that these Indians viewed with considerable suspicion, if not alarm. The evidence offered in support of this assumption is the presumed objectives of an attack on the Mohawks by a combined Mahican and Dutch force in 1626 and a letter, written by Isaack de Rasière, the newly appointed company secretary, to the directors of the Amsterdam Chamber of the West India Company.[17]

Sometime in early to mid-July 1626, Mahican warriors, accompanied by several Dutchmen led by Daniel van Crieckenbeeck, the commander at Fort Orange, marched against the Mohawks. A short distance from the fort they were overwhelmed by what seems to have been a waiting party of Mohawks. Van Crieckenbeeck, three of his men, and an unknown number of Mahicans were killed.[18]

In the earliest essay on the fur trade in New France and New Netherland, historian Jean E. Murray wrote that the Mahican attack on the Mohawks was designed "probably in the hope of clearing the way to regular trade with northern Indians."[19] Writing two months after the clash, De Rasière denounced Van Crieckenbeeck's "reckless adventure," yet, Murray claimed, De Rasière nonetheless "wanted to drive off the Mohawk unless they would give 'French Indians' a free passage through their country for trade with the Dutch."[20] Murray's interpretation of events is based entirely on the Van Crieckenbeeck/Mahican debacle and De Rasière's letter and has since been restated by nearly every historian of New Netherland and New France.[21] Furthermore, it has worked to distort, in significant ways, the history of the period, because the interpretation is mistaken.

Samuel de Champlain, the de facto governor of New France, was told of the failed strike against the Mohawks on July 26, 1626.[22] Early the following year he was given a specific reason for the attack, which evidently was related to an ongoing dispute: The Mahicans had not been willing "to allow them [the Mohawks] free passage to go and make war on a nation called the Wolves, with whom the Iroquois were at enmity." The "Wolves," or Loups, as they were often referred to by the French and others, were in all probability the Sokokis, an Algonquian-speaking group occupying the upper Connecticut Valley.[23] They and the Mohawks were on-again, off-again enemies.[24] No evidence was found to support the view that the hostilities between the Mahicans and Mohawks stemmed from attempts by one or the other to seize control of the fur trade at Fort Orange.

De Rasière's letter, and its reading by historians, is a some-what more complicated matter. In the pertinent section of his letter, De Rasière observed that "Trade at Fort Orange has been very bad, on account of the war between Crieckenbeeck and the Minquaes [read "Maquas" or "Mohawks"]."[25] He then writes:

> I must sometime perforce go up the river to see whether I can get the Minquaes [Mohawks] to come to an agreement with the French Indians whereby they may obtain forever a free passage through their country. That being accomplished, I hope to carry out my de-sign of discovering Lake Champlain, and, if this cannot be done by amicable means, I beg your Honors to authorize me to go with 50 or 60 men on an expedition against them in order to drive them off, which in the end will have to be done anyway, as they are a vindic-tive race. I shall take great pleasure in it.[26]

Murray, Allen Trelease, Trigger, and other historians have read this passage to mean that De Rasière intended to go to the Mohawks to ask them to come to an agreement with the French Indians, granting them free passage through territory controlled by the Mohawks, and thence to Fort Orange and trade with the Dutch. De Rasière also was requesting authorization to march with a large number of Dutch troops against the Mo-hawks, who apparently were near Lake Champlain, blocking or otherwise hindering the passage of the French Indians trying to reach the Dutch.[27] The syntax, however, and therefore the meaning of De Rasière's words are clear. The pronouns "they" and "their" in the sentence beginning "I must sometime per-force" refer to the Mohawks, not the French Indians. The pro-nouns "them" and "they" in the sentence beginning "That being accomplished" refer either to the French Indians or to Indians other than the Mohawks. It was the Mohawks whom De Ra-sière believed should seek "free passage" from the French Indi-ans, and it was the French Indians, or Indians that he took to be French Indians, whom De Rasière wanted to drive off.

This interpretation is supported by evidence that the French

Indians already enjoyed access to Fort Orange. De Rasière himself states that they were trading with the Dutch, writing: "I suppose your Honors sent them [copper kettles] here for the French Indians, who do not want such things from us because they can get enough of them from the French near by and because they are too heavy to carry. They come to us for no other reason than to get wampum, which the French cannot procure unless they come to barter for it with our natives in the north, just as the Brownists of Plymouth come near our places to get wampum in exchange."[28] Sometime after 1621, but before November 1624, Johannes de Laet, a director of the Dutch West India Company, reported that "our skippers assure us that the natives come to the fort from that river, and from Quebecq and Tadoussac."[29] The fort is Fort Orange, built and operational in mid-to-late summer of 1624, and the river is the St. Lawrence.[30] In an entry dated November 1626, which follows a description of the Van Crieckenbeeck affair, Van Wassenaer notes: "The nations that come the longest distance from the north known to the traders, are the Indians from French Canada. Thereabouts are the Orankokx, the Achkokx and others, both men and women."[31] Therefore, the meaning of the passage in De Rasière's letter, taken together with the knowledge that the French Indians were trading at Fort Orange in the mid-1620s, renders all previous interpretations unsatisfactory.

The sources allow a different interpretation that more accurately reflects the events of the times. In 1622 Champlain reported: "Some time ago our savages entered into negotiations for a peace with the Iroquois [Mohawks], their enemies; but up to the present there has always been some hindrance because of the distrust existing on both sides."[32] In the hopes that an accord between the warring parties would benefit the French fur trade and at the same time ensure the safety and success of Indian trappers "who go in quest of beavers, but do not dare to go into certain parts where these abound, because they are afraid of their enemies," Champlain offered to assist in the peace effort.[33]

Informal negotiations had begun at Three Rivers on June 6, 1622, with the arrival of two Mohawks. It is unclear whether the Mohawks had initiated the talks or whether they were responding to overtures made by the French Indians. Friendly discussions ensued, with the French Indians "drawing a pledge from their enemies not to injure them, nor to prevent them from hunting anywhere in the country." The French Indians offered the same assurances in return.[34] Satisfied with the turn of events, Champlain suggested that his allies dispatch an envoy to the Mohawks with instructions to invite them to Quebec to finalize the peace.[35] The task of getting all of the Indian parties to gather there, however, dragged on for another two years. It was not until June 1624 that a formal agreement was concluded, and Champlain was not there to witness it, nor do his writings make mention of it.[36]

It has been asserted that the Mohawk-Mahican war began in 1624, almost immediately after the Mohawks and French Indians had concluded their peace, but nothing has been found to support this claim.[37] De Laet, writing in the early 1620s, noted simply that the Mohawks and Mahicans were "enemies," yet a decade later, Kiliaen van Rensselaer, the founder and patroon of Rensselaerswijck, claimed that before their war, these Indians had been "friends and neighbors."[38] Furthermore, the first fully documented indication of outright warfare is the attack on the Mohawks by the joint Mahican/Dutch force in July 1626, fully two years after the 1624 peace agreement, which itself had been years in the making.[39] It is difficult then to link directly the outbreak of hostilities between the Mohawks and Mahicans to that agreement. In the absence of evidence, it is even more difficult to suggest that this war stemmed from the intentions of the Mohawks to take control of the trade at Fort Orange. The most credible explanation for the conflict is the refusal of the Mahicans to allow the Mohawks to pass through their territory on their way to the Sokokis.[40]

The peace of 1622–24 did serve a purpose. The French Indians, Champlain had learned, "were sick and tired of the wars they had had, which had lasted over fifty years." There previously had been no serious efforts made by the Indians to end the hostilities, "owing to the desire they had to wreak vengeance for the murder of relatives and friends who had been killed."[41] Nothing was said about trade or competition over the trade as driving forces behind the wars. What the peace had nonetheless confirmed were the assurances made in 1622 during the informal negotiations at Three Rivers, one of which was to allow for "hunting anywhere in the country."[42] The problem, however, was the free exercise of this right.

De Laet, Van Wassenaer, and De Rasière all report that beginning in mid-1624 and continuing into late 1626 the French Indians were trading with the Dutch at Fort Orange.[43] That this trade was a recent development, undoubtedly tied to the presence of the newly constructed fort, is confirmed by De Rasière, who remarked: "I shall know how to get wampum and to stock Fort Orange in such a way that the French Indians will never again come there in vain as they have done heretofore, according to what I hear from those who were stationed there. This is a matter that would spoil a good beginning and whereby the Indians would be discouraged, coming from so far off and that for nothing."[44]

Before 1622–24, however, everything points to the inability of the French Indians to have traveled unscathed up the Richelieu River, into the Champlain Valley, and from there to the Hudson and the Dutch. They had been, after all, at war with the Mohawks. The peace, by design or default, opened the way for the French Indians to take their furs, or at least some of them, to the Dutch. From the Dutch they could obtain wampum, which could not be had from the French. Again, on its face, the peace granted all parties the prerogative to hunt "anywhere in the country"; that is, to move freely in the region. From all appearances, the French Indians took full advantage of this prerogative and maybe then some.

What did the 1622–24 peace provide the Mohawks beyond the cessation of hostilities? They already enjoyed access to the Dutch and their trade goods, leaving no pressing need for them to venture north to do business with the French. Should the Mohawks have been tempted to go elsewhere with their furs, there was the outside possibility of taking them to English traders operating in southeastern New England and farther north along the coast, though formal trade with the English did not begin until later.[45] Yet the Mohawks may have wanted to lend their support to the Dutch and their developing trade with the French Indians. The intended payoff would have been to draw these Indians away from the French, which would then leave the French more vulnerable to raids in reprisal for their 1609 and 1610 attacks on the Mohawks. This was a strategy that the Iroquois employed late in the seventeenth century. Once the French were gone, the Mohawks could once again turn their full attention toward their Indian foes on the St. Lawrence.

Mohawk wars with the French Indians that had taken place before the peace had made risky any movement into the contested hunting and trapping grounds of the Richelieu and Champlain Valleys. Paradoxically, this situation may have become an even harsher reality after 1622–24. The evidence at hand indicates that following the peace the French Indians moved quickly into hunting and trapping territories that had previously been open to the Mohawks — the Champlain and Richelieu Valleys — and worked to deny the Mohawks further access by placing themselves strategically at the region's southern approach. In doing so, the French Indians were able to carry their pelts to Fort Orange and at the same time exploit the rich fur resources of the area. Although this may not have been a development the Mohawks had anticipated, it was nonetheless something that they could endure for a short time as they waited to see if their larger policy aims bore fruit. In any event, the peace was short-lived, and neither the expected benefits nor the unforeseen drawbacks had much effect. Hostilities resumed in 1627.[46]

The Mahicans and the Dutch

De Rasière appears to have understood that any interference with the ability of the Mohawks to hunt and trap in the Lake Champlain–Richelieu River region would spell serious trouble for the West India Company. The trade was already going poorly, he had reported, a consequence of the war between the Mahicans and the Mohawks. An escalation of hostilities would only serve to make matters worse. His immediate interests, and those of the directors of the West India Company, were to "prevent discontent and to keep *all* the [Indian] nations devoted to us."[47] It was with these issues in mind that De Rasière proposed, perhaps naively, to approach the Mohawks and persuade them to go to the French Indians and arrange for "free passage" into what formerly had been their hunting grounds, and, obviously, where they could obtain furs to trade with the Dutch. However, unfolding circumstances would render moot any attempt to deliver such an entreaty.

The Mahicans played an important role in these events, a role that has been unduly complicated by the often imaginative history that has been written around them. Brasser contends, for example, that after Fort Nassau was abandoned around 1618, Mahican "relationships with the Algonquin to the north promised a future access to the rich fur-bearing lands of the Great Lakes"; that the Mahicans controlled the trade at Fort Orange, "while in the meantime travelling throughout the hinterlands as middlemen in the fur trade"; that the Mohawks had been "subjected to Mahican taxation in trade profits"; that the Dutch joined with the Mahicans in their attack on the Mohawks in 1626 to "maintain and increase trade relations with the northern Indians"; and that, owing to a faulty translation of the Dutch by New York historians, the Mahicans, once defeated, fled not to the Connecticut Valley but to the Hoosic River near Albany.[48] None of these contentions are sustained by the primary documents.

Jennings, in turn, creates the "Mahican Channel," stretching the full length of the Hudson-Champlain-Richelieu Valleys, where "the Mahicans . . . traveled extensively up and down *their* channel on all its waterways." It was their "friendship with other Algonquian tribes along the Mahican Channel [that] gave them control over access to the fur trading that had already become institutionalized in the St. Lawrence Valley."[49] Again, these statements are not supported by the primary documents.

Mahican friendships appear to have been restricted to Algonquian-speaking groups located mostly to their east and southeast, including the Sokokis, Penacooks, and Pocumtucks. There is little to connect the Mahicans to any of the French Indians.[50] Nevertheless, Champlain reported that in the winter of 1626–27 "some of our savages went to the settlements of the Dutch, and were asked by them and the savages of that region [Mahicans] to make war on the Iroquois." To underscore the seriousness of this joint request, which, if fulfilled, would most certainly destroy the 1622–24 peace agreement, the Dutch and Mahicans were said to have "made presents to them of wampum belts, to be given to certain chiefs."[51] These belts were carried back to the St. Lawrence, where the chiefs "decided to assemble in considerable number with the Algonquins and other nations, and to go and join the Dutch and their savages so as to form a large force, and then proceed to lay waste the villages of the Iroquois, with whom they had previously been at peace."[52]

The Dutch sources are silent on this episode. Although there is no doubt that it took place, the extent to which the Dutch were actually involved is unclear. However, the Mahicans, and possibly some of the French Indians, might have been dissembling. It must be recalled that in the summer of 1626 Van Crieckenbeeck and several of his Dutch and Mahican companions had been killed in their attack on the Mohawks. Dutch officials voiced little sympathy in their recounting of Van Crieckenbeeck's actions, which were a breach of West India Company policy to remain nonaligned: De Rasière had labeled them "reckless" in his 1626 letter, even as he was in the midst of preparing an inventory of the dead commander's personal effects, and Van Rensselaer, eight years later, remarked on the "needless wars" that

Van Crieckenbeeck had caused.[53] Although the Van Crieckenbeeck episode raises the possibility that the Dutch might have sought revenge, such a move would have been foolhardy, given their few numbers.[54]

The Dutch were very concerned about the possible consequences of this incident, so much so that a few days later they sent Pieter Barentsz, a company trader with some standing among the Indians, to speak with the Mohawks. "They wished to excuse their act," he was told, "on the plea that they had never set themselves against the whites, and asked the reason why the latter had meddled with them; otherwise, they would not have shot them." Barentsz's response to the Mohawks is not known. Soon afterward he was ordered by Pieter Minuit, the recently appointed director of New Netherland, to assume command at Fort Orange.[55]

The Dutch were determined to have the fur trade continue uninterrupted and, indeed, to expand it. Toward these ends, and despite his initial saber rattling, De Rasière fully intended to avoid trouble with any of the Indians in New Netherland and beyond, by whom he meant the Mohawks and those other Iroquois who traveled to Fort Orange; the Mahicans, along with other Hudson Valley groups; Indians from southern and western New England and Long Island; and now, the French Indians.[56] In addition, De Rasière had been contacted by the Susquehannocks, with whom he expected to begin trading as soon as possible.[57]

Making matters more complicated, De Rasière reported that there were problems with his supply of trade goods. He was unable to sell a large number of "defective kettles," and the French Indians did not want the copper kettles he had on hand because, as mentioned before, they were too heavy to carry. He also was worried about the shortage of duffels that he needed "to get wampum and to stock Fort Orange in such a way that the French Indians will never come again there in vain." This concern was reinforced by the Mohawks, who had complained to De Rasière: "Why should we go hunting? Half the time you have no cloth."[58]

Having a sufficient supply of duffels warehoused also would allow De Rasière to remain "enabled to keep the sloops continually going, and thereby prevent the Indians in the north from going to the English with their skins, as they did last spring . . . likewise as regards those from the south."[59]

Given the supply and marketing problems with which the Dutch were wrestling at this time, it is a bit of a stretch to believe that they would have considered collaborating with the Mahicans and the French Indians to launch an attack on nearby Mohawk villages. There simply was no reason for the Dutch to do so; there was nothing for them to gain and a great deal to be lost. The Dutch would have put their entire trade enterprise in certain jeopardy at a time when it can only be described as precarious. They were much smarter businessmen than to risk involving themselves in an undertaking like this. It is not so difficult, however, to believe that the Mahicans were behind such a scheme, embroiled as they were in a difficult war with the Mohawks and looking for help. It may also have been the case that some of the French Indians had grown tired of the peace with the Mohawks, short as it had been, and decided to use the Mahicans' predicament as an excuse to end it.[60]

Champlain was angered by the prospect of seeing unravel the agreement he had been instrumental in fashioning. He reminded one of the headmen that it was he who had "intervened to make peace for them [the French Indians] with the Iroquois, in view of the advantage it would be to them to travel freely up the Great River, and to other places, instead of being in terror from day to day of being massacred and taken prisoners, they and their wives and children, as had been the case in the past." Moreover, he lectured, he and the French Indians "had given our word not to make war on that people [the Mohawks], unless they had first given us cause."[61]

The question still remains as to the identity of the Indians blocking Mohawk access to the Lake Champlain region, and who it was that De Rasière wanted to "drive off" at the risk of his life.

"Even if I fly into the candle," he wrote with some bravado, "only [my] reputation will be lost. My wife and children will not lose much in me, nor will they cry."[62] These Indians were not Mohawks. It is possible that they were Mahicans, or perhaps Abenakis, who inhabited the region east of Lake Champlain.[63] Still, it is more likely that they were French Indians who, at the same time that they were trading at Fort Orange, had put themselves in a position to deny the Mohawks access to the Champlain Valley and its hunting and fur resources, and who were bent on seeing an end to the peace with the Mohawks. Even the Dutch were wary of these Indians: "On entering the [Hudson] river, if they bring women with them, it is a sign they come as friends; if they visit the yachts without these, every one must be on his guard."[64]

Champlain's pleadings to his Indian allies to keep the peace were in vain. In June 1627, soon after the Mahicans had asked for assistance, "nine or ten young hot-heads" who could not be dissuaded, went up the Richelieu River and from there to Lake Champlain, where they captured three Mohawks. One escaped, but the other two were brought to Three Rivers and then back to the mouth of the Richelieu, where trading was supposed to have taken place. Instead, the prisoners were beaten and tortured.[65]

In a conference with his Indian allies following this affair, Champlain bluntly told them that if war broke out anew, "the whole river would be closed to them, and they would neither be able to hunt nor to fish without incurring great danger, and being in constant fear and anxiety; and all this came home particularly to them, since they had no fixed abode, but lived a wandering life in scattered groups, which made them all the more feeble; whereas they should all be settled in one place, as their enemies are, who are strong for that reason."[66] The assembled Indians decided to send a delegation to the Mohawks to offer compensation for their misdeeds. On August 25, 1627, Champlain received word that the delegation had reached the Mohawks and that its members had been killed.[67] The peace was over.

The resumption of hostilities between the French Indians and the Mohawks did nothing to divert the attention of the latter from their war with the Mahicans. Van Wassenaer reported that in early 1628 "war broke out between the Maikans near Fort Orange and the Makuaes, but these beat and captured the Maikans and drove off the remainder who have settled towards the north by the Fresh River, so called; where they begin again to cultivate the soil; and thus the war has come to an end."[68] Van Rensselaer and also Champlain, however, have the war ending in 1629.[69] Whatever the case, that an unknown number of Mahicans might have withdrawn "towards the north by the Fresh River" is not at all surprising. The "Fresh River" was the Connecticut, the home of the Sokokis, their Indian allies.[70] It was the attempt by the Mahicans to protect these people in the first instance that had led to their war with the Mohawks.

Citing as authority a 1633 memorial written by Van Rensselaer to the central administration of the West India Company, Trigger maintains that after the Mahican defeat the Mohawks "made it their unswerving aim never to permit the northern Algonquians, or any other northern peoples, to trade with the Dutch except with themselves as intermediaries," concluding, "if more furs were to be obtained from the north in the near future, it would have to be by way of the Mohawks."[71] No sources attest to the resolve of the Mohawks on the issue of French Indian access to Fort Orange, but here are the words that Van Rensselaer wrote:

> Are not the contrary minded well aware that their course will never increase the trade because the savages, who are now stronger than ourselves, will not allow others who are hostile and live farther away and have many furs to pass through their territory, and that this would be quite different if we had stronger colonies? Yes, that the *Maquaas*, who will not allow the French savages who now trade on the river of Canada and who live nearer to us than to them [the French] to pass through to come to us, might through persua-

The Mahicans and the Dutch

sion or fear sooner be moved to do so and that from these savages more furs could be obtained than are bartered now in all New Netherland?[72]

Van Rensselaer's memorial was a plea to the West India Company to redress certain violations of its charter, but it also was an undisguised bid to expand his fur trading rights in New Netherland, a goal that the now elderly patroon had without success pursued for years. S. G. Nissenson offers a harsh appraisal, asserting that the memorial "was a document as remarkable for illogic, self-contradiction and pure balderdash as it was luminous in illustrating Van Rensselaer's methods in actuating the accomplishment of his objectives."[73]

Yet Van Rensselaer was not off the mark in his explanation for why it had been difficult to expand the fur trade. The Mohawks and the French Indians were hostile toward each other, and as the prime mover behind the actions of these Indians, this hostility either hindered or at times halted the trade in furs.[74] The less than salutary effect on Van Rensselaer's ability, and that of other Europeans, to increase the trade was first and foremost the by-product of long-standing Indian animosities.[75]

The Mohawk-Mahican War, although important to the understanding of Indian-Dutch-French relations, was not the signal event it has been portrayed to be. It did not establish a pattern of alliances, trade, and conflict leading to the Beaver Wars of the 1640s, and it does not shed any light on the European-derived "economic motives" that many historians claim to have been their underlying origin. The Mohawks had not been poorly positioned to take advantage of the early seventeenth-century trade; they did not make a peace with the French Indians in 1624 with the intention to then attack the Mahicans and seize control of the trade at Fort Orange; and they did not blockade the Champlain Valley to prevent the French Indians from trading with the Dutch. The primary sources simply do not describe the Mohawks, or their Native foes — whether the Mahicans, the

French Indians, or New England Algonquians — as doing very much at all of what they are said to have done.

The Dutch Establish a Colony: The Founding of Rensselaerswijck

> But since *Daniel van Krieckenbeeck,* former *commis* at Fort Orange, involved and engaged these same Manhykans in needless wars with the warlike nation of the *Maquaes,* their former friends and neighbors, they lost in the beginning their general chief named *Monnemin,* and subsequently were so hard pressed from time to time, especially by the defeat they suffered in 1629, that they resolved in the years 1630 and 1631 to sell and transfer their said lands with all their rights, jurisdiction and authority to and for the behoof of *Kiliaen van Rensselaer.*[76]

The 1630 and 1631 purchases from several Mahicans, most of whom were identified as "owners and proprietors," excepting one Papsickene (var.), who was also named a Mahican chief, established the founding land base for the patroonship of Rensselaerswijck.[77] Well-connected and wealthy persons — patroons — were authorized by the West India Company to acquire from presumed rightful owners land on which they were to settle, within a four-year period, fifty persons above fifteen years of age. In return, the patroon was granted administrative, executive, and judicial rights over his colony and allowed to pass the patroonship on to his heirs. In short, this was an attempt by the West India Company to privatize the colonization of New Netherland, a costly endeavor that the company could not bear on its own.[78] What would eventually become a one-million-acre agricultural colony, comprising roughly present-day Albany and Rensselaer Counties, was administered by Kiliaen van Rensselaer, a highly successful merchant in Amsterdam and one of the directors of the West India Company. It was Van Rensselaer who had directed Bastiaen Jansz Krol, his representative in New Netherland, and at the time the commissary at Fort Orange, to acquire land for the patroonship.[79] There was a third purchase made in 1637, and then, following Van Rensselaer's death in 1643, through to the end of the Dutch period, several others, all in the name of the patroonship or its heirs.[80]

Information on Mahican activities during the early years of the patroonship is scarce. The participation of these Indians in the fur trade can obviously be inferred by their proximity to Fort Orange, and by the appearance of trade goods on a few nearby sites discovered on the Hudson. Documented evidence of trade is from the record of an encounter between Jacob Jacobsz Eelckens, an important figure in the first decades of New Netherland, and authorities in New Amsterdam and Fort Orange.

Eelckens, a Dutchman, had been supercargo on the 1613–14 voyage of the *Fortuyn*, which led to the building of Fort Nassau, a post he would command in 1615–16. Leaving his command, Eelckens returned to the Netherlands, sailing back to the colony in 1618, only to discover the fort abandoned, which forced traders to do their bargaining from yachts or temporary quarters on shore. Eelckens would be on the Hudson in 1620 and again in 1621 on the ship *Witte Duyf*. All indications are that he had early on forged and then maintained a serviceable level of amicable and profitable trade relations with the Indians in the region, including the Mahicans. Further confirmation of his abilities comes from a 1633 dust-up he had with Dutch authorities while serving as supercargo on the English ship *William*.

The *William* and its crew had been sent to the Hudson to challenge Dutch claims to New Netherland and their control of the fur trade, reaching the river in late April. With his considerable experience in the region and familiarity with its Native residents, bolstered by his own motives obviously divorced from any loyalties to *patria*, Eelckens was key to the mission. After a stopover of several days in New Amsterdam, where there was a to and fro with the newly arrived director Wouter van Twiller over trading rights, the *William* sailed upriver to just below Fort Orange, soon trailed by a Dutch-manned caravel and one or two smaller craft.[81] For about two weeks, Eelckens carried out a lively trade with the Indians from a tent he and his crew had pitched on shore until "there came about a dozen dutch men, with half pikes, swords, musketts and pistolls" led by the commander of Fort Orange, Hans Jorisz Hontom. In the ensuing tumult Eelckens's tent was pulled down, a portion of his merchandise was confiscated, and, for good measure, the soldiers beat some of the Natives who had come to trade. As soon as the situation quieted, the *William*, with Eelckens on board, was accompanied downriver to New Amsterdam and, after further questioning of its crew by Dutch officials, sent out to sea.

In a deposition given in regard to the incident, Eelckens was described as "being well acquainted with the said Indians, having often traded with them and speakinge theire language." A second deponent added that Eelckens "was much beloved of them; and that they were a greate deale more willinge to trade with him then with the Dutch." Trade indeed. One deponent allowed that if the *William* had been permitted to stay longer on the upper Hudson, "a nation, called the Maques [Mohawks], would come downe, and bringe with them fower thousand beaver skinnes. And another nation, called the Mahiggins [Mahicans], would come downe thither with three hundred skinnes more."[82]

As best as can be determined, this is the only known statement on the numbers of furs taken specifically by the Mahicans, although there is no indication that these pelts ever made their way to Dutch traders. More disappointing, however, is that little documentation exists that would shed much light on not only Mahican trading activities, but also their settlements, economy, or other aspects of daily life from the 1630s to the English takeover in 1664, and then well into the next century. What there is tends to reflect, in virtually all instances, tension and conflict, and often outright warfare, with European interlopers and surrounding Native people alike.

The Mahicans and the Dutch

Seven

The Mahican Homeland

The Mahican Homeland

Establishing the extent—the boundaries—of the Mahican homeland at contact, and for the period of these Indians' occupancy
of the upper Hudson and upper Housatonic Valleys and environs, is a task fraught with difficulties. The basis for the earliest published description of Mahican territory is obscure and
lacks an explicit statement on sources. Those that followed are
commonly little more than unattributed restatements of this
work. The most frequently cited history of these Native people
offers no evidence for the boundaries it describes. More recent
attempts uncritically maintain that the limits of Mahican territory can be extrapolated from the large number of land sales
that took place over the course of a century and a half, that is,
between 1630 and the final decades of the eighteenth century.
This argument, however, discussed later, is absent a theoretical
framework; is shot through with anachronisms; does not take
into full consideration the motives and agendas of not only the
Dutch purchasers but, equally important, the Native sellers; and
finally, fails to reconcile or make accommodations for the movements—the shifts in location—of Mahican people through time.
Adding to the complexity of the problem is the relative weakness and thus ineffectualness of the archaeological record as a
mechanism with which to fix boundaries.

The earliest known account to situate what may have been the
main body or core area of the Mahicans is found in a passage

from the 1624 section of Van Wassenaer's *"Historisch Verhael."* The "Maikans," it reads, were "a nation lying 25 leagues on both sides of the [Hudson] river."[1] Assuming that Van Wassenaer's estimate followed the line of the river, it remains that the starting and ending points of this distance are not specified. At this early date, however, the Dutch knew next to nothing about the Hudson above Albany, which was where navigation ended. Thus, it might be reasoned that this was the northern point of Mahican occupancy insofar as the Dutch understood things. Applying the standard conversion factor of about three statute miles to a Dutch league (*mijl*), the downriver boundary of the Mahicans would have been near Newburgh, deep in Munsee country.[2] Modern scholars would agree, then, on the inutility of Van Wassenaer's acknowledged secondhand views and look elsewhere for depictions of the lands the Mahicans might have controlled, even nominally.

What in all likelihood is the first general description of the Mahican homeland, absent supporting documentation, has it that, at contact, these Indians possessed "the east bank of the [Hudson] river from an undefined point north of Albany to the sea, including Long Island; that their dominion extended east to the Connecticut [River], where they joined kindred tribes; that on the west bank of the Hudson they ran down as far as Catskill, and west to Schenectady; that they were met on the west by the territory of the *Mohawks,* and on the south by chieftaincies acknowledging the supremacy of the *Minsis* [Munsees], a totemic tribe of the *Lenni Lenapes.*"[3]

A century later a second historian, setting aside certain of the exaggerated boundaries claimed by the first, especially as they concerned the Connecticut Valley and the line drawn from Albany south to the sea, confined Mahican lands to "eastern New York and adjacent portions of Massachusetts and Connecticut in historic times."[4] In the 1970s, however, this expanse was again broadened amid claims that Mahican occupancy had extended "from Lake Champlain southward into the western part of

Dutchess County, New York, and from the valley of the Schoharie Creek in the west to south central Vermont in the east."[5] Although it is these boundaries that have been repeated by other historians, it remains unclear how they had been determined.

In his short history, written about 1790, Hendrick Aupaumut explained that the people at Stockbridge, whose lands were "partly in the State of New York, partly in Massachusetts and Vermont," had hunted moose in Vermont's Green Mountains. However, he said nothing about boundaries or to what extent any of this area had been occupied by his people.[6] Other assessments of the late precontact limit of Mahican territory are based on the distribution of archaeological sites, but they too have their limitations, rendering the setting of boundaries essentially unattainable.[7]

To approach anew, then, a consideration of the Mahican homeland, it must first be acknowledged that the documentary record, including period maps, is weak. But this has not precluded the use of what little exists in ways that are, at best, questionable. For example, on Adriaen Block's 1614 map, the earliest to depict what would be called New Netherland, the word "Mahicans," in large block Roman letters, is drawn at midvalley, straddling the river (map 3). Its position on the map, without any additional information, has been interpreted by Shirley Dunn as indicating the presence of Mahican settlements well south of the upper Hudson. When, on the 1616 Henricksen map, the word "Mahicans" appears in smaller letters farther north on the east side of the Hudson, opposite the designation "Nassau" (Fort Nassau) at the mouth of the Normans Kill, Dunn concludes that "the Mohicans [sic] could not have moved upriver so easily, unless they remained in their own territory" (map 4).[8] Needless to say, equating words on a map created by persons who were hardly familiar with the region much beyond the banks of the river with the movement of Native people or with the presumed bounds of their territory is a dubious exercise indeed. Nonetheless, it is possible to portray in a general way the extent of the Mahican homeland.

The western boundary of Mahican country was most likely formed by the eastern edge of the Catskill Mountains. The thickly forested peaks of this part of the range, which rise sharply out of the Hudson Valley, would have presented a formidable natural barrier to settlement by Native people. In fact, there is little evidence to suggest that these rugged highlands were frequented by Indians at any time during the early decades of the seventeenth century or afterward. In addition, the region would have been poor habitat for white-tailed deer, an important game animal that supplied Indians not only with meat but also with hides for clothing and footware.[9]

Late precontact and early postcontact Mahican sites are found on both sides of the Hudson Valley, stretching from Albany, about Papscanee Island, to the Schodack Islands, and then continuing south to just inside Dutchess County. Mohawk villages sat directly west of Albany, beginning at about Schoharie Creek, so the western boundary of Mahican lands north of the eastern Catskills had to have rested somewhere between the Schoharie and the Hudson River at the time the Dutch arrived. Yet De Laet, whose *Nieuwe Wereldt* was published in 1625, had the Mahicans dwelling on the east side of the Hudson, while the Mohawks were on the west side, suggesting that the boundary between these two peoples was the river.[10]

In all probability a significant portion of the land lying between present-day Albany and Schenectady early on constituted a buffer zone between the Mahicans and Mohawks and, following contact, may have been contested by them. That is, none of this land appears to have been exclusively occupied, or had access to it controlled, by either group. This situation may best be explained by examining relevant environmental and geological factors. Lying generally south of the Mohawk River, and north of the Normans Kill and the precipitous Helderberg escarpment, this area contains pine barrens and sand dunes that took form on a delta built by the discharge of the ancestral Mohawk River into glacial Lake Albany approximately thirteen thousand years ago. As such, the deep, sandy soils of what is today called the "Pine Bush" were of little use to Native farmers, nor did these appropriately named barrens support adequate numbers of white-tailed deer or other game sought by the Indians.[11]

That Mahican territory is believed to have extended north of the Albany-Troy area, and thence to Lake Champlain, appears to be based, in part, on certain land sales, the first taking place in 1683 of what would be called the Saratoga Patent. Although these lands—which lay on both sides of the Hudson River in present-day Saratoga and Rensselaer Counties—were sold by Mohawks to several prominent Albanians, a memorandum attached to the deed reads as follows: "That the Mahikans were present at the aforesaid purchase of the land at Sarachtogoe [Saratoga] and saw the Maquas [Mohawks] aforenamed receive the payment. Being asked if they had any right or claim to the said land, that they must now speak or forever keep silent, they declared they renounced all rights and ownership which they had therein, leaving it to the purchaser's discretion to give them something as an acknowledgment or not, inasmuch as in old times it was their land before the Maquas won it from them." Then, releasing the purchasers from any and all further demands, the four presumed Mahican signatories, one of whom was identified solely as a witness to the proceedings, received seven pieces of duffel, two half casks of beer, and two small casks of wine.[12]

The circumstances of this sale, in particular the unusual renunciation by the Mahican participants of any further claims to the subject lands, raises doubts about any pretensions to past "ownership." That their land had been "won" from them as a result of a war with the Mohawks, assuming that the wording of the memorandum accurately reflects what the Mahicans had said, does not accord well with consensus understandings surrounding the reasons underlying Native warfare in the region, which had nothing to do with territorial expansion or the conquest—the taking of land.[13] More to the point, neither of the Mohawk-Mahican wars, which took place in the 1620s and again in the 1660s, were fought over land.[14] Finally, it is noteworthy that the Kayaderosseras patent, a much larger tract of land north of the Saratoga patent on the west side of the Hudson, a petition for which is dated April 1703, was also purchased from several Mohawks. There is no indication, however, that Mahicans were involved or mentioned in this transaction.[15] This leaves up to question, then, how far north of the Albany-Troy area—that is, in the direction of Lake Champlain—actual Mahican occupancy or "control" can be demonstrated with any confidence.

There is no question, however, that the Mahicans occupied the lands east of and close by the Hudson River, on a line south from about Troy to the Schodack Islands, and from that place to about northern Dutchess County. Archaeological sites associated with Mahican residency in the region are firmly rooted in a sound historical record that begins shortly after the arrival of the Dutch.[16] The distance east, toward the Taconic Mountains and the Berkshires, that their lands may have reached in the early seventeenth century, however, is unknown, except for the Mahicans' occupancy of the upper Housatonic Valley. Residing there at an early date were the ancestral communities to those that would settle at Stockbridge in the 1730s, along with others that were likely established in the Westenhook region of southwestern Massachusetts, in far-eastern New York, and in northwestern Connecticut. There is no evidence to suggest at any time during the seventeenth century and afterward that the Mahicans maintained a presence in the Housatonic Valley and environs south from northwestern Connecticut to Long Island Sound. This region was populated by Munsee, Quiripi, and Wampano-speakers.[17]

As mentioned before, materials collected from the eighteenth century and later demonstrate that the Indians of the upper Housatonic Valley spoke Eastern Mahican, often referred to as Stockbridge Mahican. It was the language of the Stockbridge Mission and previously was spoken at Wnahktukook (town of Stockbridge, Massachusetts) and Skatekook (Sheffield, Massa-

The Mahican Homeland

chusetts). It also was the language of the nearby communities of Weataug (Salisbury, Connecticut) and Wechquadnach (Sharon, Connecticut), thereby establishing the region as part of the Mahican homeland.[18]

The Roelof Jansens Kill, which along its southernmost stretch inland meanders a short distance into northern Dutchess County, is generally considered to mark the downriver boundary of Mahican territory on the east side of the Hudson Valley.[19] The strongest evidence in support of this view comes from the place-names listed in a deed to land purchased by Robert Livingston (1654–1728) from several Mahican Indians in July 1683, land that would form the bulk of the manor and lordship of this notable businessman, colonial official, and politician. Place-names in the deed, used to describe the metes and bounds of the parcel, refer to that section bifurcated by the kill where it flows through cleared land at a point southeast from its mouth. A 1714 map of the tract lists several other place-names. All are detailed, local onomastics, considered to be good evidence for identifying the Native people who may have occupied the area. And they are written phonetically in Mahican, thus lending support to the longstanding presence of these Native people in the area.[20]

In June 1688 a patent was obtained for land in the far northwest corner of Dutchess County, called the Schuyler Patent, lying to the east of Magdalen Island (aka Goat Island, Cruger Island). The north boundary of the patent abutted the Livingston purchase of 1683, that is, it was at the present-day Columbia-Dutchess County line. The southern boundary ran east from the Hudson River beginning about the vicinity of the Saw Kill, Annandale, and Barrytown. Of the three place-names associated with the patent, two are not distinctive. The third, "Waraughkameek," is clearly Munsee and not Mahican. Farther south, into central and southern Dutchess County, place-names associated with purchases of Indian lands are also Munsee.[21]

The southernmost limit of Mahican lands on the west side of the Hudson, as suggested by Van Wassenaer and others, appears to have been at about Catskill.[22] Here, however, place-names are of little help in determining who were the Indian people occupying this locality. For example, those mentioned in a deed transferring certain Indian lands on Catskill Creek to one Jacob Lokermans are not assignable to either the Mahican or Munsee languages.[23]

Occupying the Land: Territory, Title, and Alienation

A thesis, first presented in 1994, maintains that the boundaries of the lands occupied by the Mahicans can be fixed with confidence by examining land transactions that took place between these Indians and colonials in the seventeenth and eighteenth centuries.[24] Although attractive on its face, this thesis, beyond lacking a theoretical framework, fails to contemplate or address the most elemental questions about the manner in which Native people viewed land and then, by extension, how these views may have changed over time. The literature makes it clear, however, that a first question, one contemplating forms of Indian land tenure, has been answered—namely, that Native people lacked entirely a concept of land ownership, nor did their systems of land tenure approach anything like the jurisdiction and control assumed by European nation-states over their territories on the other side of the Atlantic.[25]

It is understood that the world of Indian people was absent metes and bounds. In their place stood the recognizable civil law doctrine, obviously applied retrospectively, of "usufruct," normally construed as "use right," a claim laid and limited to lands on the basis of how they were managed and to what ends. Usufruct is not a private or absolute right to the land. Instead, individuals or collectives might use or extract resources from a given territory, for an unspecified period of time, that they did not and could not hold in perpetuity. It is from these considerations that the contemporary notion of "communal ownership" most likely evolved and, by extension, the existence of recognized "rights" of community members—persons—to collect or oth-

The Mahican Homeland

erwise acquire a range of resources from the land for their own use. Such "rights" would have been an expression of or shifted with a range of ecological uses as determined by Native people themselves.[26]

From the outset, there exists little evidence in the seventeenth-century record that would shed light on how Mahicans, or the neighboring Munsees, regarded "property" or, for that matter, "ownership" of any kind. One of the few hints is found in Adriaen van der Donck's midcentury *Description of New Netherland*, wherein he observed: "Of all the rights, laws, and maxims observed anywhere in the world, none in particular is in force among these [Indian] people other than the law of nature or of nations. Accordingly, wind, stream, bush, field, sea, beach, and riverside are open and free to everyone of every nation with which the Indians are not embroiled in open conflict. All those are free to enjoy and move about such places as though they were born there."[27]

The "law of nature or of nations" that Van der Donck mentioned may be less a comment on Native perceptions and behaviors toward land and its constituent components than a reflection on certain legal theories as described by a fellow attorney and countryman, the influential Dutch jurist Hugo Grotius (1583–1645). In 1604 Grotius had drawn a distinction between common or public property and private property, maintaining that the former, given that it was not susceptible to occupancy or being occupied, was destined for the use of all humankind. Private property, on the other hand, was anything subject to seizure and possession by a person, something that is peculiarly one's own. "Common," maintained Grotius, was the simple antonym of "private."[28]

Whether the Mahicans had made use of such categories of land tenure prior to or soon after the arrival of the Dutch is unknown. Comparative data, however, suggest that for Indians throughout the region, land, rather than being owned or subject to purchase, sale, or other forms of formal conveyance, was seen as a geographical expression of social structure. That is, land was allocated as an extension of kinship through "usufructuary privilege," which was discharged primarily through families and corporate groups such as lineages or clans.[29] An often overlooked detail is that access to lands was acknowledged not only by members of these social units but, equally important, by adjacent, unaffiliated, and potentially uncongenial communities or groups. There is no reason to believe that the same acknowledgment of access did not hold for Dutch (and then English) colonial officials, whose position from the beginning was that Indians were the true "owners" of the land and that possession could be obtained only through regulated purchase. As Grotius explained, "discovery imparts no legal right save in the case of those things which were ownerless [*res nullius*] prior to the act of discovery." Thus, he reasoned, from a wholly Western, legal perspective, and certainly without having consulted with Native people, that they nonetheless "enjoyed public and private ownership of their own property and possessions, an attribute which would not be taken from them without just cause."[30]

But this idea of ownership, which importantly included the ownership of land, did not originate with Grotius. It was, he acknowledged, "expounded by the Spaniard [Francisco de] Victoria with irrefutable logic and in agreement with other authorities of the greatest renown."[31] It was Victoria whose lectures in 1532 set out the proposition that Native people "possessed natural legal rights as free and rational people," leading to the "Doctrine of Discovery" and the methods by which their lands could be acquired.[32] The Dutch, however, could not rely easily or solely on claims of first discovery and thus unrestricted access to the lands alleged to constitute New Netherland in the face of aggressive counterclaims by England. It remained, however, that under such a legal theory, land could be acquired only by purchase from Indian possessors.[33]

Discerning, creating, or depicting the boundaries defining Mahican territory for the precontact period is impossible. And unless there exists a significant and rigorously generated and tested archaeological record — there is none — along with strong demographic data — also absent — it does not get any better for the early years and decades following contact. What is demonstrable, however, is that, for any number of reasons, the Mahicans were relatively mobile, their settlements often shifting location, a practice that would have given rise to fluid boundaries, however defined.[34]

Among the most critical variables to affect intergroup boundaries would have been related to the exploitation of game animals, in particular the white-tailed deer. Competition for these critical and heavily utilized animals may have led to hostilities between Indian communities, predicated on the fact that deer populations and densities are known to expand and contract from season to season and year to year. Accordingly, so would the extent of hunting territories.[35] After contact, similar sorts of competition developed around the beaver, or more precisely, beaver hunting territories.[36] In addition, a significant but poorly understood factor affecting land use and occupation was the impact of European-introduced diseases, which began to strike Native people in the Hudson Valley shortly after the Dutch arrived.[37] The high levels of mortality that resulted had an unknown although assuredly devastating effect on, for example, political and social organization, with the loss of leaders and other influential members of a community. As a consequence, tasks associated with subsistence, the maintenance of settlements, and the oversight of lands doubtlessly were reconfigured and modified and thus adapted to rapidly changing events and their aftermath.[38] But again, the relevant data for seventeenth-century Mahicans — archaeological and documentary — are either non-existent or weak, making any assessment of boundaries problematical.

The acquisition of Mahican lands by the Dutch began with the 1630 purchase that would usher in Rensselaerswijck, the patroonship at the northern extreme of the Hudson Valley. Patents to land in the midvalley were secured in the 1640s and 1650s.[39] Of note is that all of these transactions were conducted under Dutch law as specified in the *Freedoms and Exemptions* of 1629.[40] Most informative, however, are the 1625 instructions to Willem Verhulst, the Dutch West India Company's first director in New Netherland, which detailed views on Indian lands and how they could be best and most appropriately acquired. For instance, in the search for a suitable place to build a settlement on Manhattan, company officials indicated that any land so chosen would first have to be "abandoned by the Indians or unoccupied." If no such lands could be found, then it would be necessary to deal directly with the Indian proprietors and "for trading-goods or by means of some amicable agreement, induce them to give up ownership and possession to us, without however forcing them thereto in the least or taking possession by craft or fraud, lest we call down the wrath of God upon our unrighteous beginnings, the Company intending in no wise to make war or hostile attacks upon any one."[41] These instructions reflect, to a great degree, important elements of the Doctrine of Discovery and how, in accordance with this doctrine, Indian lands might be obtained; that is, through a just war, which was not an option for the Dutch, or, if said lands were either unoccupied or had been abandoned. The third option, which the Dutch consistently chose, was through purchase.

How Indian lands were acquired by the Dutch and under what circumstances presents a complex and often confounding history. The first and most reasoned work to address these issues, by Robert Grumet, began by asking what on its face was a straightforward question: Why did Munsee-speakers sell their lands in present-day northern New Jersey to the Dutch?[42] The answers that Grumet proposed or that he discovered in the literature, however, are more in the way of after-the-fact exculpations for what allegedly transpired than anything else. The foremost of these, invariably reiterated in subsequent historical studies, is "that the Native parties to the conveyances did not fully understand the meaning of the documents they affixed their marks to." Others include the "misunderstanding hypothesis" where transfers of land meant something different to Native people than to the European purchasers; and the suggestion that Indians were "naturally guileless" or that they disposed of land or "sold it cheaply, as a gesture of friendship, high regard, or at worst, pity." Grumet also points to the explanation that accidental or deliberate mistranslations of deeds and related documents may have interfered with the Indians' understanding of land conveyances. The counter-argument he offers is that the widespread use of a trade jargon (or a pidgin), which purportedly "conveyed full understanding to the parties to the deeds," Indian or Dutch, was an important mitigating factor.[43]

On the other hand, the language of the deeds in nearly all cases adheres to a form or style, a legal protocol, that is remarkably consistent and thus, on its face, transparent. What nonetheless remains little understood is to what extent the Indian "proprietors" were told of the precise wording in a deed, deeds that in all likelihood they could not read for themselves.[44] Francis Jennings offers a strident view in the context of what he derisively coined "the deed game," seeing little more than trickery and fraud in land transfers that took place in colonial New England.[45]

Whatever the case, many of the questions first raised by Grumet, and then by historians who followed, have not been satisfactorily answered. Others have yet to be asked. They all bear directly on the question of whether the information found in deeds is of any use in determining the boundaries of Indian lands, in particular, Mahican lands. For example: Who were the Indians who signed the deeds? Did they have the right to do so, and even if they did have the right, how would we know? More to the point, would it have made a difference to either party? What was it that the Indians believed they were, in fact, "selling"? What were the motives of the Natives who were involved in selling land? And once the land was sold, did its location have anything at all to do with a Native group's territory or boundaries? Finally, no matter how one might define ownership, was the land that the Indians — individually or collectively — sold to the Dutch actually theirs to sell? But no matter. In light of the weakness of the documentary record and the inability to be certain of or understand at any level what was in the minds of Indian people, or even the Dutch, virtually none of these questions can be answered with anything resembling confidence. What merits further consideration, however, are alternative explanations or possibilities.

The process by which land was sold by the Indians and purchased by the Dutch in New Netherland appears to have been straightforward. Dutch officials needed to find potential, willing "sellers" or, perhaps less likely, were approached by Native "proprietors." Surviving documents do not allow for an easy determination of who initiated what or much at all about how arrangements to transfer land might have been made. The resulting deeds or other forms of conveyance contained information sufficient to fulfill the legal requirements of the colony: the names and frequently the office or title of the parties involved, Indian and Dutch; a description of the metes and bounds of the land conveyed; occasionally something of the quality and character of the land; and what was given or received in payment. Assertions made in the language of the deeds that the Native "proprietors" were representatives authorized to transfer land on behalf of their communities or other social units; or were leaders, headmen, of their communities; or indeed, "owned" the land, cannot be confirmed. For example, in his research on Munsee and Mahican deeds, Grumet has conceded that it cannot be known for certain whether such alleged influential persons actually possessed authority, although he points the finger at European ignorance of Indian political systems rather than consider the possibility of Native resourcefulness or self-promotion.[46]

What might be suggested as an alternative to this lack of confirmation is that Indians were quick to discern that the Dutch were intent on purchasing the land on which they may have or did live, subsist upon, or otherwise frequent, and that, in turn, they would be the recipients of valuable and needed goods in exchange for that land. And among the possibilities is that, in their desire to adhere to stated policy, what mattered most to the Dutch was that deeds were drawn up, signed, and secured to fulfill the requirements of that policy, and if challenged, would be brought into one of their own courts for adjudication. There was no known equivalent forum in Native communities. In the end the Dutch may have been unconcerned about from whom the land was actually purchased. It was the deed—a legal agreement, an instrument—that counted, one that could not easily be countermanded unless malfeasance could be proved. The Indians, on the other hand, fully understood that the Dutch wanted to buy land, and taking the position that there were economic and perhaps social advantages to be gained, sold whatever land the Dutch wanted. Did the Indians "own" or manage the land they sold? Were they authorized to sell the land? These questions are not answerable. There remains the possibility, however, that whatever Native land tenure practices existed before the arrival of the Dutch, they were rapidly transformed to address and accommodate changing circumstances. Moreover, both parties, Dutch and Indian, saw these changes as mutually beneficial, an advantage to be had.

Mahicans, sometimes leaders or those who may have ingratiated themselves to the Dutch or who had close connections with local officials and saw opportunities in the making, were likely the sometime initiators of these changes. The familiar view that Indians were simply and usually the victims of the colonial land-taking juggernaut need not prevail. There is no reason to believe that Native people were incapable of the kinds of expedient adaptation suggested here. Indeed, there is sufficient evidence in the literature that a bias has been operating among historians, a consequence of which has been a long-standing but wrong-headed assumption that Indians in fact could not adjust to the change taking place around them. Just how quickly and skillfully the Indians moved from their own system of land tenure to accommodate themselves to and even exploit that of the interlopers is demonstrated by the midcentury activities of several Mahicans, in particular, the headman Skiwias (var.), more commonly known by his Dutch sobriquet, Aepjen (var.).[47]

In fall 1648, and then in the following spring, three large tracts of land were purchased from certain Mahicans: the first on the east side of the Hudson River on the Muitzes Kill, opposite the Schodack Islands, then called Paponicuck or Paponikack; a second west of the village of Catskill, encompassing parts of the drainage of Catskill Creek and several surrounding flats; and a third at about Claverack and the city of Hudson.[48] All of these conveyances involved Brant Aertsz van Slichtenhorst, who the same fall had been appointed director and *schout* of the patroonship of Rensselaerswijck, and, on the Indians' part, Aepjen.[49] Van Slichtenhorst's tenure in the colony, however, was short-lived. In 1652, following disputes with Petrus Stuyvesant, the colony's director-general, Van Slichtenhorst was arrested and shipped back to the Netherlands.[50] Once released, he brought a lawsuit against the heirs of the patroonship to recover expenses he claimed he had incurred in negotiations with the Indians for the above-mentioned land purchases.[51] Passages translated from the court proceedings, where the Mahicans were subjects of interest, reveal much about the roles they played in these transactions.[52] Aepjen served as a broker in two of these negotiations and as a witness in the third. "[Aepjen was] always running errands concerning the purchase and the arrival of the sellers, and the price, and providing the same with food and good beer, together with 2 to 3 römers of brandy each day, which he himself demanded, and if I [Van Slichtenhorst] gave him white or middle beer, he demanded black beer. . . . [and he] would not leave until they saw the barrels and bottles with brandy were empty; and I also had to have more barrels of beer fetched."

As the "principal broker" in the Catskill purchase, Aepjen,

The Mahican Homeland

along with the other Indian participants, had taken to marking the metes and bounds in a way that most certainly did not reflect anything of Native practice—he used chalk. Also noteworthy is that the Indian brokers, along with others who were party to the sale, asked that they be paid at the time the agreement was signed. Moreover, Van Slichtenhorst reported, they kept the "best booty for themselves" and asked to receive their payment "separately and alone," that is, out of sight of the other Indians.

A major source of friction between Indians and Europeans in the Northeast, whenever and wherever lands were transferred, was the differing views held on the degree of closure of a sale. Where the Dutch (and also the English) presumed the transfer of "ownership" of lands to be complete and absolute with the signing of the deed, Indians often did not. For Native people, the purchase of their lands, that is, securing rights of access and use, was an open-ended affair, frequently subject to demands for renegotiation and amendment.[53] This was a situation that Van Slichtenhorst said he had faced firsthand, reporting to the court that "if the lands are not immediately occupied upon payment, then gifts have to be given [to the Indians] whenever one comes; even though other Christians are waiting for the lands." A decade later (1650), Cornelis Melijn, who in 1641 had purchased from the Indians Staten Island, where he established a patroonship, found himself in similar straits. As he described it, "the Indians began then of to speak of buying ye Island again; I then demonstrated to them ye aforesd. Sale & agreement, which they acknowledged they knew very well, & that they did not speak of that, but they supposed that ye Island by reason of ye war, by killing, burning & driving us off, was become theirs again."[54] Melijn refused to buy the land a second time, telling the Indians, "ye Dutch will not pay twice for any thing, which they have once bought." Finally, however, Melijn gave the Indians "a small gift gratis to maintain good friendship."[55]

Van Slichtenhorst described Aepjen's involvement in the sale of the lands at Claverack as follows: "Whereas Aepien [*sic*] was also the broker in the purchase of Klaverack [*sic*], he marked off the boundaries and land with chalk 8 to 10 times, both before and after the purchase, with his 7 to 8 wives. Or he brought news of the seller's appearance, or then he would go and fetch them; it was always something, so that he repeatedly remained several days with all those people, and Slichtenhorst had to furnish him and his with everything." In addition, "Aepien was the broker and was also 4 days at Katskil and Klaverack, and was the guide for Slichtenhorst, his honor Hoges, and the Dom[ine], and for this was given a coat with cords, a piece of garment cloth, an axe, an adze, a glass of brandy."[56] The ubiquitous Aepjen, it seems obvious, had forged good relations with the Dutch authorities and he may have spoken enough Dutch or a jargon so that his value as a broker was secured. Furthermore, he clearly had become a valuable resource for other Mahicans interested in selling lands.

Nothing of what Van Slichtenhorst described reflects what is known or has been inferred in regard to Native — that is, aboriginal — land tenure practices in the region. What is instead evident from his testimony, in addition to the extensive record of land transactions that took place beginning shortly after contact, is that the Mahicans who sold land, and certainly brokers such as Aepjen, had very quickly made a number of creative adjustments to meet the needs of the Dutch and, not surprisingly, their own needs. For starters, these Indians moved from not possessing or holding land, other than through usufructuary privilege, to alleging to "own" the land, to the extent that it could be sold by them to the Dutch. What is more, this "ownership" was not at all communal. The lands sold were never declared to be the lands of "the Mahicans," but from what the deeds spell out, they were lands "owned" by individual Mahicans: headmen or sachems, the kin of headmen or sachems, or simply named persons and, now and again, their kin.[57]

It is also apparent that the Mahicans understood that the

The Mahican Homeland

Dutch not only desired land and were prepared to purchase it according to directives issued by the authorities, but that they would, at the same time, not question the Indians' "ownership" of the lands they were prepared to sell. Once the Dutch purchasers obtained title to the land, its validity, if it were to be challenged, would be tested in a Dutch court and nowhere else. This continued to be the case even as an unknown number of Mahicans, for various reasons, moved farther east, inland from the Hudson River later in the seventeenth century, where they occupied and often sold lands upon which they may not have previously traveled, resided, or held in usufruct.[58]

For their part, the Indian sellers received whatever payments they were able to negotiate with the purchasers in goods, wampum, and sometimes food and drink.[59] Such commodities had previously been obtained by trading furs with the Dutch, the supply of which in much of the Hudson Valley was greatly reduced within two decades after contact.[60] Ultimately, it must be said, land sales fulfilled not only the immediate economic needs of both the Mahicans and the Dutch, but they also must have satisfied for each the notion of having profited from the transaction. It is doubtful that either party saw itself at a serious disadvantage; that is, for all intents and purposes, neither considered itself, nor could otherwise be perceived, as an easy mark.

Once fully considered, there is little in the historical or ethnological record that would support the notion that Mahicans "owned" land in the region, either before or after contact. Moreover, there is no evidence that any of the land individual Mahicans sold in the seventeenth century was actually theirs to sell, a fine point that the Dutch, perhaps by design, never seem to have raised with these Indians. Yet, in the end, maybe none of this matters. What did matter was that the Dutch wanted to purchase land in accordance with the prevailing law, and that the Mahicans made themselves available to sell it to them. Finally, it cannot be determined with any confidence what broad expanse of land the Mahicans may have controlled or occupied at any time from before the arrival of the Dutch, through to the seventeenth and eighteenth centuries, excepting the environs where their communities were established. These points, taken together, raise formidable, possibly fatal questions about whether land sales and associated deeds can reasonably be assumed to have anything to do with defining the boundaries of a Mahican territory.

Eight
A Century of Mahican History

In the beginning of this year [1628], war broke out between the Maikans near Fort Orange and the Makuaes, but these beat and captured the Maikans and drove off the remainder who have settled towards the north by the Fresh [Connecticut] River, so called; where they begin again to cultivate the soil.

—NICOLAES VAN WASSENAER, *Historisch Verhael*, in J. Franklin Jameson, *Narratives of New Netherland, 1609–1654* (NNN)

This excerpt from Van Wassenaer's *Historisch Verhael* offers the only hint as to where an unknown number of the Mahicans might have withdrawn two years after some of their warriors, aided by Daniel van Crieckenbeeck and his men, had been routed by a party of Mohawks, and in their turn the Mohawks had been forced by marauding Mahicans to abandon their easternmost village.[1] It remains, however, that there is nothing to establish that such a retreat took place. If the Mahicans along the Hudson River, most likely those nearest Fort Orange, did remove themselves, it is impossible to securely identify the location or locations where they may have taken up residence. The single claim or account to suggest their whereabouts—that they had moved into the upper Connecticut River Valley at about Newbury, Vermont—turns out to be "legend."[2] This is not to deny a general drawback of Mahicans east from the Hudson, perhaps to seek temporary refuge among their countrymen on the upper Housatonic or with their allies the Sokokis, Penacooks, or other Western Abenaki groups farther inland. After all, it had been the refusal of the Mahicans around Fort Orange to permit the Mohawks to cross the river and launch an attack on the Sokokis that had precipitated the conflict in the first place. Whatever the case, not all of the Mahicans left the Hudson Valley. A number remained about the Schodack Islands, their presence there confirmed by land sales made to the Dutch.[3] Moreover, there is no evidence to suggest that the other known Mahican communities at Catskill and on the upper Housatonic had been emptied of their inhabitants.[4]

Widely acknowledged is the close and longstanding relationship that existed between the Mahicans and the Western Abenaki groups to their east, especially those in the mid- and upper Connecticut Valley, one that may predate the arrival of Europeans. It endured through the turmoil and displacement of Native groups following King Philip's War (1676) and beyond, in spite of the differing accords that had been reached with European powers: the Mahicans, first with the Dutch, and after the takeover in 1664, with the English; the Western Abenakis with New France and later, if only nominally, with the English. Their common enemy and the impetus behind their often joint ventures were the Iroquois, most notably the Mohawks. What muddles the history of this relationship, however, is the precarious position the Mahicans held, located, as they were, next door to the Mohawks. Further complicating matters was an amicable trade that the Mahicans, by necessity, had to maintain at Fort Orange and the town of Beverwijck, renamed Albany with the takeover.

For the Dutch and, after the takeover, the English, the Mohawks were absolutely key to keeping the fur trade on track and as profitable as possible. Without their cooperation and the furs that they funneled into Fort Orange, in addition to their engagement and influence with interior groups of other Iroquoians and the Algonquians on the St. Lawrence and about the eastern Great Lakes—military, economic, and political—the trade

A Century of Mahican History

would undoubtedly have foundered.[5] The Mahicans were of lesser concern, certainly to the Dutch, who seem to have accepted the everyday presence of these Indians while maintaining a robust trade with them and, more important, acquiring their lands. For their part, there is no reason to doubt that most Mahicans, as did other Natives who packed their furs to Fort Orange, saw gain to be had as participants in the trade and, for a number of enterprising individuals, in the sale of lands over which they ostensibly held control. With the exception of the now and again theft, assault, and, rarely, a killing at the hands of either a Mahican or Dutchman, the relations between these two peoples were short on violence. The Dutch, it seems, never figured the Mahicans to be a threat to the future of their colony, although matters were quite different with the Munsees farther down the Hudson River and around Manhattan. The Mahicans, however, continued their sporadic warring with the Mohawks, turning frequently to the Western Abenakis for both protection and direct assistance when the need was felt.

Kieft's War

Gordon Day put it best in his observation that "few topics in northeastern ethnohistory have been more confused than the course of Mohawk-Mahican relations" in the years that followed their wars of the 1620s.[6] The same can be said for what transpired between the Mahicans and New England Algonquians. Acknowledging the meagerness of the record, historians have nevertheless held that clashes between the Mahicans and the Mohawks, the latter on occasion aided by the Oneidas and Onondagas, their confederates to the west, went on past midcentury. Still, there appear to have been periods of uneasy but peaceful coexistence. A first glimpse of this cycle is on the activities of the Mahicans and Mohawks during the brutal and destructive Kieft's War (1643–45) fought in the lower Hudson Valley. Most agree that this conflict was triggered by a levy on the Munsees, "in peltries, maize or wampum," that the colony's controversial and often reckless director, Willem Kieft, had sought to impose in 1639 to pay for the protection he claimed his government was providing these Natives.[7] The Indians must have raised strong objections to this new policy, reflected in Kieft's directive that each man in the colony was to take up arms and be placed under a local military command, and that a system of alarms warning of Indian threats be established. All this in the midst of an already tense situation generated by the Indians' increasing resistance to the presence of Dutch colonists on their lands. Quarrels that arose between the Dutch and Natives over the killing of livestock, the sometimes unchecked wanderings of which laid waste to the Indians' crops, disputes over trade, the heavy-handedness of colonial authorities, and undoubtedly other altercations escalated into retaliatory, bloody raids that soon plunged the entire region into a full-blown war.[8] In the end reported figures of Indian casualties — men, women, and children — were in the hundreds, and scores of Dutch met equally violent deaths.

The single known military involvement of Mahicans during Kieft's War was their attack on the Wiechquaeskecks (var.) in 1643. Inhabiting the lower parts of Westchester, one of these Indians two years before had murdered Claes Cornelissen Swits, an elderly wheelwright living on Manhattan. Demanding satisfaction from the Wiechquaeskecks, Kieft instead found himself rebuffed by a defiant headman who claimed that the killing had been in revenge for the death of one of his people at the hands of the Dutch years earlier.[9] Although there were calls to immediately punish the Wiechquaeskecks, others urged restraint, to wait until what they believed would be a crushing surprise attack could be mounted after the harvest and during the Indians' fall hunt. However, disagreements between Kieft and a committee of advisers he had appointed about how and when an attack would take place forced weeks of delay. And when in early 1642 a decision was made to go against the Wiechquaeskecks, the Dutch force became lost on the trail and, giving up the chase,

A Century of Mahican History

made its way back to New Amsterdam without having encountered a single Indian.[10]

In late February 1643 some eighty to ninety Mahicans, "each with a gun on his shoulder," launched an attack on the Wiechquaeskecks for reasons that are not fully understood.[11] According to De Vries, the Mahicans had traveled downriver from Fort Orange to "levy a contribution upon the savages of Wick-quas-geek and Tapaen [Tappan], and of the adjacent villages." But what De Vries meant by a "contribution" is unclear, although some have interpreted this to mean to collect "tribute," a term (and cultural process) that is often mentioned in the primary sources. Historians of the period, however, have never satisfactorily defined "tribute," nor are they in agreement about its application or cultural context.[12] But why would such a deadly attack have been undertaken if the question revolved solely around what was to be a straightforward "contribution," and why was it made against just the Wiechquaeskecks and not the Tappans or adjacent villages? More interesting is its timing, coinciding with Kieft's at-the-moment thwarted aim to avenge the death of Swits. De Vries, to whose plantation many Wiechquaeskecks fled after the attack before they moved on toward Manhattan and Pavonia, was nonplused, wondering how it was that a few score of Mahicans could cause Indians "so many hundred strong" to turn tail.[13]

De Vries's account, published in 1655, was compiled from contemporary notes on the Wiechquaeskeck episode he had made in 1643. It is one of three on the attack. The second is under the heading "Report and Advice on the Condition of New Netherland, drawn up from documents and papers placed by commission of the Assembly of the XIX., dated 15th Decr 1644, in the hands of the *General Board of Accounts*." Mentioned first is the 1641 killing of "an old man in his own house with an axe," which had set in motion a plan by Kieft and his advisers to strike back against the Wiechquaeskecks. "But nothing was done at that time in consequence of missing the enemy, who, observing what was designed against them, sued for peace." Then came the Mahicans' move against the Wiechquaeskecks, where "full 70 of them" were slain and many women and children taken away as captives. Others fled in the direction of Manhattan.[14]

The third account is "Journal of New Netherland, 1647," by an anonymous author sympathetic to Kieft and his administration. Offering additional detail on the incident, it nonetheless borrows from the 1644 report mentioned above, with two exceptions. In the journal the Mahicans are said to have killed seventeen Wiechquaeskecks, not seventy, which is likely the result of a slip by a copyist or a typographical error made in printing the translation. But there is also the more interesting demurral that the Mahicans' attack had taken place "without our knowledge."

John Winthrop (1588–1649), at the time governor of the Massachusetts Bay Colony, saw it differently. In a journal entry made shortly after the assault on the Wiechquaeskecks, he wrote: "It fell out that the Mowhawks [sic], a people that live upon or near Hudson's river, either upon their own quarrel, or rather, as the report went, being set on by the Dutch, came suddenly upon the Indians near the Dutch and killed about 30 of them, the rest fled for shelter to the Dutch."[15] Winthrop's number of casualties is at variance with the seventeen and seventy found in other accounts. And while he also got it wrong in attributing the attack to the Mohawks, his suggestion that the Dutch had been the instigators may not be far from the truth.

De Vries is known to have had intimate knowledge of the Indians of the Hudson Valley. That he would have misidentified those who had moved on the Wiechquaeskecks, even as he stood in opposition to Kieft and his policies, is not credible. Moreover, when the fleeing Wiechquaeskecks pleaded for his protection, De Vries's response was that "the Indians from Fort Orange were also our friends, and that we did not interfere in their wars."[16] He could not have been talking about anyone other than the Mahicans. The two other accounts may have taken some of their information from De Vries, although there is no unambiguous evidence that they did. There are, however, several interrogatories that were prepared by officials on Manhattan following the deadly Kieft-directed assaults on the Wiechquaeskecks and others who had gathered at Pavonia and near Corlear's Hook on the lower east side of Manhattan. Drawn up to be presented to and elicit responses from the fiscal Hendrick van Dyck, council member Johannes La Montagne, and secretary Cornelis van Tienhoven, they all state that the attack on the Wiechquaeskecks had been at the hands of the Mahicans.[17]

Making the Mohawks the culprits in this affair, assuming for the moment that Winthrop was right, is a stretch. It is true that they sometimes acted as intermediaries for the Dutch in their interactions with the Hudson Valley Indians or brought pressure to bear on these groups to come to the negotiating table. Yet there is little in the record that establishes for the Mohawks a vested interest in engineering a strike against the Wiechquaeskecks. Certainly Kieft, whose own efforts to launch an attack against these Indians had for months been frustrated by his advisers, had reason enough to have his people at Fort Orange arrange for assistance from the Mohawks. But making this highly unlikely, if not impossible, was the person of Arent van Curler, who in 1639 had been appointed by his uncle, Kiliaen van Rensselaer, the patroon of Rensselaerswijck, manager of his holdings on the upper Hudson, and who had served as the commissary at Fort Orange from 1642 to 1644.[18] Even though Van Curler had developed a rapport with the Mohawks, his ready access to and influence among these Indians had not been enough to cause them to give up three French captives on whose behalf he had interceded in 1642, much less convince them to attack the Wiechquaeskecks.[19] Also at Fort Orange was Adriaen van der Donck, the rather obstreperous chief legal officer of Rensselaerswijck, who in 1649 would join the opposition to Kieft's administration. It is hard to believe that either one of these men would have acted on Kieft's behalf.

But this leaves open the question of Mahican involvement. Why would such a large force march more than one hundred miles overland, made necessary due to the risks posed by taking canoes down the upper reaches of a river that, in February, was entirely closed or mostly frozen over and filled with ice floes, to attack the Wiechquaeskecks?[20] There are no signs that there had been any previous hostilities between the Mahicans and Munsee groups on the lower Hudson, nor any noticeable contact. For any number of reasons, including the season, De Vries's comment about the matter of levying a contribution rings hollow. Were there one or more confederates of Kieft at Fort Orange who were able to convince these Mahicans to go against the Wiechqueskecks, perhaps in exchange for more guns, other coveted trade goods, or wampum? Did these Mahicans decide to ingratiate themselves to whomever they were talking with in the hope, or perhaps with the false promise, that they would receive aid in their ongoing disputes with the Mohawks? Absent documentation, these and other suppositions will doubtlessly remain such.[21]

The scores of Indians who had fled to Pavonia and Corlaer's Hook offered the Dutch the opportunity to exact the revenge they had long planned. The ferocity of their assaults, recited in grim detail, left between 80 and 120 men, women, and children dead.[22] Now began a series of reprisals, raids by the numerous Indian communities of the lower Hudson Valley and western Long Island, on Dutch settlements there, interrupted for a short time by peace agreements negotiated with Long Island groups and those in eastern New Jersey.[23] But unrest flared anew in Westchester, where Indians burned out several farms, killing some Dutch and losing numbers of their own. The violence soon spread to Pavonia and again to Long Island, forcing the Dutch to withdraw from the countryside and to seek refuge behind the walls of Fort Amsterdam. Soon companies of Dutch and English troops, the latter dispatched by a competing but acutely apprehensive Connecticut colony, launched a series of attacks on Wiechquaeskeck villages in eastern Westchester and southwestern Connecticut with devastating effect. The deaths and deso-

A Century of Mahican History

lation wrought, undoubtedly attended by a mutual war-weariness, left both sides ready for peace, at least for awhile. It was in this climate that in midsummer 1645, Kieft journeyed north to Fort Orange with the objective to negotiate a treaty with Hudson Valley Indians who since his arrival had stood in deadly opposition to the Dutch presence and the authority he presumed to exercise over their country and their very lives. There, he and Johannes La Montagne, one of his counselors, met with the Mohawks "in order to bring to a peaceful conclusion the disaffection and wars between Director Willem Kieft, on the one hand, and the neighboring Indian nation, on the other."[24]

In late August 1645, headmen from a number of Hudson Valley groups and Dutch officials gathered at Fort Amsterdam to confirm a peace. Also present were Mohawk "ambassadors" who had been asked to attend the talks "as mediators." With them came their interpreter and "co-mediator," one Cornelis Antonissen.[25] Although not stated, Kieft's choice to have the Mohawks attend seems to have been related to the influence he evidently believed they held with these Munsee peoples, stemming from his earlier meeting with them at Fort Orange.[26]

Speaking at the treaty for the Wappingers, the Wiechquaeskecks, the Sintsincks, and the Kichtawanks, all Munsee groups on the east side of the mid- to lower Hudson Valley, was Aepjen, aka Skiwias, identified as "Sachem of the *Mahikanders*." His presence there is unexplained, as well as how it was that he spoke for these Natives. There is nothing known of his life before the treaty. His name next appears among materials tied to a 1648 land sale, and a few years later in a court case associated with this and other land transactions where he is identified as a Mahican "chief."[27] There is no further trace of Aepjen after 1665. Throughout, Aepjen comes off as less a leader of people than a man whose activities were charted largely for his own benefit. This is plainly the case when the surviving record of his activities — the land sales in which he participated and the mentions of the role he played in Mahican politics — is considered.[28]

As discussed before, when it came to the sale of land, Aepjen was on a number of occasions the broker between Dutch purchasers and other Mahicans. Everything points to his being, at some level, trusted by his Dutch clients and also by some of his own people in these and perhaps other kinds of transactions. There is no sign, however, that he was party to anything other than private sales entirely unrelated to a polity that could be referred to as "*the* Mahicans." Instead, he acted at the behest of specific persons and also family members wishing to dispose of land. Although he was one of several Mahican headmen whose names are found in Dutch administrative records and correspondence for the period, Aepjen's primary role as the "go-to" person for land sales seems well placed. He was very much the entrepreneur and opportunist.[29]

The scope of Aepjen's participation in the political arena is less clear. His attendance at the 1645 treaty cannot be assessed through other contemporary documents, for there are none. It seems doubtful that the groups for which he is said to have spoken would have acquiesced easily to such an arrangement. This would seem to have been the case especially for the Wiechquaeskecks, who not only had borne the brunt of the war but had previously been attacked by Mahicans and were not, as the Dutch would soon discover, defeated people. That is, not unless Aepjen's role was more that of an emissary, a go-between — that he had been tapped by the Dutch to ensure that what was said among the gathered Indians, and what the Dutch might have wanted these Indians to hear, was accurately conveyed. This assumes, of course, that as a translator, Aepjen did not shade meanings in a deliberate way. In any case Aepjen may already have developed a cozy relationship with the Dutch, one that he would quickly work to his advantage in the land sales that he brokered between 1648 and 1665.[30] Still, he did put his mark on the treaty document, apparently in the stead of the headmen of the groups for whom he spoke, the meaning behind which is obscure.[31]

Aepjen and other Mahican headmen continued to be party

A Century of Mahican History

to the political dealings of the time, which included, in particular, the warfare that had erupted in 1655 and then three years later would begin anew between the Dutch and the Munsees of the lower valley. These Indians' activities, however, were limited to acting as couriers and mediators for the Dutch, in the latter role, sometimes alongside Mohawks. Other than these occasional mentions, which do not begin in the records until just before 1660, the Dutch appear to have paid the Mahicans scant attention, and they the Dutch. A mutually beneficial tolerance seems to have been the order of the day.

Challenging the Iroquois

As Allen Trelease explains it, Kieft's War was followed by a period of relative quiet in New Netherland.[32] Other than their attack on the Wiechquaeskecks, the Mahicans had avoided the wider conflict, their activities being restricted largely to the trade in fur, selling land, and the workaday tasks of maintaining their communities. Missing from the record, unfortunately, are descriptions of Mahican society for any time during the last half of the seventeenth century and into the first decades of the eighteenth, information that would obviously furnish a much needed portrait of these Native people. And while these Indians remained caught up in their on-again, off-again conflicts with the Mohawks, which would not end until the last quarter of the century, they did not go against their neighbors alone, joining with or joined by the Western Abenakis.

The "relative quiet" in New Netherland that Trelease spoke of characterized the upper Hudson for a longer period of time than it did the downriver stretch. Notwithstanding, the Mohawks found themselves under threat from the Onondagas, their sometime confederates to the west. In mid-1657, Mohawk headmen went to the authorities at Fort Orange asking for horses to haul timber out of the woods to repair village fortifications, a cannon for each village to be used as part of a warning system, and for the Dutch to provide shelter for their women and children in the event of an attack. At this meeting the Mohawks told the Dutch that "they had called on us [the Dutch] in passing through on their way to the *Mahikanders,* to renew the old friendship between us and them [the Mohawks]."[33] Whatever business the Mohawks intended to conduct with the Mahicans is not specified. It is likely, however, that it had something to do with intrigues to the east and the hostilities between the Iroquois and Western Abenaki groups, the Mahicans' allies. There are hints that these New England Indians, having learned of the Iroquois' destructive campaigns against the Hurons and the Algonquians of the St. Lawrence Valley, feared they might next be targeted.[34]

In September 1650, the Jesuit Father Gabriel Druillettes (1610–1681), acting at the behest of the government in New France, traveled into New England.[35] His mission was first to enlist the assistance of New England's colonies in a campaign against the Iroquois, who had long been a thorn in the side of the French and their Indian allies and fur trading partners on the St. Lawrence. Moreover, Druillettes would argue, Iroquois attacks on the Abenakis posed a serious threat to English trade in the region.[36] Druillettes's task was facilitated by his familiarity with the Abenakis and their language and, to a limited degree, by the rapport he would fashion with important New England personalities such as John Winslow, William Bradford, John Eliot, and John Endicott. In April 1651, following meetings with these and other influential men, Druillettes sat for a second time with the Penacooks, Sokokis, Pocumtucks, and the Mahicans, whom he asked to join with the New England colonies. These Indians, Druillettes would report, "resolved to risk it against the Iroquois." The colonies, however, rejected Druillettes's proposal out of hand.[37]

There are only hints of what happened next. In a letter from the Council of Quebec to the Commissioners of New England, dated June 1651, the Iroquois were said to "kill the Sokoquis and the Abeenaquis your [the commissioners] allies" in a war.[38] It may be that the Iroquois had learned of the attack being planned against them, as Druillettes described it, by several Abenaki villages, assisted by the Mahicans and backed by a force of French and Montagnais. This, in part, would be in retaliation for an even earlier raid by the Iroquois that had left thirty Abenakis dead.[39]

Day has speculated on the reasons behind the Mahican–Western Abenaki efforts to challenge the Iroquois, beginning with the geographical proximity and unsteady truce that marked Mahican-Mohawk relations. Whether the Sokokis were unhappy with the Mohawks' demand for "tribute" or the badly functioning alliance between the two, as Day surmised, is up to question. Nor is it evident that the complex and shifting alliances of the Mohawks with the Natives in southern New England played a part in the enmity that marked their encounters.[40] It is likely, however, that the hostility is traceable to the historically close ties of the Western Abenakis to the Algonquians of the St. Lawrence Valley. It was with the Algonquians that the Iroquois had warred for uncounted decades, a belligerency that was exacerbated by these Natives' alliance with the French, who became yet another Iroquois enemy.

The Peach War and the Esopus Wars

News of sporadic Indian attacks on the Dutch living around Esopus reached Petrus Stuyvesant, the colony's director-general, at Fort Amsterdam in the spring of 1658. In response to the settlers' request for assistance, yachts carrying Stuyvesant and a detail of sixty soldiers sailed upriver, arriving at the mouth of the Esopus Creek in late May. After meeting with the inhabitants there, most of whom were farmers, Stuyvesant proposed that they could either move as a group to a suitable place where he could post soldiers to protect them until "further arrangements are made," or they could relocate to New Amsterdam or Fort Orange "so as to prevent further massacres and mischiefs." A third alternative, in the face of the settlers' concerns about leaving lands in which they were so heavily invested, was offered with much less grace: "If they could not make up their minds to either, but preferred to continue in such a precarious situation, they should not disturb us in future with their reproaches and complaints." The settlers opted to form a combined community.[41] What this episode points to, however, is that Fort Orange and the surrounding area was free from strife and, importantly, belligerent Natives who might pose a threat to the Dutch living there.

August 1658 brought with it the rumor that Indians on the Esopus were planning to go to war with the Mahicans. "But God only knows, what will become of it," Andries Louwrensen, a sergeant posted there, wrote to Stuyvesant.[42] From all indications, nothing did, although there was "some mischief and fighting" on the Esopus with the Indians there, news of which the Dutch made certain the Mahicans were made aware. In expressing their gratitude for being told of these developments so promptly, the Mahicans assured the Dutch that when "the *Esopus* or other River savages should come to them with presents and ask for assistance, to fight against us [the Dutch], they would kick them and say, You beasts, you pigs, get away from here, we will have nothing to do with you."[43] But a short time later the Mahicans would find themselves in the middle of a real war, that between the Iroquois and the Western Abenakis, while the Dutch and several Munsee groups — in particular, the Esopus Indians — faced off in another series of bloody conflicts.

The so-called Peach War, and the first and second Esopus wars, were violent engagements that took place between the Indians and the Dutch in the lower Hudson Valley and also the environs of Manhattan, Staten Island, New Jersey, and western Long Island from the mid-1650s to the early 1660s.[44] Although devastating to all involved, unrelenting Dutch military actions once and for all ended the dominance of Natives in these regions. The Mahicans were never directly involved in the hostilities; instead, some of their number at times fulfilled the roles of go-betweens, often joined by the Mohawks.

In October 1659 unnamed Mohawk and Mahican headmen traveled to the Esopus to ransom Dutch captives and arrange a truce. A few days later Nitamoret (var.), a Mahican headman, carried a letter about these same matters from Johannes La Montagne, vice-director at Fort Orange, to Ensign Dirck Smith (also Schmidt, Smit), the commanding officer at the Esopus. At about the same time, two Mahicans delivered another letter to Smith detailing Stuyvesant's order to complete the armistice. They had in their possession strings of wampum from the Mohawks, from the Mahicans, in all likelihood those nearest Fort Orange, and also from the Mahicans living at Catskill, signaling a peace offer to the Esopus Indians. These Mahican emissaries, no doubt together with the Mohawk headmen, had spent several days among the Esopus, returning with a Dutch soldier and a "free man," both of whom had been held prisoner there. Accompanying this party, at the insistence of the Mohawks, Mahicans, and Catskill Indians, were several Esopus headmen, who requested of the Dutch "an armistice," to which they guardedly agreed, "for as long a time as it shall please the Honble General."[45]

The armistice between the Esopus and the Dutch was not as it seemed. Ensign Smith, complaining to La Montagne about the behavior of the Mahican headman "Nietonnoret" (Nitamoret), who had passed off his courier duties to "another savage," trusted neither the Esopus Indians nor the truce that had been arranged some two weeks before. *"We behave ourselves as friends,"* he wrote, *"but they show themselves as rascals."* Although two Dutchmen had been ransomed, Smith maintained that the Esopus still held a boy and had killed their remaining captives. As for the armistice, *"none of their principal Sachems have been present,"* a situation that, insofar as Smith saw it, raised questions about the good faith shown by the Esopus, not to mention the legitimacy behind the arrangement. "We remain however watchful, as we have been before," he assured La Montagne in late December.[46]

Mohawk and Mahican couriers continued to carry letters back and forth between Fort Orange, the Esopus, and New Amsterdam. "Some well-known *Mahikanders*" also provided the Dutch with valuable intelligence about activities on the Esopus. In January 1660, when "the *Esopus* savages keep very quiet now," Mahicans reported "that they [the Esopus] do so, in order to carry out their intentions so much better and are watching for the chance of surprise, when the *Dutch* will not expect it and then to kill every body, whom they can. They have also stated to the aforesaid *Mahikanders* in plain words, that they would not allow the *Dutch* to live any longer on the *Esopus,* only one house on the bank of the Kil close to the river for their own convenience, to get some necessaries for their own use."[47] And the fighting continued. On March 25, 1660, the Dutch, "having suffered many massacres, affronts and unbearable injuries," declared war, "offensive and defensive," on the Esopus Indians.[48]

In April Stuyvesant directed La Montagne, from his vantage at Fort Orange, to "inquire if possible, but cautiously" into whether the Mahicans there or at Catskill "do not assist the *Esopus*." He was also to remind these Natives of their promise that "they would not favor the *Esopus* savages and would not allow them to remain among them nor give them any assistance." The reaction of the Mahicans was immediate. Several of their number, requesting safe conduct from the Dutch, traveled to the Esopus in a bid to end the hostilities. Shortly thereafter Catskill headmen, "in the name and on behalf of the *Esopus* chiefs," and in the presence of other Mahican headmen, delivered the message that the Esopus Indians were prepared to surrender and then leave all of their lands. Moreover, they intended to make restitution for the losses and damage caused to Dutch settlers and to release the prisoners they had taken. "Finally, they ask for a firm and permanent peace for all times." In their turn, the Mahicans, reminding Stuyvesant of their disposition to remain peaceful, asked him to respond positively to the Esopus proposals and, while arrangements were being made, to maintain a truce. They then gave Stuyvesant "a large present of wampum" as a sign of their gratitude.[49]

In late May 1660, Stuyvesant met with three Mahican head-

A Century of Mahican History

men acting as emissaries for the Esopus Indians. They brought with them the same message that the Esopus had earlier sent with the Catskill Mahicans, namely, that they "were no longer willing to make war, but wished to live as friends and that they would leave the *Esopus* altogether and convey it to the Dutch." The emissaries also asked twice during the discussions, the second time increasing the measure of wampum from two strings to twelve, that the Dutch release the prisoners they had taken, a matter that was of the utmost importance to the Esopus. Stuyvesant, however, would not release the prisoners "before or until the Sachems of the *Esopus* came themselves here [Fort Amsterdam] or at least to *Fort Orange*, to consider the conditions of the peace." An entirely new twist to events was the Mahicans' fear that the Dutch might go to war against their people, to which Stuyvesant replied: "As long as they kept quiet and lived in peace with us, we would do the same and not make war against them." Concluding the conference, the Dutch gave each of the emissaries a blanket, a length of duffel, an axe, a knife, a pair of socks, a pound of powder, two small kettles, and sent them on their way.[50]

From this point forward, the Dutch took an even harder line against the Esopus. Acknowledging that a lasting peace would not be reached without releasing their Esopus prisoners, Dutch officials nonetheless decided to send all but two or three to their colony of Curaçao, where they would be placed "with the negroes in the service of company." The others, regarded as murderers, would receive their punishment in due course. Meanwhile, Dutch forces "would continue a defensive and offensive war against the *Esopus* savages and inflict all possible harm upon them, until such time, that we can obtain a peace with them on favorable conditions."[51]

The Mahicans and Mohawks were not alone in their efforts to intercede on behalf of the Esopus Indians and end the war. Joining them were lower Hudson Valley groups — the Wappingers, the Hackensacks, and the Haverstraws — in addition to the

Natives on Staten Island. But the Dutch would not have any of it until the Esopus headmen themselves appeared before them "and submitted to us some security and reasonable conditions in this regard." These headmen, it was claimed, had on at least two occasions set out to go to the Dutch but had turned back, even as their people, including their young men, wanted peace.[52]

On July 15, 1660, following a series of indirect negotiations between the Dutch and the Esopus Indians, a peace was finally concluded. Present were headmen who had "asked for peace in the name of the *Esopus*," including Mohawks; the Mahicans Aepjen and Ampumet from the upriver community; Keseway and Machaknemeno from the Mahican community at Catskill; then Wappingers, Hackensacks, Susquehannocks, and a headman from the Indians on Staten Island. The Dutch regarded all of these Indian people as "our friends" and "friendly tribes." The Esopus sent their headmen Kaelcop, Seewackemamo, Neskahewan, and Paniyruways. Dutch officials present to sign the treaty were the burgomaster and former burgomaster of New Amsterdam; Arent van Curler, deputy of Rensslaerswijck; and Petrus Stuyvesant, the colony's director general.[53]

But once again, the peace was less than what the Dutch had hoped for. Six months after the treaty was signed, the Mohawks met with officials at Fort Orange, informing them of their intention to go south to the Delaware River (the South River) on a path directly through the Esopus country. It seems the Esopus Indians had put out the word that "when the *Maquas* would go to the *Southriver* and would pass there, they would kill them." The Mohawks were determined to show they could not be intimidated, although they did tell the Dutch they would not stop to speak to the Esopus "because the latter have said, the *Maquas* were the cause, why they had lost so many men in the war against the *Dutch*." The threats of the Esopus were not lost on Stuyvesant. In a report to his superiors in Holland, he expressed deep concern that "when they [the Esopus] see an opportunity they will take advantage of it to strike a blow and revenge themselves;

A Century of Mahican History

we are, indeed, almost constantly warned against them by other savages and are made very uneasy and circumspect." Doubts abounded as to whether the peace would hold.[54]

Then, on June 7, 1663, the Esopus Indians struck, destroying New Town (Nieu Dorp) on the Esopus, killing and wounding many of its inhabitants while taking others prisoner. The Indians also mounted an attack from inside the older settlement of Wiltwijck, their men having earlier entered the village under the pretense of wanting to trade, and engaged the Dutch in hand-to-hand fighting. All told, more than twenty Dutch were slain and a larger number wounded, captured, or reported missing.[55] There was no accounting of Indian losses.

The Dutch first attempted to obtain a release of prisoners taken by the Esopus employing the services of a métis headman who the Dutch called Smits Jan (aka Smiths Jan, Smiths John, and the Flemish Bastard, of Mohawk-Dutch ancestry, fl. 1650–1687), along with Aepjen.[56] Both Mohawk and Mahican headmen also continued with the task of carrying messages back and forth between the Esopus and the Dutch. About the same time, the Dutch voiced their concern that some Esopus, apparently limited to women and children, were living near the Catskill Mahicans and planting corn there. In an effort to control the situation, Stuyvesant asked the authorities at Fort Orange to inform the Catskills and also the Mohawks "not to suffer any *Esopus* among themselves," adding, "because we shall be obliged to hunt them up." And given how it was "difficult to distinguish one tribe from the other," he warned, he did not want to see other Indians attacked by mistake.[57] Fears that the Esopus might draw surrounding Native communities to their side, fueled mostly by rumors, kept the Dutch on high alert, even amid strong denials of such complicity from the Catskill, Minisink, Wappinger, and Highland Indians. The Dutch, however, would remain wary of the close bond that existed between the Esopus and the Wappingers, "who still keep together," a bond, incidentally, that would survive into the next century.[58]

Raids by both sides continued, with the Dutch receiving some assistance from Long Island Indians. In early fall 1663 an Esopus fort was attacked, leaving more than thirty Indians dead or captured. Then, in the first week of October, a force of Dutch and Long Island Indians returned to the scene. Finding the place deserted, they proceeded to destroy what remained. The rest of the year and into the next was spent in confused negotiations, with both sides working cautiously toward a final settlement. Again the Mohawks, along with "the *Mahikanders* and *Katskil* savages, *Aepje* and *Keesien Wey*," played the part of go-betweens in arranging a peace.[59] But none of these Natives was in attendance, nor was their presence required, for what would be a final treaty concluded between the Esopus Indians and the Dutch at Fort Amsterdam on May 15, 1664. The Esopus wars were once and for all ended.[60]

The Iroquois, Mahican, and Northern Indian Wars

Other than the participation of one or two of their headmen as emissaries in the extended effort to end the wars between the Dutch and the Esopus Indians, there is no evidence that the Mahicans had been drawn into these conflicts. Their principal interests, it seems, were with New England Algonquians to their east, while at the same time keeping a close eye on their ancient adversary, the Mohawks. So too did the Dutch, who in March 1651 learned that a party of Mohawks "had invaded the territory of the *French* in *Canada* and captured 8 or 9 Christians." War broke out the following year, continuing into the mid-1650s, causing the Dutch, not wanting to see any disruption of the fur trade, considerable worry. Indians they referred to as "the *Canada* savages," planning to attack the Mohawks in their home territory, had asked Dutch authorities for "permission to cross over the North River" to do so. This suggests, however, that many, if not all of these Indians, were Abenakis rather than Algonquians out of the St. Lawrence Valley, a supposition that is borne out by subsequent moves of the Mohawks against the

Abenakis on the Kennebec River in the early 1660s.[61] For the Dutch, these and other Natives comprised the "Northern Indians," sometimes called "North Indians," routinely undifferentiated groups that resided in northern New England and the upper Connecticut Valley. Wars between the Mohawks, at times aided by their brethren the Oneidas and Onondagas, and the Northern Indians, most often those in the Connecticut Valley, continued through about 1670.[62]

Evidence that the Mahicans were sometimes party to these hostilities is first documented in mid-October 1663. Following several encounters between the Mohawks and the Algonquians to their east, Stuyvesant had directed one of his officers "to go to *Fort Orange* before the winter and speak with the *Maquaas*, to see whether peace can be made between them, the *Mahicanders* and the Northern savages, so that each tribe may go quietly hunting beavers."[63] Three days later, however, vice-director La Montagne at Fort Orange, joined by Jeremias van Rensselaer, the director of Rensselaerswijck, reported that "a party of *Sinnekus* [presumably Oneidas and Onondagas] and *Maquaas* has left, to march against their enemies [*left blank in the original*], they took their course above the *Cahoose* [Cahoes Falls], that neither the *Dutch* nor the *Mahikanders* should know or get information of it." Their enemies, in this instance, were the Sokokis. A short time later came a cryptic letter from La Montagne to Stuyvesant, describing the "flight of the *Mahicanders*, who have left their land and corn, as well as the strange and unheard of disposition of the other savages."[64] The Mahicans on the upper river had undoubtedly retreated east toward the Housatonic and Connecticut Valleys and their allies residing there, under pressure, immediate or anticipated, from the Iroquois.

The reason behind the Mahicans withdrawal is reflected in the strong protestations of virtually all other Northern Indians on the Connecticut, put in writing to the Dutch by trader John Pynchon the previous July. Among the Indians listed were those from "*Agawam, Pajassuck, Nalwetog, Pacomtuck,*" that is, Springfield, Westfield, Northampton, and Deerfield, all in Massachusetts colony, in addition to an unidentified group, the *"Wissatinnewag."*[65] These Indians first acknowledged that the Sokokis had killed several Mohawks, which evidently led to the Iroquois' October attack. Then, they insisted, "they are very much put out" and did "repudiate the deed and swear at the *Sowquackick* because they had killed the *Maquaas* and they will have nothing to do with them." They appealed to the Dutch to offer, on their behalf, assurances to the Mohawks that "they had no knowledge of it, they were at too great a distance," and that they would remain their friends. The Dutch did not reply until near the end of October, noting that they did not receive Pynchon's letter until late that same month. The next day, however, the Dutch delivered the Northern Indians' message to Adogodquo (var.), "alias *Big Spoon*," a Mohawk headman. "It was well," he said, that the Northern Indians would have nothing to do with the Sokokis, his peoples' enemy. "But if the savages, their friends," speaking of the Indians from the Connecticut Valley, "would send hither some of their people with presents, then the friendship and peace would be so much firmer and he says, that he will then do his best." Thus, it appears, 1663 marked a new period of some level of enmity between the Mohawks and the Mahicans, who were allied with the Northern Indians, as they had been in the 1620s.[66]

It is unclear, however, whether from the beginning, Mahicans and Mohawks actually took the field against each other—that is, whether they were directly engaged in combat. In one of the largest full-scale clashes of the Iroquois–Northern Indians wars, which took place in December 1663, there is no evidence of Mahican participation.[67] Indeed, the following May, three Mahicans were enlisted to serve as interpreters or go-betweens for a party of Mohawks and Dutchmen traveling to Pocumtuck territory in the middle Connecticut Valley, whose intent was to obtain the release of prisoners taken in that engagement and to arrange a peace. The following June a Mohawk headman and his delega-

A Century of Mahican History

tion, on their way to the Pocumtucks to ratify the peace, were murdered on the trail. Mahicans, apparently those close to Fort Orange, "who appear to be knowing thereto, are fled from the Mohawks," suggesting they had been complicit in the killings. Yet the Mohawks did not hold them responsible, blaming instead the Pocumtucks.[68] Complicating the situation, however, was the July burning of a house in Claverack, down the Hudson, leaving a farmer dead and his wife and young son missing, along with the killing, injuring, or theft of a number of cattle, all by unidentified Indians, whom at least one historian has assumed to be Mahicans.[69] But there is nothing to link these actions to the Mahicans, who had nothing at all to gain and much to lose by attacking their Dutch neighbors and, not incidentally, by being readily identified in the process. Jeremias van Rensselaer, who was in a position to know, plainly stated the facts: "Our greatest trouble here is that the Mahikans side with the northern Indians, who now do us the greatest damage," going on to provide details on the death of the farmer at the hands of these Northern Indians.[70] Besides, the Mahicans were supposed to have fled the area, probably with the expectation of being accused in the murder of the Mohawk peace delegates. But this was only the beginning.

On September 6, 1664, Petrus Stuyvesant transferred New Netherland to Richard Nicolls, commander of English forces and governor-designate of what would become the colony of New York.[71] A short eighteen days later, Mohawk and "Synicks" headmen, among the latter, in all probability, Oneidas and Onondagas, met with Colonel George Cartwright, acting on behalf of Nicolls, at Fort Albany, the renamed Fort Orange. The purpose of the meeting was to facilitate and formalize the transition from the Dutch to the English administration. Thus, assurances were given the Indians that the fur trade and access to trade goods would continue as before, and that offenses committed by any "English Dutch or Indian (under the proteccôn of the English)" would receive "due satisfaccôn" on all accounts and for all parties. Although no other Indians were present, Cartwright none-theless extended the "Articles of Agreement and Peace" to include the Wappingers and Esopus Indians, and "all below the Manhattans."[72]

For their part the headmen offered their own set of demands, to which Cartwright consented. Among these was a pledge by the English not to provide assistance to the enemies of the Iroquois—the Sokokis, Pennacooks, or Pocumtucks. Next, acknowledging that they were engaged in a war with their equals, and maybe then some, the Iroquois asked that if they "be beaten by the three Nations above mencôned, they may receive accommodacôn from ye English." Finally, what on its face seems to have been an unnecessary request, given the relatively untroubled history of Iroquois-Munsee relations and the outcome of the Esopus wars, was for the English to arrange a peace, on behalf of these Iroquois, with the Indians living downriver from them. Trelease has suggested that the Iroquois' request was made because some of the Munsees appear to have been drawn into the conflict between the Mohawks and Northern Indians. However, this peace may also have been a strategy meant to neutralize one or more of the Munsee groups, keeping them at a distance from the war that the Iroquois had for many years been fighting with the Susquehannocks of southeastern Pennsylvania.[73]

Within the month, Nicolls would meet with a number of Esopus headmen in New York to finalize a peace accord with these Indians. As had been the case with the Iroquois, it was agreed that there would be no further hostilities, and that any and all offenses committed by Indians against colonists, or the opposite, would be dealt with to the satisfaction of both peoples. Among other provisions, the Esopus agreed to grant the English "a certaine Parcell of Land" called "*Kahankson*."[74] Curiously, there was no mention of a peace having been made with the Iroquois or any other Indians, nor of the conflict involving the Northern Indians.[75] But of great interest is that the English did not think it at all necessary to sit with the Mahicans and forge

A Century of Mahican History

an agreement similar to those it had with the Iroquois and the Esopus Indians. This was in spite of these Indians' alliance with the Northern Indians, whose war with the Mohawks was of considerable concern to much of New England.[76]

Throughout the wars between the Mohawks, joined by other Iroquois, and the Northern Indians of the Connecticut Valley, the Mahicans seem to have played a cautious, self-protective, and, to many historians, often baffling role. There is certainly reason to believe that part of the difficulty in searching out the details of their activities in these conflicts is a consequence of a spare and scattered historic record. However, perhaps unappreciated is the peculiar and precarious position in which Mahicans found themselves, and this may have allowed them little latitude in their interactions with either the Dutch or their Indian enemies and allies.

Immediately to their west lived the Mohawks, a longtime foe whose population in the third quarter of the seventeenth century is estimated to have been just under 2,000 persons, at least 400 of whom would likely have been warriors. To their west were the Oneidas, with some 100 men, and then the Onondagas, with perhaps 250 more.[77] To the Mahicans' east were their allies, the Northern Indians, composed primarily of Western Abenaki communities in and around the Connecticut Valley, whose combined population equaled and may have exceeded that of the three mentioned Iroquois groups. It is impossible to assess Mahican numbers for the same time period although their presence in their homeland may have remained relatively substantial.[78] In any case it is doubtful whether, in most circumstances, they alone would have been a match against Mohawk or united Iroquois forces. Still, the Mohawks and other Iroquois had their hands full, their forces stretched to the limit, fighting wars not only against the Northern Indians but also the Maryland-supported Susquehannocks southward and the French-allied Algonquians to their north. This may have leveled the playing field, although to what ends is unknown.

On the other hand, the few mentions of Mahicans in the primary documents, when compared to what was recorded about the Iroquois and Northern Indians, suggest neither a large population nor one over which the Dutch or the English expressed much worry. At first glance, then, the Mahicans seem to have been a withdrawn and quieted people, wisely maintaining a low profile. And given the circumstances of their nearness to the Mohawks, and not incidentally, to the Dutch upon whom they were to a large degree economically dependent, this makes sense. It may also be that their warriors melted into, became lost in, the larger force of "Northern Indians," acquiring for European observers a generic identity. Nonetheless, most likely at the level of individuals or small parties of warriors, Mahicans do seem to have taken some part in the engagements that were recorded between these enemies, and there are hints of Iroquois fears — real or perhaps feigned — of their strength. This conclusion, however, it based primarily on circumstantial evidence, for the Mahicans are seldom named in the accounts of the conflict.

The English takeover was followed by a series of military engagements between the Iroquois and Northern Indians that did not end until the 1670s. The most intense fighting followed a campaign launched in January 1666 by a large and well-trained force, led by Sieur Daniel de Rémy de Courcelle, to destroy the Mohawks, who had resisted French proposals for a general peace. Although the army failed to directly engage these Indians, mistakenly marching to near Schenectady instead of the intended Mohawk villages farther west, its mere presence made an impression. In April, in an obvious effort to forestall further French invasions of their homeland, the Mohawks asked the authorities in Albany to intervene on their behalf. In exchange for his assistance, Governor Nicolls insisted that they first negotiate a peace with the Mahicans and the Northern Indians, known allies of the French, an undertaking that was torpedoed by a Mohawk raid near Hadley, Massachusetts. This attack was answered by a counter-raid by Northern Indians, which may have included some Mahicans.[79]

A Century of Mahican History

In mid-July, 1666, the Mohawks met with English authorities at Fort Albany, warning that "the French are really coming now," followed by the apparent non sequitur "you spoke and told us also that we should stop bothering the Mahikanders, in which we obeyed you." Although their main concern was the French, who, the Mohawk headmen complained, "want to fight," they also were looking over their collective shoulders, letting the English know that "we do not want to sleep on the hillside tonight, for we do not want to be killed by the Mahikanders." Fully aware that they would soon face French soldiers, the Mohawks were not about to have their backs to Mahicans ready to take advantage of the situation. That September Alexander Prouville, Seigneur de Tracy, led more than a thousand troops into the Mohawk Valley. Forewarned, the Mohawks fled their villages, which, along with a vast stored harvest, the French burned.[80]

In mid-August, shortly before the raid, Mohawk and French envoys assembled at Fort Albany for a council held in the presence of English authorities. Explaining that "the war was not their fault," the Mohawks made it known that "they would very much like to see a good lasting peace made between them and the French." They offered to release a number of the prisoners they had taken, pledging to return the remainder when a peace was finalized, with the expectation that "the Maquase who are prisoners of the French will be set free." Metaphorically throwing their guns away, they assured the French that "they would not begin any trouble" and "will keep the peace."[81]

At the end of August, again at Fort Albany, Mohawk and Mahican headmen met, also to arrange a peace. The council was opened by the sitting justices of Albany. Addressing the Mahicans and "the other nations of Indians," a reference to the Northern Indians, who "from time to time attacked our brothers, the Maquase," they asked that "a good, lasting, and true peace" be the outcome. Joining in the agreement were the Mohawks' confederates, the Oneidas and the Onondagas. "You people are thoroughly tired of all wars and hostilities," the justices told the gathered Indians, "and will dig a grave of forgetfulness and will put a heavy stone on the grave so that evil will not come out of there again." The peace, however earnestly agreed to, would not hold.[82]

In 1667, after the brief lull engendered by the treaty, raids on the Mohawks resumed amid Northern Indian worries about waning French support. Two years later, in summer 1669, at a time when the "Loups," here the Northern Indians, were said to "infest the roads" on which the Onondagas, the Mohawks' allies, traveled, there took place what to all appearances was a turning point in the wars.[83] A force of several hundred men from the allied Northern Indians attacked the easternmost Mohawk village. Unable to penetrate their enemy's defenses, the attackers withdrew, only to be waylaid on their journey home by pursuing Mohawk warriors. Losses on both sides were reported to have been heavy, with the final victory, such as it was, going to the Mohawks. There is no clear indication that the Mahicans were involved in this battle, although it is possible that numbers of their men fought alongside the Northern Indians. Whether they participated or not, the Mahicans were again a party to the peace talks that followed.[84]

In October 1669, in correspondence with his magistrates in Albany, Governor Francis Lovelace reported on certain "propositions" that he had received from the Indians. Transmitting this information to Connecticut's governor Winthrop, he wrote that they reflected "ye Earnest desire of ye *Maquases* to conclude a firm peace with ye *Mohicands*." Wary of the "Jelousy ye *Mahicanders* Conceive of ye *Maquesyes* by reason of some former misactings," Lovelace nonetheless believed that through "a Treaty *de novo* it is possible a good issue may be Expected." Winthrop, however, was planning a voyage to England, bringing to a halt any further action on the Mohawks' proposal.[85] However, a peace would be reached two years later when events in Europe resulted in the two competing powers — France and England — joining

A Century of Mahican History

forces against the Netherlands. During this brief respite Canada and New York were able to bring the Mohawks and Mahicans to the table, where, Albany officials promised, "we will take care that the peace will remain steadfast and force the Mahicans to come here."[86] But "steadfast" was only a word.

The surviving, if slim, record suggests that small parties of Mohawks continued their raids into the mid-Connecticut Valley, even as yet another peace was "newly made or renewed by them at the ffort betweene ye *Maques* and *Mahicanders* Indyans" in October 1675.[87] No matter the accord, in April 1676 New York's governor Edmund Andros, who had arrived in the colony two years earlier, reported that as the Mohawks returned from another fight with the Northern Indians, the Mahicans had fled. "But hee [Andros] sent to them to come backe," and as "some of them were come backe upon the Go[v]. promising the protection if they should come, & stay if they wanted land that hee would supply them."[88]

The Mahicans' flight implies, once more, a well-founded fear of their ancient enemy who, joined by their Iroquois confederates, was again engaged in wars with the Northern Indians. And it was with the Northern Indians that the Mahicans had steadfastly remained allied, although indications are that not all had gone well. In an April 1677 meeting, for example, the "Mahikanders and other River Indians" expressed their thanks to John Pynchon, "for wn we were formerly in warr, (pointing towards ye West where ye Masquasse live) yn Major Pinson did as it were Take us in his armes & ptected us." As a preface to their gratitude, the Indians emphasized that "of Late years ye Govr. Genl: is become or father, *we being now butt a very few.*"[89] Andros's efforts to draw the Mahicans back toward Albany, amid assurances that he would shelter them and provide them with land, is further proof that despite their generally untroubled relationship with the Dutch and now the English, they had come out of the colonial experience and their wars with the Mohawks badly weakened. This is not to mention having lost much of their land along the way. "Those who remained near Albany," Trelease correctly observed, "ceased to be a major power factor, and their subsequent relations with both the Mohawk and English were marked by greater friendship and increasing dependence."[90] That the Mahicans no longer occupied a position of strength is further demonstrated by Iroquois assurances to the French in late 1674: They would "prevent the Mohegans of Taracton [the Catskill Indians] . . . continuing hostilities against the Outawacs [Ottawas]."[91] In May 1676 Andros sent word "by some good *Mahicander* Eastward . . . that all Indyans, who will come in & submitt, shall be received to live under the protection of the Government."[92]

Noteworthy is that in December 1675 a large number of "Northern Indians" were already on the Hoosic River, causing considerable unease, if not panic, among Albany's citizens. As Andros reported it, about one thousand warriors, led by King Philip, Metacom himself, were encamped some forty miles northeast of Albany.[93] There is little to shed light on the reasons why Metacom had moved so close to Albany, although Douglas Leach, following Increase Mather's reading of events, suggests that Metacom wanted to enlist the Mohawks to join his insurrection. But his method for doing so, it seems, was to secretly kill some Mohawks and then blame the deed on the English, a plan that backfired. Instead, Mohawks and other nearby Iroquois chased Metacom and his forces out of New York and back into New England. For the next several months, at least until July 1676, they continued in their pursuit. Escaping the Iroquois, Metacom would die in a fight at Mount Hope, near Bristol, Rhode Island, the next month, ending the war bearing his name.[94] Andros, a man Francis Jennings described as "loyal, intelligent, and bluntly aggressive," had been appointed by James Stuart, duke of York, to bring order to and expand the boundaries of the duke's province.[95] All this on his way to becoming royal governor-general of the Dominion of New England in 1686. Andros's move "to 'civilize' the locals, Native and European alike," began by at-

A Century of Mahican History

tracting Natives — those on the Esopus, at Albany, and "most warrlike Indyans neare a hundred miles beyond Albany" — to his side, setting in motion the establishment of the Indian town of Schaghticoke near the mouth of the Hoosic River northeast of Albany.[96] Although there is no contemporary account, including anything by Andros himself, it is believed that shortly thereafter he met with the Indians who had gathered at Schaghticoke. There he is assumed to have concluded a treaty styled "a great Tree," "a Tree" or "tree of Welfare," whose extended branches, metaphorically New York colony, would provide them protection. The flip side of Andros's largesse, however, was his intention to stop the exodus of these displaced Indians to New France, from which they could potentially do New York harm.[97] At the same time, Andros had taken a great interest in events in New England, here warning Connecticut authorities of a rumored Indian attack on Hartford, and there working to expand his province by seizing the western part of the same colony. This, added to allegations that he had something to do with contraband powder and lead that had made its way to Indians fighting in King Philip's War, made Andros a controversial figure indeed.[98]

By the turn of the century there were reported to be just under 100 men in what was considered Albany County, which included Schaghticoke, suggesting a total population of about 400 Indians, a number that had been reduced over the previous decade from 1000. Even so, in mid-1701, the "River Indians" declared that they could muster some 200 warriors, representing a total of perhaps 800 Indians. The next year there were 197 "fighting men" in the same area, of whom 110 were "Indians at Skachcock," thus, a population of around 400.[99]

The Alleged Mahican Confederacy

An important sidebar to the Iroquois–Northern Indian wars is the assertion that a Mahican confederacy was formed and functioning during the last half of the seventeenth century. To this can be added the contemporaneous claim for a Wappinger confederacy composed of a number of lower Hudson Valley and Connecticut Valley communities. However, the question of whether there had been a Wappinger confederacy has previously been addressed and dismissed, first by Ives Goddard in 1871 and then by Robert Grumet a decade later.[100]

The belief that a Mahican confederacy once existed begins with, or is predicated upon, the same nineteenth-century source that maintained there had been a Wappinger confederacy. But unlike that now-deceased entity, the notion of a Mahican confederacy is alive and well. Rachel Wheeler speaks not only of a Mahican confederacy but also a River Indian confederacy. James Oberly provides for lowercased Mahican confederacies. Ted Brasser's oft-cited monograph on the Mahicans, in addition to his earlier, virtually identical essay in *Handbook of North American Indians*, also contains references to a Mahican and River Indian confederacy.[101] Finally, there are any number of Internet websites that repeat similar claims, including those at Clark University, Bard College, and several online dictionary and encyclopedia entries.

The originating source for a Mahican confederacy is Edward Ruttenber's 1872 *Indian Tribes of Hudson's River*. There Ruttenber applied the term "confederacy" to the Mahicans and also to the Indians he called "Lenni Lenape." He further maintained that until his book "the several nations composing the confederacy have never been designated." Thus, he identified "certain general divisions [that] appear under the titles of the *Mahicans*, the *Soquatucks* [Sokokis], the *Horicons*, the *Pennacooks*, the *Nipmucks*, the *Abenaquis*, the *Nawaas*, the *Sequins*, and the *Wappingers*." Ruttenber classified these different groups that, he declared, operated in "confederated action," under the general name "*Abenaqui, or Wapanachki*," in his words, "Men of the East." "The representative nation of the confederacy of the Hudson, the *Mahican*," Ruttenber continued, "appears to have taken original position there, and to have sent out subduing colonies to the south and east, originating other national combinations." Furthermore, he divided the Mahican division into five subgroups, beginning

A Century of Mahican History

with the Mahicans; then "The *Wiekagjocks* [Wiechquaeskecks] . . . The *Mechkentowoons* . . . The *Wawyachtonocks* . . . [and] The *Westenhucks*."[102]

Ruttenber's view of things is breathtaking in its historical sweep—especially the business of "subduing colonies" fanning out from the Mahican homeland—all of which sounds very much like what his contemporaries had to say about the Iroquois. But there is little in what Ruttenber wrote that bears any semblance to historical fact, including his putting several of these groups in places where they never were. What bears scrutiny is how Ruttenber managed to find himself in the midst of telling such a story. It is also worth examining how it is that equally strong statements on the Mahican or River Indian confederacies have found their way into the historical literature of the twentieth century and beyond. Accordingly, the state of historical and ethnological thought of the mid- to late nineteenth century is considered and then, briefly, the practices of historians writing in the twentieth and twenty-first centuries.

Grumet has linked something of what Ruttenber wrote about confederacies to the geographer and ethnologist Henry Rowe Schoolcraft, in addition to a number of selected colonial sources and a statement made in 1762 by Daniel Nimham, the Wappinger headman and descendant of western Long Island Indians.[103] In support of what Grumet concluded, it must be said that by the mid- to late nineteenth century, finding confederacies among Indians of the eastern woodlands was considered to be the thing to do.

Still, much of the idea for confederacies in the region can be traced to the military and political fame of the Iroquois and their highly touted league of five, then six, Indian nations. Ruttenber had easy access to a host of nineteenth-century sources on these Indians, including the work of the estimable Lewis Henry Morgan, published collections such as the *Documentary History of New York*, and most of the *New York Colonial Documents*. Ruttenber also cites materials that were archived at the New York

State Library, many of which were lost in the 1911 fire. It is perhaps no surprise that where historians found one documented confederacy—that of the Iroquois—they reasoned that there could or should be others. Also worthy of consideration is the extent to which Hendrick Aupaumut's (1790) formal structuring of Mahican culture may have turned Ruttenber's head, especially when it came to sociopolitical processes and organization where these Native people came to resemble the Iroquois in ways that are not expressed or borne out in the primary documents that the Dutch and English left behind.[104]

Ruttenber's 1872 assertion that there had been a Mahican confederacy is repeated by subsequent authorities, including Frederick Hodge in his 1907 *Handbook of American Indians*. But it was Brasser in the 1970s who appears to have sought to strengthen Ruttenber's position by citing a document in the *Livingston Indian Records*, first published in 1956, a collection that had been unavailable to historians for 170 years. From these materials Brasser drew upon an excerpt from a February 1675 conference in Albany held between Mahican headmen and colonial officials. It was here, Brasser contends, where the Mahicans "gave explicit evidence of the existence of a confederacy."[105]

During the conference, a Mahican spokesman offered the following: "The English and the Dutch are now one and the Dutch are now English. Thus we Mahikanders, the highland Indians, and the 'western corner' Indians are now also one. Thus they pray that they will not be exiled or destroyed by the English, something they have never done to the Christians."[106] From the headman's words, "are now also one," Brasser concluded that "the neighbouring Wapping and Housatonok had become divisions of a larger unit, and subsequent data reveal the supremacy of the Mahican Chief Sachem"—that is, these Indians had formed a confederacy.[107]

Fully considered, this is thin evidence from which to argue for the establishment of something as politically complex, not to mention obvious, as a confederacy. More baffling is that there

A Century of Mahican History

is nothing in the endnotes Brasser provides that supports any of his contentions. Indeed, the sources he does cite either restate what is found in Aupaumut's history; quote from Mahican John Quinney's 1854 Fourth of July address in Reidsville, New York, where he said that the confederacy comprised the geographically widespread Delawares, Munsees, Mohegans of Connecticut, Narragansetts, Pequots, Penobscots of Maine, and "many others"; or are simply of no consequence to the question at hand.[108] For example, Brasser cites a page in Beauchamp's 1907 *Aboriginal Place Names of New York*, containing this sentence: "This was a tradition of the Delawares that the northern door of their long house, or confederacy, was at Gaasch-tinick or Albany, and the southern on the Potomac."[109] Beyond the fact that Beauchamp used the word "confederacy," and that what he conveyed to his readers sounds suspiciously like a take-off on the Iroquois confederacy's western and eastern doors-to-their-longhouse motif, his statement is of no relevance. Moreover, subsequent to the 1675 conference in Albany, there are no suggestions of anything resembling the concerted political or military actions one would expect from a Mahican confederacy. On the contrary, the proposals by the Mahican headmen at that conference are those of Indian people fearful of being "destroyed" — their word. They had just come out of a serious dust-up with the Mohawks and other Iroquois, and events to their east, involving their Northern Indian allies, along with the portent of King Philip's War, could not have made them feel at all comfortable about the present or future. In the absence of evidence, then, Brasser's declaration that "the events during the past wars, however, suggest wider liaisons, which appear to find corroboration in the oral tradition of the Mahican, Munsee, and other coastal tribes," rings hollow.[110]

But how is it that this tale of a Mahican confederacy persists into modern histories? The answer may be that historians, while they have finally and prudently set aside much of Ruttenber's writings, nonetheless rely on Brasser, never thinking to check his endnotes or his sources. Brasser wrote uncritically, and usually without acknowledgment, around Ruttenber, in addition to a few of Ruttenber's contemporaries. Ruttenber's contemporaries, however, had in their turn used Ruttenber, something that seems to have entirely escaped Brasser. Where Brasser did not use Ruttenber, he seems to have drawn his information on the Mahicans out of the ether, yet he found precisely what he was looking for, however unconfirmed it was by the historical record.

Fin de Siècle

Neither the 1675 peace accord nor the end of King Philip's War seems to have completely closed the chapter on the animus that marked relations between the Mahicans and Mohawks. But at the same time, it becomes increasingly difficult to know anything of the details surrounding their encounters. A large part of the problem is, once again, a sparse documentary record. Equally challenging are the designations — the names — given Indians in European accounts, whether by design or default, and then the consistency, or more commonly lack thereof, in these designations.

At first blush, names appear to have been carefully ascribed to Native groups in the Hudson Valley. In early 1690 the "River Indians" were said to be those living at "Beere Island and Catskill." Given this location in what was the core area of their homeland, there is no doubt that they were Mahicans. Above Albany were "ye Indians of Skachkook [Schaghticoke]."[111] As discussed earlier, most of this settlement's original residents were known to have been Western Abenakis. Yet on other occasions there are differences of opinion. Written three days apart, in 1695, are two reports, one of which refers to "the Mahikanders or River Indians," while the other mentions "River Indians & Mahikander[s]."[112]

There is also some divergence in attaching names to Indian groups when the research conducted by present-day scholars of the period is examined. In one instance, the River Indians were considered to have Mahicans among their members, while not a single "tribe" was "chiefly Mahican." In another, the name is considered to be equivalent to—that is, interchangeable with—Mahican. Others have concluded that the Mahicans and River Indians "seem to be geographically and probably politically distinct populations," separate also from Munsees, a position opposite to that where the term "River Indians" is used as a generic for all Native residents of the Hudson Valley.[113] In their turn the Indians at Schaghticoke are considered by some to be exclusively Mahicans or a population of New England Indians founded on what may have been an earlier Mahican community. Noteworthy, however, is a remark by Soquans, a spokesman for the Schaghticokes, made at a conference in Albany in 1700. "Schakkook," he said, was "that place being allotted for us," suggesting that it had been a newly established town.[114] Finally, while infrequent, there are mentions of other River Indians, meaning those Natives living in a part of the Connecticut Valley. Much of this lack of correspondence is due to what is found in European accounts. Nevertheless, the outcome has been a mostly understandable lack of clarity and precision in the attempts by historians to attribute a particular activity or engagement in period events to one group or another.

March 1677 brought a "Notice & Order" delivered to the Mohawks "to send no more partyes farre Eastward" against the Northern Indians and to recall those already in the field so that Governor Andros might "settle things there." The Mohawks, however, paid the order scant attention. That July, Andros reported, strangely enough, that Mohawks, *together with* Northern Indians, had acted with "Insolence and violence . . . upon the Mahicanders."[115] But Andros had either been misinformed or was confused about what he had been told. In June "some *Mahicander* Indyans" told officials in Albany that they were "afraid of the *Maques* Indyans." Within days, undoubtedly describing what actually had happened, and making more sense, came word that eighty to one hundred Mohawks had "fallen upon some *Ma-*

hicandrs & *North* Indyans at *Phillip Peiters* Bowery and the [area of] *Halfe Moone*, robbing the *Mahicandrs* and carrying the Others away Prisoners."[116] In the meantime, Father Jacques Bruyas, from his mission post in the western Mohawk village, sent word to Albany that "forty *Oneydas* designed to fall on our River Indyans at *Catskill*," where there was another Mahican community. There is nothing to confirm that such an attack took place.[117] But the year 1677 was the last time that the Mohawks and other Iroquois, finally triumphant, would war against the Mahicans, leaving these Natives a minor power in the region.

Although occupied with events close to home and adjacent New England, numbers of Mahicans had made their way into Canada and west to near Lake Huron, where they hunted beaver, no longer abundant in the Hudson Valley. Their pursuits to the north, where they were joined by Indians from elsewhere in the Hudson Valley, were chiefly meant to assist the English in their conflict with the French. Yet Bruyas believed that Andros would nonetheless voice disapproval of some of their conduct. In July 1678, for example, a party of "*Mahingans Taraktons* [Catskill Mahicans]" had passed through Mohawk country with "two prisoners of the *Algonquins*," this after Andros "did forbid those Indyans [Mahicans] to make warre in those parts."[118] Even so, Trelease points out that into the 1680s, the River Indians—in this instance Mahicans—played but a subsidiary role there, linked to their now settled relationship with the Mohawks, who were and would ever remain a staunch English ally.[119]

That the River Indians' role in Canada was a subsidiary one appears to be contradicted by information contained in a letter to Joseph-Antoine le Fèbvre de la Barre, governor of New France, in September 1684. Its writer, the Jesuit Father Jean de Lamberville, reported that "six or seven hundred Mohegans (*Loups*) were preparing to go to the assistance of the Iroquois," against whom the French were planning an invasion. "Mohegans [Mahicans]" is the translator's interpretation of "Loup," which may be incorrect. It is difficult to imagine the Mahicans fielding such

A Century of Mahican History

a large force of warriors at this late date, even if the Indians at Schaghticoke were included in the total. Either Lamberville was mistaken about or had exaggerated his figures, or his information was wrong.[120] Instead, the Mahicans seem to have served primarily as scouts or, operating in small raiding parties, as interceptors of French Indians making their way toward English settlements.[121]

New York officials, however, became increasingly concerned with the influence that they believed the French were exerting on an unknown number of Mohawks, along with the "North Indians with the River Indians." It was alleged that the French were attempting to draw these Natives to their side by giving them land and "4 Forts," and by putting "a head[man] over them." In response, the Albany commissioners ordered that the Mohawks at home "may bee underhand advised to give all Encouragement to draw back the Indyans that are gone to *Canada* whether *Maques*, North Indyans or *Mahicandrs*," with the promise of "land assigned them to build forts together or a part in some convenient place if desired in ye Governmt."[122]

New York's efforts to bring back the Mahicans from Canada and return them to the fold did not meet with immediate success. In a conference with the five Iroquois nations in August 1687, Governor Dongan asked that "you ought to doe what you can, to open a path for all the North Indians and Mahckanders that are att Ottowawa and further Nations, and I will endeavour to doe the same to bring them home." The Mahicans and Northern Indians, it seems, feared to pass through Iroquois country on their return from the eastern Great Lakes, while, at the same time, Dongan warned the Iroquois that the French wanted to keep them as allies "on purpose to joyne with these further Nations against you for your distruction."[123] The reply of the Iroquois is informative, clearly suggesting that not all of the Mahicans were open to French overtures. The "Mahikanders and other River Indians" who resided in New York colony were, the Mohawk spokesman reminded Dongan, along with all the Iroquois, "subjects of the Great King of England, whom his Excellcy will be pleased to make use off and send to the Farr Nations of Indians to help to effect the peace."[124]

Early the next year, French agents, among whom was the Jesuit Father François Vaillant (1646–1718), traveled to Albany to "compose the difference" with Dongan. Once there, they complained of having been set upon by "some Indians called Mahingans subjects of the Government of New Yorke." These Indians were among those "who returned out of Canada," obviously having rejected whatever invitation the French may have extended to join them in their wars against the Iroquois.[125] Earlier, in 1685 and 1686, however, Dongan had strengthened the Iroquois' hand by licensing trading expeditions into the Ottawa country, intending to divert the fur trade to Albany. The Iroquois enthusiastically supported this endeavor as it would not only draw Great Lakes Indians to their villages on their way to trade at Albany, but it would deny the French vital economic and military bases. Irritated by Dongan's attempt to undercut the western trade, the French decided to end by force the competition over furs and punish the Iroquois for warring against their colony and its Indian allies.

In June 1687, nearly 2,000 French and Indians moved against the Senecas, scattering their warriors and burning their villages and stores of food. Well armed by New York, the Iroquois retaliated in kind, raiding French settlements along the frontier. Then, in late 1689, during the first days of the War of the League of Augsburg, in the colonies called King William's War (1689–1697), a force of 1,500 Iroquois warriors destroyed Lachine, the French settlement near Montreal, seriously disrupting the trade. The expected retaliation by the French was met by counterraids by the Iroquois, a pattern of violence that continued into the 1690s.[126]

Only a limited amount of this activity seems to have involved the Mahicans. Notable, however, was the participation of Schaghticoke Indians in a bungled land and sea assault on Canada by

A Century of Mahican History

New York and the New England governments in summer 1690. A promise from Mohawk headmen for 1,000 men—Mohawks, other Iroquois and their Algonquian allies—never materialized, the mission derailed by a smallpox epidemic in their towns. Instead, a small force led by Johannes (John) Schuyler, joined by some 120 Mohawks, Oneidas, Onondagas, and Schaghticokes, struck out for La Prairie de la Magdeleine, opposite Montreal. Arriving at the French fort there, Schuyler was told that "the folks were leaving the fort of La Prairie to cut corn." Unable to control either his troops or the Indians, about twenty prisoners were taken along with six scalps. It was only then that Schuyler discovered the enemy garrison of 800 men had slipped out of the fort, which he nonetheless decided to take. But Schuyler "could not move the savages to give their consent to help us." Denied a fight, Schuyler ordered the killing of nearly 150 head of cattle; the torching of homes, barns, and hay; "and everything else which would take fire," and with that he returned to Albany.[127]

The following summer, a larger party of Mohawks and "River Indians," among whom were Mahicans, marched with a company commanded by Major Peter (Pieter) Schuyler, Johannes Schuyler's brother, to once again launch an attack on La Prairie.[128] There, it was rumored, the French were gathering men and supplies for an assault on Albany. In an indecisive to-and-fro struggle that took place on August 1, the English and Indian force of 266 men lost 21 "Christians," 16 Mohawks, and 6 River Indians, while leaving about 200 Frenchmen and their Indian allies dead on the field of battle.[129]

At the same time that Mahicans, whether from their communities below Albany, linked to Schaghticoke or elsewhere, were playing a relatively minor role in King William's War, if only due to their small numbers and vulnerability, a few were occupied elsewhere. There is nothing in the record that reveals what the Mahicans on the upper Housatonic might have been up to. As mentioned before, however, some Mahicans had been drawn to the eastern Great Lakes by the fur trade, and beginning in the early 1680s others made their way into northern Illinois and Indiana—Miami country—where an unknown number would remain in anonymity.[130] Mahicans also appear to have joined the Mohawks and Esopus Indians in raids against the Piscataways and other Indians in Maryland and Virginia.[131] A decade later River Indians (here Schaghticokes), along with Minisinks, entered the Ohio Valley, possibly with English backing, to open the trade with the Shawnees.[132]

In August 1692 a party of Shawnees that had been approached by several Minisinks and Mahicans traveling in their country appeared in the upper Delaware Valley. They were met by Arent Schuyler, who had been dispatched with orders to bring them to Albany.[133] After conferring with colonial officials and Iroquois headmen there, these Indians, who above all wanted access to the trade, were escorted back to their homeland by one Arnout Viele and a party of eager fur brokers.[134] After two years in the west, of which little is known, Viele led about a thousand "Showannees Farr Indians," evidently most of those then living in Ohio, toward New York colony. Along with these Natives, it was said, came "seaven Nations of Indians with women and children." Schuyler, in turn, reported that "seaven hundred of ye Shawans Indians loaden wth beavor and peltries" would arrive in midsummer. Whatever the case, reaching their destination in July 1694, many of these Indians remained in the upper Delaware Valley to live among the Minisinks. Others would settle on the Susquehanna and Potomac Rivers. Records indicate that the Shawnees, and likely those Indians who traveled with them, were received as friends of the Iroquois and placed under the protection of Governor Fletcher.[135] Evidence of significant Mahican involvement in these actions, however, is slim, although in his history Hendrick Aupaumut has it otherwise. Much of what he offers, however, is difficult to verify.[136]

Mahicans continued their now close relationship with the Mohawks and other Iroquois as the century drew to an end, taking part in the now and again foray against New France and her Indian allies. Nevertheless, they and the Schaghticokes maintained their historic friendly ties with their brethren, the Northern Indians, who themselves were firm allies of the French.[137] There were, however, the shifts in ground by both Native and European actors as England and France vied for political and economic control of the region, their efforts thoroughly bound up in their and the Natives' struggles over the trade in furs. Historian Daniel Richter has it right in his description of the "many-headed political culture" of the Iroquois, where "localism, factionalism, voluntarism, and individualistic patterns of leadership operated paradoxically within a system stressing consensus."[138] Much of the very same can be said for the Mahicans, along with their neighbors the Munsees and the New England Algonquians, where individuals or groups of individuals within the same people tended to go their own ways and for their own reasons.

In the tumult of the period, it becomes increasingly difficult to sort out the sides taken and the strategies employed by all concerned, amid the blurred loyalties and ever-evolving intrigues. For example, in early 1695, Seneca and Cayuga messengers brought news to the Onondagas that plans were afoot for a French force, commanded by Governor General Louis de Buade de Frontenac, to attack them in the spring. Complicating matters, however, was Frontenac's improbable expectation that "the other four [Iroquois] Nations to be sylente." His reasoning was that "Dekanissoré," an Onondaga headman, "had broke his word in not returning to Canida" and that he "had gon' to Albany to meete Cayenquiragoe [Governor Fletcher], & has given defyance to all the strength of Canida." The Iroquois quickly moved to inform the "Mahikanders or River Indians" of this turn of events, whom the Onondagas then asked to assistant them in repulsing the anticipated assault.[139]

In July 1695 Major General Fitz-John Winthrop led Connecticut colonials and "Maquaes, Saktaco [Schaghticoke], and River

Indians" on a military expedition to Canada from Albany, intending to catch up with a company of Dutchmen that had left two days earlier. Hobbled by short provisions and the spread of smallpox among his troops, Winthrop got no farther than Wood Creek, near Lake Champlain. He nonetheless managed to send forty of his own men—"Christians"—and a hundred Indians north, where they raided what had become a convenient target, La Prairie de la Magdeleine, killing twelve and taking nineteen prisoner.[140] These and similar such raids continued to occupy Mahican, Schaghticoke, and Munsee warriors—the oft-labeled River Indians.

Mahicans were obviously involved in more than trade and warfare during the last quarter of the seventeenth century. Sales of their lands continued apace, especially in the acknowledged core area of their homeland—the Hudson Valley south of Albany and the environs of the Schodack Islands.[141] Not surprisingly these and earlier conveyances led to an ever-shrinking land base, restricting the ability of Mahicans to farm and leaving them to rely on what was left of the trade in furs or to seek their fortunes elsewhere. For most of these Natives, however, survival was dependent on selling more land, which nonetheless diminished even further their economic and political independence. Still, the Mahicans seem to have maintained their communities around Catskill Creek, the Schodack Islands, on the upper Housatonic, and here and there in the vicinity of Albany. The River Indians, as Governor Fletcher saw them in 1696, whose numbers may have included some Mahicans, "are much dispersed and scattered upon the River, in so much that I can not see a body of you, by this you become weak and a prey to your Enemies." He then directed these Indians "to settle together," undoubtedly at Schaghticoke, "that I may see you in a body as the Five nations, by which you will be stronger, and better able to secure yourselves and do service for the Country."[142]

In August and September 1700, months before the commencement of Queen Anne's War, as the War of the Spanish Succession

A Century of Mahican History

(1702–1713) became known in the colonies, New York's governor Richard Coote, earl of Bellomont, met with the five Iroquois nations in Albany. Also present was a contingent of River Indians, who brought to the table their own concerns. This conference would lead directly to the 1701 treaty at Albany and another at Montreal, both of which represented an Iroquois initiative to secure their hunting territories and to neutralize their longtime foes, the French and their Indian allies. Bellomont's first order of business was to dismiss widespread and troubling rumors of an Anglo-French plot to destroy the Iroquois. To this issue was attached what was for New York the unsettling prospect of French influence on these Indians through the efforts of Jesuit priests, who were actively engaged among the Iroquois. Iroquois interests, however, were to protect their hunting territories north of Lake Ontario, and moreover, to ensure that their promises to the Western Indians—the Mississaugas, Ojibwas, and others—that they would have access to the trade in Albany, were kept.[143]

Well into the conference, Soquans, the River Indians' representative, stood to address Bellomont. Soquans's opening statement described a time when the Christians had first come to the region that would become "Renselaer's ys [sic] land," whom, he said, "wee lov'd as soon as wee see them." Although the Indians of which Soquans spoke must have been Mahicans, he then suggested something different—that it had been twenty-six years "since wee were allmost dead when wee left New England and were first received into this government." That is, these were the Indian refugees from King Philip's War, invited by New York's government to establish Schaghticoke. The thrust of Soquans's speech, however, was largely meant to assure Bellomont that the Indians at Schaghticoke would remain there and not be a cause of worry to the colony, as the Iroquois had become. "Wee are unanimously resolved to live and dye under the shadow of that Tree [of Welfare planted at Schaghticoke] and pray our Father to nourish and have a favorable aspect towards that Tree, for you need not apprehend that tho' any of our people goe out a hunting they will look out for another Country, since they like that place call'd Schakkook so well."[144]

Soquans went on, "Your Lordship is so belov'd of us all," lauding Bellomont's treatment of Indians as "ravishing and agreeable." For these reasons, he concluded, "the farr Eastern Indians [in adjacent New England] are desireous to be link'd in our Covenant Chain as well as the Five Nations." Nonetheless, accompanying these niceties were Soquans's telling and twice-repeated words, which reflected the precarious position in which the River Indians—Mahicans and others—after years of war, land loss, debilitating epidemics, and economic uncertainty, found themselves: "therefore wee begg your Lordps protection in this government" and that "our young Indians . . . will alwayes return to their habatacôn at Schakkook under your Lordships protection."[145] Five years earlier, December 1685, the same Soquans (Sachquahan) told the Albany magistrates that "All ye Indianes upon ye north River are dead & ye Indians yt Live upon this river are but few in number."[146]

Bellomont's reply was somewhat off topic. Although he would welcome the Schaghticokes' invitation to "your friends the Pennekoke and Eastern Indians to come and settle with you," and promised "you and them the King's protection and favour," he voiced other more pressing concerns. "You have not the same good disposition that the Five Nations have express'd of becoming Protestants and being instructed in the true Christian Faith," he chided. "If you intend to convince mee of your affection and duty to the King," he instructed, "you must resolve to renounce all sort of correspondence with Canada," including religious schooling by the Jesuits, and equally important, "nor carry on any trade with the French of Canada or their Indians." And he pointed to the problematic disposition of Hawappe, one of the Schaghticoke headmen, who was "false to the King's interest and makes it his business to debauch as many of your nation to the French of Canada." He should be disowned, Bello-

A Century of Mahican History

mont told the Indians, "unless you can reclaim him from so ill a custome." With that, the governor presented the assembled Schaghticokes with "40 Gunns 40 Bags of powder of 6lb. each 400 lb. Lead 500 Flints 20 Hatchets 40 Knives 8 Kags of Rum 40 Shirts 2olb. Tobacco 1. Cask of Pipes 1 Dozen Hatts."[147]

Bellomont died in March 1701, and was replaced by John Nanfan. This was just prior to the treaties of 1701, the meetings for which would be held simultaneously in Montreal and Albany in July and August. Over one thousand Indians would eventually assemble on the St. Lawrence, including the Iroquois, the Ottawas, Wyandots, Winnebagos, Sauks, Potawatomis, Miamis, Mascoutens, Nipissings, Foxes, Ojibwas, and others. There was no known Mahican or River Indian presence. The 1701 conference in Montreal would put to an end the wars between the Iroquois and New France. Iroquois objectives there were to reaffirm the commitment to peace they had previously made, to extend the peace to those Native groups not present at the initial peace settlement, and, most important, to secure their beaver hunting lands north of Lake Ontario.[148]

The primary goal of the 1701 treaty conference held in Albany was for the five Iroquois nations and the English to stabilize their relationship and to resolve issues outstanding from what had been a contentious June meeting at Onondaga. Representing New York, in addition to Governor Nanfan, was Secretary for Indian Affairs Robert Livingston, Peter Schuyler, and other local officials. The Iroquois delegation included nine Mohawk headmen, five Oneidas, twelve Onondagas, four Cayugas, and three Senecas. Unlike at Montreal, River Indians were in attendance.[149] What they had to say to Nanfan, however, was little different from what Bellomont heard a year earlier.

"Itt is now twenty six years agoe since our father the then Govr Planted a great tree under whose branches wee now shelter ourselves," said Sacquans (Soquans), the River Indians' speaker, duplicating much of his speech from the 1700 conference. "When wee first come here from New England wee were poor mager [*sic*] and lean," but now the River Indians had "flourished and grown fatt." Responding to an inquiry by the colony, they could field "two hundred fighting men belonging to this County of Albany from Katskill to Skachkook," the heart of the Mahican homeland.[150] Moreover, they hoped to have three hundred men under arms in a year's time, recruited, it is presumed, from the arriving Penacooks and the so-called Eastern Indians. It is obvious that, whatever they called themselves or were labeled by others, the River Indians or Mahicans resident in the upper Hudson Valley were a mixed population of local and New England Algonquians.

In his reply, Nanfan planted "another Tree" for the River Indians, who once again confirmed their firm attachment to the English, and also to the Mohawks. The tree "shall be soe large and flourishing that the branches will shade and cherish as many of your friends as will be perswaded to come and live peaceably" at Schaghticoke, he assured them. Moreover, he promised that they would be kept fully informed "of all publick matters relating to Indians," and that they, in turn, would "doe well to communicate whatever news you have to the Gentn of Albany," meaning the Indian commissioners. "Itappuwa," or Hawappe, as his name appeared in the proceedings of the 1700 conference with Bellomont, seems to have resisted the "temptations" of the French and had returned to the fold. Finally, as had his predecessor, Nanfan extended the king's "Royall protection and favour" to the River Indians, an act that was accompanied by gifts of guns, powder and lead, kettles, knives, mirrors, blankets, tobacco, hatchets, shirts, stockings, loaves of bread, kegs of rum, and vats of beer, "besides what presents was given to particular Sachims [headmen] privately."[151]

The Indians at Schaghticoke, however, many of whom were Abenakis (Northern Indians), were torn in their loyalties. For many years these Natives were, at least nominally, tied to the French and frequently had fought against the Iroquois, the Mohawks in particular. The end of the wars between the Iroquois and the Mahicans, along with the turmoil wrought by King Philip's War, brought the Northern Indians and others in New England to accept Governor Andros's invitation to settle there beginning in the mid-1670s. However, the ascendance of the English colonies and the Iroquois' achievements in forging a peace with New France and its Indian allies in 1701 seem to have made Schaghticoke a much less attractive place to be. It had become, after all, a place soddened with alcohol amid abject poverty, its people preyed upon by unscrupulous Albany traders. Moreover, the heavy losses these Indians suffered in the Anglo-French wars had brought them to a point of exhaustion.

By the turn of the century, then, the Indians at Schaghticoke began a slow but steady drift northward, first settling on the east side of Lake Champlain and joining with the Abenakis at Missisquoi (Swanton, Vermont), just south of the Canadian border. Getting ahead of the story somewhat, by 1723, many joined Grey Lock, a leader of the Missisquoi Indians. Grey Lock, it turns out, may have been among those Indians taking refuge at Schaghticoke after King Philip's War. From there he moved to Missisquoi, where he organized and led raiding parties against English settlements on the Connecticut River, especially those in Massachusetts. And the exodus from Schaghticoke continued, with the Indians moving north from both this town and Missisquoi to the mostly Abenaki community of Odanak and the Jesuit mission of St. Francis on the St. Lawrence. The migration out of New York colony was completed in 1754.[152]

Returning to the first years of the century, by 1703 the situation at Schaghticoke had deteriorated to the point that numbers of their people decided to journey west to live in one of the Mohawk villages. Reaching Schenectady, they were intercepted by Peter Schuyler and a number of officials and military officers, most of whom were from Albany. When questioned about their having left Schaghticoke, the Indians, through Awanie, a Mohawk headman, first argued that, after entering into a covenant with the colony, the English could not "pretend to have any Command over Us." Furthermore, the Indians reminded Schuyler that "in ye Late Warr You gave us ye Hatchet In hand to strive for your Countrey And wee were always obedient To all Your advises and Directions." The result, they pointedly told him, was that they had "Become a Small Nation the flesh taken from our bodyes." In their apparent desperation to continue their journey, the Schaghticokes asked that they not be delayed, that where they were going was "The Place where our Nation formerly Dwelt and kept there fyre Burning there so Now wee are Goeing Up to Setle & Kindle our fyres there again." This tale did not convince Schuyler, who replied: "wee Never heard that they had had a setlement With ye Mohogs," that they instead had been removed by Andros from "The Lake Towards Canida [Lake Champlain] and Planted at Schaakook." Schuyler ordered the Indians to return to Schaghticoke, but "They would Not hearken But Rose Up in a Passion & Went on There Journey up To ye Mohogs Countrey." There they would remain until at least November 1704, when they were the subject of an attempt by the French to send them "back to their ancient abode near Orange."[153] It is not known whether they ever returned, perhaps instead becoming a part of the Mohawk presence that the soon-to-arrive Palatine Germans would find in the Schoharie Valley.[154]

Pressures on the Mahicans, nearly all of whom had lived outside the confines of Schaghticoke, continued, marked by further land loss, hunger, poverty, and the bane of all Indian communities, alcohol. "Wee are very Glad to see You," the "Mahikanders or River Indians" told Peter Schuyler and a host of colony officials in August 1720. They had come to the conference without the customary gifts, explaining that they were "very poor haveing not been out a hunting," adding, "we had some presents from you Last Year but they are all wore out and we are Naked and bare." And they voiced regret for not having the language to understand the minister, "haveing a Great Inclination to be Christians and turn from the heathenish Life wee are bred up

A Century of Mahican History

in." Schuyler was not sympathetic. He first admonished these Indians, along with the Iroquois, as having allowed themselves to be "Deluded by the french and their Emissaries." What they needed to attend to, Schuyler lectured, was to "behave your selfe as Dutifull Childrin and keep your selves sober and eat Drink Hunt and Plant in Peace." Given that there was no question as to the Indians' loyalty to his government, and "since [you] Complain of your Poverty and are so bare & nake[d] which must be ascribed to your Drinking and Laziness," Schuyler supplied them with ammunition and clothing. Even so, facing as they did an increasingly difficult, even uncertain, future, with little reason to believe that things would improve, the Mahicans, for one, would soon be forced to weigh their options.[155]

Nine
Stockbridge and Its Companions

Spaces

The second and third decades of the eighteenth century found
Mahicans at several locations in the Hudson and Housatonic Valleys. A small number, it is generally believed, resided at
Schaghticoke until its abandonment shortly after 1750, leaving
these Indians to seek shelter elsewhere in the region. Although
there is little *direct* evidence that at the turn of the eighteenth
century Mahicans lived in the Schodack Islands area, the traditional core of their homeland, the continued sales of lands there
suggest otherwise. This, even as Dutch settlement was rapidly
expanding, putting pressure on however many Mahicans were
there. Even so, a hamlet of these Indians was reported to be on
Moesmans (Lower Schodack) Island in 1730. And in June 1744
Alexander Hamilton, M.D. (1715–1756), in his famous itinerarium, entered the following observation: "Att five we sailed past
Musman's Island, starboard, where there is a small nation of the
Mochacander Indians with a king that governs them."[1] But Mahicans also lived in other places, although the time when these
communities were first established is impossible to fix.

Some twenty-five miles east of Rhinebeck, in the highlands
of the town of Northeast, Dutchess County, was Shekomeko
(map 8).[2] This was a mixed community of Esopus, Wappinger or Highland Indians, Minisinks, and also Wompanoos from
the Housatonic Valley, dominated in voice and number by Mahicans. Its importance is tied to the fact that in 1740 it became the
first Indian mission of the Moravian Church in North America.[3]

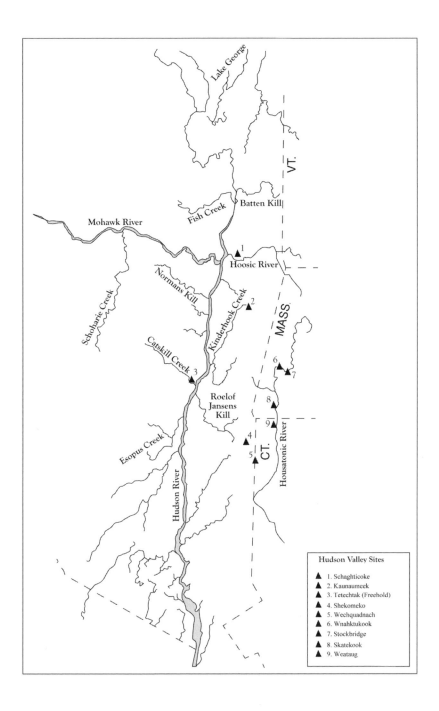

Labels on map:

Lake George

VT.

Fish Creek Batten Kill

Mohawk River

Hoosic River

Normans Kill

Schoharie Creek

Kinderhook Creek

MASS.

Catskill Creek 3

Roelof Jansens Kill

Esopus Creek

Housatonic River

CT.

Hudson River

Hudson Valley Sites

▲ 1. Schaghticoke
▲ 2. Kaunaumeek
▲ 3. Tetechtak (Freehold)
▲ 4. Shekomeko
▲ 5. Wechquadnach
▲ 6. Wnahktukook
▲ 7. Stockbridge
▲ 8. Skatekook
▲ 9. Weataug

MAP 8. Eighteenth-Century Mahican Locations.

Shekomeko does not seem to have been a recently built place, perhaps having been occupied for a decade or two, yet little is known about it before the Moravians' arrival. In 1724 a one-mile square of land, "Shekomakes," is mentioned, likely containing an Indian community, although this cannot be verified.[4] There is, however, much more known about Shekomeko from 1740 to its demise in 1746, information tied directly to the Moravians' presence and the community's political and social relationships to Indians in other areas. It was from Shekomeko that the Moravians made their way to Mahicans living at Wechquadnach, in the town of Sharon, Connecticut, and also to those resident in the large praying town of Stockbridge, discussed later.

A 1745 drawing of Shekomeko by Moravian John (Johannes) Hagen shows a line of fourteen houses with three others close by (fig. 2). Another house is a short distance away. A cluster of three buildings outside of the village is assigned to a non-Indian, "Hendrijsens" (Hendricksen). Also depicted is the mission house and church, a workshop, two root cellars, a fenced garden, a four-pole hay barrack, and a cemetery.[5] Except for the portrayal of a single dome-shaped wigwam, all of the Indians' dwellings are bark-covered half-pole frame structures with vertical or near vertical walls and pitched roofs. Incorporated here and there are rough-hewn planks. Most houses have a smoke hole on the roof ridge, indicating a central hearth. At least one has an external chimney. Similarly constructed houses are known from elsewhere in the Northeast, such as at mid-eighteenth-century Pachgatgoch, a Wompanoo village and the location of a second Moravian mission a short distance east near Kent, Connecticut, and in the several refugee villages on the upper Susquehanna and Chenango Rivers in New York Colony.[6]

The population of Shekomeko is difficult to estimate, as Indians from neighboring communities — Freehold, Pachgatgoch, Wechquadnach, Stockbridge, a couple of poorly known settlements in western Dutchess County, and Potatik, farther down the Housatonic — came and went, visiting relatives and acquain-

Stockbridge and Its Companions

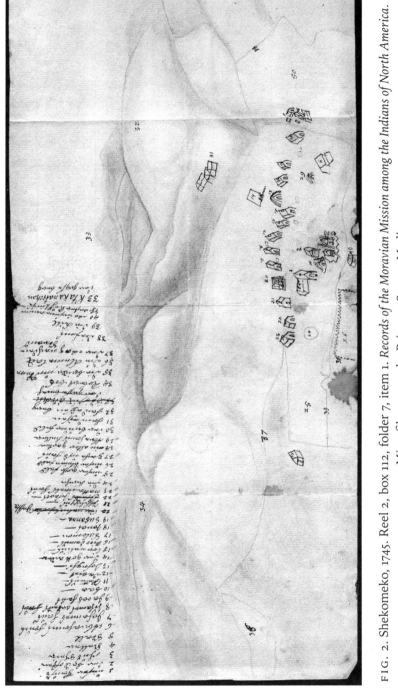

FIG. 2. Shekomeko, 1745. Reel 2, box 112, folder 7, item 1. *Records of the Moravian Mission among the Indians of North America.* Microfilm, 40 reels. Primary Source Media.

tances but also becoming curious about the Moravians. The number of houses in the hamlet, however, suggests a resident population of sixty to seventy persons, who together pursued a subsistence economy based on raising corn, to which was likely added beans. The Indians supplemented these foods by hunting deer, occasionally taking fish and waterfowl, and with seasonal maple sugar making. The Moravians did much the same, lending to the mix of crops turnips, beets, wheat for making flour, and cabbages, from which sauerkraut was made. There is no indication, however, that the Indians consumed root vegetables or cabbages in whatever form. Other economic activities of the Indians at Shekomeko included manufacturing brooms and baskets, which they traded or sold to nearby colonists, and hiring themselves out to local farmers as field workers.[7]

Shekomeko was an active mission and training ground for Moravian workers and ministers who would travel from there to Iroquois country, primarily to learn the Mohawk and Onondaga languages; or cross the mountains into the Housatonic Valley and to the Wompanoo Indian town of Pachgatgoch, where they would serve for some thirty years; or pay visits to the few other Mahican communities in the region. Beyond the effects of their religious message, the Moravians exercised considerable influence on the people of Shekomeko, which worked to some degree to alter traditional Native practices and behaviors. For example, although there were several headmen identified in the community, the Indians, at the Moravians' prodding, "elected" an Indian "overseer" to act in their stead on "external matters," that is, relations with the surrounding colonists — in particular, the farmers for whom they worked.[8] Unfortunately, other than the sketch of Shekomeko, the Moravians had virtually nothing to offer about the Native society in which they lived and worked, nor of the Indian people themselves, save for their presumed secular and religious character.[9]

Life at Shekomeko for all concerned was hard, with frequent food shortages, illnesses, the fallout from Indian drinking, and

Stockbridge and Its Companions

interference, some of it bordering on violence, from local colonists. Further complicating matters was the beginning stages of King George's War (1744–1748) and talk among the local citizenry of possible Indian attacks, one of which had 500 Indians gathered at Shekomeko, joined, if not led, by the Moravians. These and other allegations brought county and colony officials to Shekomeko to investigate rumors of an Indian uprising and also that contraband guns and ammunition were stashed there. Added to this were the grumblings about Moravian intrigues amid suspicions of their being "disaffected to the Crown," a charge linked to their alleged papist sentiments. Called to muster with the local militia and later asked to swear the oaths required under "The Act of Naturalization" (rev. 1715), the Moravians refused. They soon found themselves facing a panel of judges, bound over and ordered to appear at a hearing in New York City before Governor George Clinton and other high officials, and questioned about their political and religious leanings.[10]

On September 21, 1744, "An Act for Securing of his Majesties Government of New York" was signed into law. It contained the pointed proviso that "no Vagrant Preacher, Moravian or Disguised Papist, shall Preach or Teach Either in Publick or Private without first takeing the Oaths appointed by this Act, and obtaining a Lycence from the Governour or Commander in Chief." The following November the governor directed the sheriffs of Albany, Ulster, and Dutchess Counties to give notice to the Moravians to halt all of their activities "and to depart this province." In January 1745 the congregation of the Moravian Church in Bethlehem received word from Shekomeko that the brethren had been ordered to leave. Thus, it was on July 25, 1746, that the mission at Shekomeko was officially closed. Those few Indians who, invited by the brethren, had chosen not to move with their countrymen, first to Friedenshütten and then to Gnadenhütten, Moravian praying towns in Pennsylvania, continued to live at Shekomeko and in the neighborhood. Insofar as the documentary record is concerned, however, Shekomeko ceased to exist.[11]

The lower watershed of Catskill Creek, that portion nearest the Hudson River, was a longtime home to Mahican people. It remained so through the 1740s, in particular about the hamlet of Freehold, some fifteen miles northwest of Catskill. There, in the Indian community called variously Tetechtak, Teteching, and Letechgoth, a Moravian missionary, Christian Heinrich Rauch, accompanied by his wife Anna, was posted for one year beginning in spring 1743 (map 8). Nothing more is known of the community, although its population was large enough to merit two Mahican headmen and, of course, to attract the attention of missionaries. One of these headman was "Corlaar," a person who may possibly have figured in a number of land transactions in Connecticut in the 1720s and 1730s. "Corlaar" (Corlaer and var.), a name derived from Arent van Curler, the founder of Schenectady, was also the honorific the Iroquois had bestowed upon Governor Andros, the king's appointed official.[12]

Southeast of Albany, some eighteen miles from Stockbridge, was the Mahican village of Kaunaumeek (map 8). Patrick Frazier puts Kaunaumeek at New Lebanon, New York; Dunn puts it on Kinderhook Creek, close to the Columbia-Rensselaer county line. Philip Colee has Kaunaumeek in the vicinity of Old Chatham and East Chatham, New York, Old Chatham probably being the most likely location. It is at the distance just given to Stockbridge, and also fifteen miles from Kinderhook and twenty miles from Albany, the intervals provided by the Reverend David Brainerd, who lived off and on at Kaunaumeek for about a year.[13] As with Freehold, this community is poorly known, although it had first been noticed a few years earlier in 1737. That September the Reverend John Sergeant of Stockbridge preached to a gathering of "thirty hearers," although "there were but few *Indians* that properly belong'd there," a hint that it was not very large community. Two years later he would preach to "seven new Hearers from *Kaunaumeek* & the Neighbourhood." In mid-1739 Sergeant wrote that ten families were living at Kaunaumeek. By 1744 the number had risen to fifteen—forty to six-

Stockbridge and Its Companions

ty persons — whose headmen were Aunauwauneekhheek (var.) and Wautaunkumeet (var.). In April 1744 the Indians at Kaunaumeek left and joined the mission community at Stockbridge.[14]

The Mahican settlement of Wechquadnach (var.), meaning "wrapped around by the mountain," located adjacent to Indian Pond on the New York–Connecticut border, had been occupied for an unknown number of years before the 1720s (map 8).[15] In 1726 Metoxson, alleged to be "ye Chiefe Sachem of the indians in these parts," and other Indians, sold a large tract of land that included the western part of Sharon where Wechquadnach was, to the land speculator Richard Sackett, a partner in the Little Nine Patent of New York. With the final adjustment of the New York–Connecticut boundary in 1731, a part of Sackett's land, now determined to be in Connecticut, was confiscated. In 1738 an agent for the colony of Connecticut repurchased from the same Metoxson and others the land that had been deeded to Sackett. The Indians at Wechquadnach, however, insisted that they should retain the right to live where they were, in the northwest corner of the purchase, suggesting that not all of them had been involved in or agreed to the sale in the first place. The matter of lands reserved to the Indians, however, remained unresolved. By the late 1740s the Indians at Wechquadnach found themselves left with only a small portion of their original holdings while the land around them continued to be sold, all of which placed the community under certain threat.[16]

Soon after their arrival at Shekomeko, the Moravians were visited by Indians from Wechquadnach, whose population at this time may have been about forty-five.[17] In October 1742 these Natives went to Rauch with the news that, after conferring among themselves, they had agreed to ask the Moravians to come and minister to them as well. To facilitate this new relationship, they decided to move their houses to the west side of Indian Pond, closer to the mission. But the pressures on their lands, the relentless encroachment of colonists, and doubts about what the future would bring, took their toll. In April 1749, with the support of the Moravians, a few families and individuals began the exodus from Wechquadnach to Pennsylvania. Four years later, also in April, "all the baptized ones" decided to move to either Gnadenhütten or Wyoming, also in Pennsylvania. The last of Wechquadnach's residents were reported to have left by July 2, 1753. Wechquadnach was no more.[18]

That there was a Mahican village called "We-a-taug" (Weataug and var.), situated on the Housatonic River in the far northwest corner of Connecticut, is first reliably documented by Joseph Talcott, the colony's sitting governor, in 1725 (map 8). How much earlier the village had been there is unknown. With a reported population of fifty Natives, it lay ten miles south of a second settlement, unnamed in the records, having thirty residents.[19] Talcott provides no other details on these places or their locations, although Weataug is generally believed to have been on the Housatonic River between Washining Lake and Canaan, Connecticut, which would place the second village north of Sheffield, Massachusetts.[20] Benjamin Trumbull's assertion that "in 1740, there were seventy wigwams, all in a cluster, at Weatog," representing somewhere between 200 and 250 Indians, does not seem credible.[21] It is unlikely that a Native population of this size would have escaped the notice of the Congregationalists at Stockbridge, or perhaps the Moravians, even at this early date. Of course, this is not to say that there was no village. In the preface to a sermon he delivered at John Sergeant's ordination in 1735, the Reverend Nathanael Appleton (1693–1784) reproduced a letter written by a colleague, the Reverend Stephen Williams (1693–1782). Mentioned therein, absent any additional details, is the Mahican village of "*Weteoge* (that is the North-West of *Connecticut* government)."[22]

What appears to have been the case is that, with the incorporation of Salisbury township in 1741, what remained of the Indian holdings at Weataug—actually a tract of land—was lost. A few Mahicans may have stayed in the area, with the majority probably relocating to Wechquadnach, Shekomeko, or Stock-

Stockbridge and Its Companions

bridge, although this cannot be documented. The idea forwarded that a *village* called Weataug was in place early in the last quarter of the seventeenth century is probably mistaken, based as it is on misreadings of the primary sources and questionable local histories.[23]

Stockbridge

Founding

The story of Stockbridge, the praying town in southwestern Massachusetts, has often been told (map 8).[24] There are in print full-length historical studies of the community, critiques of the sources on which such studies are based, narratives on the Stockbridge in the Revolution, analyses of the impact of Christianity on the community, a chronicle of land loss, and micro-histories on some of its citizens, Indian and non-Indian alike. It is primarily the community's beginning and end, however, that are of interest here.[25]

The most important source on Stockbridge, Samuel Hopkins's *Historical Memoirs* (1753), provides nearly all of what is known about the community's founding.[26] The value of this work, as Philip Colee concluded, is tied to its reliability as a secondary source, based as it is on the record kept by the Reverend John Sergeant, in addition to allied correspondence.[27] Moreover, Hopkins (1693–1755), a graduate of Yale College and ordained in 1720, played a central role in the beginnings of the mission, although his involvement after that was minimal.

John Sergeant (1710–1749) also attended Yale, graduating in 1729. He received a second degree in theology in 1732 and was ordained three years later. In October 1734, at the invitation of the Society for Propagating the Gospel Among the Indians of North America, Sergeant traveled to the Housatonic Valley and the Natives there. His obligations as a tutor at Yale, however, required his presence in New Haven, but in spring the following year he returned to the Housatonic, where he would serve as missionary until his early death.[28]

One of the first mentions of the Housatonic Mahicans is from 1676. That August the Indian Menowniett (var.), a Mohegan-Narragansett who had been taken captive near Farmington, appeared for questioning before members of the Connecticut colonial council. At the end of his interrogation he was asked which Indians were at that time living on the Housatonic. "None," Menowniett answered. "They are all gon[e] to Paquiag ye West side of Hudson's River."[29] And so had the Indians about Hadley and Springfield. Paquiag (in the same document called Paquayag and Powquiag) is Packquiack or Pachquyak (and var.), a flat at Leeds, New York, a few miles upstream from Catskill on the west side of the Hudson. Purchased in 1678, this tract became part of the Catskill patent of 1680 and was home to the Catskill Mahicans.[30] That the Housatonic Mahicans had chosen to temporarily join their brethren in the Hudson Valley was undoubtedly a reaction to King Philip's War, which had Indians throughout New England on the move, either as participants or, in this case, fleeing from the violence.

In his 1735 letter Stephen Williams wrote that the Mahicans, "the River Indians," lived below Albany, that is, at the Schodack Islands; had a settlement called Weteoge (Weataug) in northwest Connecticut; and were on the upper Housatonic in southwestern Massachusetts. Hopkins repeats what Williams described, but adds important information on Native holdings prior to the establishment of Stockbridge.[31] It was in 1724 that a number of Mahicans, "all of Housatonack alias Westonook," conveyed a large section of land to the General Court of Massachusetts, one that encompassed the present townships of Sheffield, Great Barrington, and the southern part of Stockbridge. They reserved for their own use a parcel called Skatekook, in Sheffield, where a village by the same name apparently stood. Ten miles farther upriver (at what would be Stockbridge), was a second settlement, Wnahktukook, meaning "at the top of the river." Skatekook may be the village that Talcott reported was in the vicinity of Sheffield in 1725, mentioned before. In each of

Stockbridge and Its Companions

these communities, Hopkins observed, lived four or five Indian families, suggesting a total resident population of some forty or fifty persons.[32] This is in contrast to the numbers of Indians, primarily Algonquian-speakers, but not always Mahicans, who were and would be drawn to the mission over the course of its first decade, only later to be joined for a time by Iroquoians.[33]

It is important to recall that, based on linguistic evidence, the Indians of the upper Housatonic Valley spoke Eastern Mahican, a dialect distinct from that spoken by Mahicans in the Hudson Valley. As Goddard has shown, Eastern Mahican was originally spoken at Skatekook and Wnahktukook, and probably by the Indians at Weataug and Wechquadnach in northwestern Connecticut. The presence of the two dialects — Western and Eastern Mahican — could only have evolved through a process of isolation, where the Indians in the upper Housatonic and Hudson Valleys lived to some degree not only geographically but also socially separated from each other. Moreover, it would also have been the case that these Indians had been in their homelands for a considerable period of time to allow the dialects to develop.[34]

In January 1735 Hopkins, accompanied by Stephen Williams and John Ashley, a man who would become a wealthy land owner in the area of Stockbridge, traveled to Housatonic to meet with the Indians about establishing the mission. A year earlier, at Sergeant's request, the Indians had built "a *publick House*" at this place, situated between Whahktukook and Skatekook, "to serve them, both to meet in on the *Sabbath*, and to keep the *School* in; round which they built small Huts for their several Families to dwell in." The Indians occupied what was a shared settlement during the winter of 1734–35, while continuing to maintain the two villages.[35] But before any discussion on plans for a mission could go forward, these Mahicans felt it necessary to first confer with their countrymen living in the Hudson Valley. The Housatonic Mahicans' concerns, it seems, stemmed from the resentment they understood to exist among the Hudson Valley Indians for having welcomed a minister into their midst without seeking "approval," and rumors that, as retribution, their headmen would be poisoned. A few days later the party of Mahicans living near Albany arrived at Stockbridge, although without incident. On the following Sabbath Williams preached to a gathering there of some 150 to 200 Indians, "great and small." In attendance were Konkapot (var.) and Umpachenee (var.), the headmen of the autonomous communities of Wnahktukook and Skatekook, respectively, and *"Corlair,"* said to be "the Chief sachem of the whole Nation."[36] To the satisfaction of most, Sergeant assumed the post of resident missionary in July 1735, assisted in his duties by schoolmaster Timothy Woodbridge (1709–1775).

As mentioned before, the Mahicans practiced a farming economy, growing corn and beans, supplemented by hunting and fishing. At Stockbridge, they also hired themselves out as field hands to nearby colonial farmers.[37] These activities seem to have been more efficiently carried out from their villages, each of which was several miles from Housatonic, where they spent the summer. However, according to Hopkins, this "laid them under Disadvantages, as to attending upon the publick Worship, and the School, in the Summer." The intention all along, he pointed out, was to provide the Indians of Skatekook and Wnahktukook with land so that they could "settle in one Place, and that there might be Accommodations also for others of the *Tribe,* who might be dispos'd to come and settle with them."[38]

The land selected for Stockbridge, then in the hands of the colony, an outcome of the 1724 conveyance, was "the great Meadow, above the Mountain of *Housatunnuk.*"[39] At a meeting in Deerfield in August 1735, Governor Jonathan Belcher informed the Mahicans about what steps would be taken to put the land in their possession, afterwards bringing the matter before Connecticut's general assembly and then the general court. Over the course of these proceedings, the Indians at Wnahktukook and Skatekook, led by their headmen Kunkapot and Umpachenee, held discussions not only among themselves but also with Sergeant and colonial officials about their options. These were difficult negotiations, marked in particular by Umpachenee's wariness about Christianity and his place in this new religion and, importantly, also having to do with the practical matter of the title to land that the Housatonic Mahicans would hold. Then, in early May 1736, Umpachenee's people moved from Skatekook to a six-mile square of land adjacent to the Housatonic River, granted by the colony. Within this tract was Kunkapot's village. There, in the vicinity of Wnahktukook, Stockbridge was built. In 1739 the village and mission — that is, the praying town that had taken form — was incorporated, becoming the township of Stockbridge.[40]

People

The numbers of Mahicans and other Indians at Stockbridge not unexpectedly varied with time. Hopkins, in a letter written before the Indians were settled on the six-mile square of land on which was the praying town, describes succinctly the fluidity of their movements: "the River Indians (of which those at *Houssatonnoc* are a part) frequently visit their Brethren at *Houssatonnoc*, take great notice of what is doing there; none of them oppose it, they generally approve of it: and many of them express their designs of coming to settle there; and some have put such a design in execution already, and are upon the spot."[41]

In June 1736 Sergeant counted fifty-two Indians baptized among Stockbridge's resident population of "upwards of 90." By 1740 the total had risen to 120.[42] Among other topics, Sergeant described the demographics of Stockbridge in a lengthy letter to philanthropist Captain Thomas Coram (1668–1751) in January 1747. "When I came into these Parts first," Sergeant wrote, the Indians "were much dispersed, four or five Families in a Place, and often moving from Place to Place." Now, eleven years later, and settled at Stockbridge, they "are much more fixed than they used to be." No longer living in wigwams, the Indians occupied seventeen "*English* Houses," undescribed, nearly all of which they had built themselves and furnished with "House-hold Stuff."[43] Some fifty Native families, "besides Old people & transient young Persons," resided then at Stockbridge, representing a population of perhaps two hundred persons. Sergeant observed, however, that Indian families "are but small, as is common among the Natives," a condition that he attributed to "their Manner of Living, and want of suitable Medicines in Time of Sickness." As was the case at nearby Pachgatgoch, and certainly Native communities throughout the region, infant mortality was high, and so were rates of death in childhood as influenza and other maladies took their toll.[44]

Referring to a letter he had received from Timothy Woodbridge shortly after Sergeant's death in 1749, Hopkins reported that there were fifty-three Indian families, that is, 218 Natives at Stockbridge, living now in eighteen houses they owned, "built in the *English* Mode." Baptized Indians numbered 129, of which forty-two were communicants. There also were twelve or thirteen English families living in the community.[45]

Virtually all of the growth in the Native population at Stockbridge can be linked to in-migration, a phenomenon that Sergeant identified as early as spring 1740. "Our number is increased by the addition of new families," he said, although he made special note of how, if only births and deaths were factored in, "our number is somewhat lessen'd."[46] As mentioned before, in 1744 as many as fifteen families, about sixty persons, had moved to Stockbridge from Kaunaumeek, while over time, others relocated from the Sharon and Salisbury areas of northwest Connecticut, perhaps beginning shortly after 1739. They came from "Wukhquautenauk," Sergeant's spelling of Wechquadnach, where the Moravians were at work, and also Weataug. Additional newcomers in the 1740s were Mahicans from Hudson Valley communities.[47]

Other additions to the Native population at Stockbridge were boarding school enrollees. Their stay, however, was temporary. The school was completed just before Sergeant's death, in late July 1749, and the first pupils were twelve Indian boys who had

Stockbridge and Its Companions

been under the tutelage of Martin Kellogg (1686–1758) in New-
ington, Connecticut. Kellogg, widely regarded an incompetent,
failed to properly clothe, feed, and treat the boys while they were
in his care at Stockbridge, and they soon left. Also prior to his
death, Sergeant had contacted William Johnson, Crown agent
for the northern Indian department, asking for his help in per-
suading the Mohawks to send their children to Stockbridge. By
the end of 1751 some ninety-five Mohawk, Oneida, and Tuscarora boys were enrolled in the school. However, disputes between
those involved in running the school, who used and misused the
Indians in their political battles, caused many of them to leave
Stockbridge. In spring 1753, the Mohawk headman Hendrick ordered all of the Iroquois there to return to their communities.[48]

By far the largest number of immigrants to make their way to
Stockbridge followed from the displacement of Hudson Valley
Munsees. In December 1755 the second year of the French and
Indian War, New York's governor Charles Hardy had directed
authorities in Ulster and Orange Counties to warn the Indians
in the area to avoid "Back Settlements, where they might be
mistaken for enemies, and to advise them to seek safety in the
local towns." On March 2, 1756, a party of men led by a Samuel
Slaughter attacked Indians who had encamped on the Wallkill
near Walden, New York, killing several men, women, and children.[49] Three weeks later, following a request from now Sir William Johnson, the Mohawks agreed "to go and bring those Indians living or left about that part of the Country to settle among
us at the Mohawks." These Munsee-speakers were primarily
Esopus Indians from the west side of the Hudson and the environs of Ulster (including present-day Sullivan) and northern
Orange Counties. They arrived in the lower Mohawk village at
the mouth of the Schoharie Creek shortly before May 21, 1756.[50]

A second group of Munsees from the Hudson Valley also joined
the Mohawks at about this time. On May 28, 1756, Johnson wrote
to the magistrates of Fishkill: "The River Indians whose families are at Fish Kilns, have had a Meeting with the Mohawk In-

dians, and it is agreed that they Shall remove and live with the Mohawks." At a conference the following July the total number of River Indians and Mahicans "sent for the 28 may last," was nearly two hundred.[51] Although the record is suggestive, it is nonetheless unknown whether any of these Munsees found their way to Stockbridge.

However, in late spring 1756, 227 Indians identified as Wappingers, under the leadership of Daniel Nimham, who was descended from Long Island Munsees, found their way to Stockbridge.[52]

> About the year one thousand seven hundred And fifty Six, by Order of his Excellency Sr William Johnson, all the Males belonging to said Tribe, that were fit to bear Arms, chearfully entered his majesty's Service: And (having Removed their Females, their aged men, and such as were unfit for Duty to a Place called Stockbridge, for the sake of their being more easily accommodated in their absence) were conducted forth into the wars by their brave Sachem aforesaid himself, continued in his majesty's Servic [sic] as it is said chiefly at their own Expence during the whole Term of the last Warr, behaved themselves valiantly, and were eminently Serviceable in the Reduction of Canada to the British Crown.[53]

Life at Stockbridge

Native life at Stockbridge is not easily reconstructed. As with many praying towns, those who created the record, whether in the form of journals, reports, correspondence, or the like, had little interest in things ethnological. The same was the case at nearby Shekomeko and Pachgatgoch.[54] As James Axtell has written, the oft-stated purpose of English missions and missionaries was to "'*reduce*' the Indians from savagery to 'civility.'" As the English saw it, this meant correcting certain deficiencies in the Indians and their societies along the lines of "order, industry, and manners." This also meant altering, as much as could be expected, Indian economies, systems of governance, tenets of morality and religion, in addition to their "'scattered and wild course of life,'" the last statement being code for removing any Indian claim to the lands that the English so coveted.[55] Thus, the general aim of missions, hand-in-hand with colonial governments, was to dismantle Indian societies and reconfigure them so as to facilitate the intromission of Christianity and the full range of its principles. As a consequence the limited documentary evidence on the Indians at Stockbridge, except for that on the teaching of Christianity and their responses to it, leaves but a narrow window through which to view events there.

Leadership, at least in the early years of Stockbridge, remained with Konkapot and Umpachenee. Each man appears to have occupied a larger house — "*Wigwams*" — than did other families. Indeed, in early 1735 some forty Indians gathered in Umpachenee's house for a ceremony, seating themselves along both sides of the interior and leaving an open space of five or six feet at one end. Hopkins estimated the house's overall length to be fifty or sixty feet.[56] Over the next decade, the familiar wigwam would disappear. And following the deaths of Kunkapot (c. 1766) and Umpachenee (1751), and presumably that of the peripatetic Metoxson, who allegedly flourished from 1704 to 1748, traditional forms of leadership at Stockbridge were disrupted, and then supplanted, by "indirect rule."[57] This was a commonly used tool of colonial governments — to bestow titles and offices on selected, sometimes co-opted, persons or even self-promoters in the Indian community, along with the responsibility and authority to act, at least on the face of it, on its behalf. Thus, the Native political system would be transformed to accommodate the political, economic, and in this instance missionary agendas of the colony. The identical process was introduced and made effective in nearby Pachgatgoch.[58] Arguably the first indication of the colony's attempt to infuse indirect rule over the Indians who would soon populate Stockbridge were the commissions of captain and lieutenant that Governor Belcher awarded to Kunkapot and Umpachenee in 1734. The underlying reasons for granting these commissions have not been reconstructed. However, Colee points out that they came at the same time that plans were being made for the mission, leaving open the strong possibility that they were intended to garner the support of both men in this effort. As Hopkins observed, "When the *English* made Settlements there, they became acquainted with those *Indians*; and *Kunkapot*, the principal Person among them, was soon taken Notice of by the *English*, and spoken of as a Man of Worth." Within a few short years, Indian men in Stockbridge would assume posts such as hog reeve, constable, surveyor, and selectman.[59]

Active in and about the Indian community at Stockbridge was the enigmatic figure of Metoxson, sometimes also known as Corlaer (var.). That is, in spite of claims to the contrary, a one-to-one link between the Indian Metoxson and the name Corlaer has not been historically consistent, suggesting that some other agency was at play.[60] Although it has been claimed that Metoxson was a signatory to a land sale in northwestern Connecticut in 1704, no primary document has surfaced as proof. A "Correlaer," identified as a Mahican Indian, along with his unnamed wife, is found listed in the accounts of an Albany fur trader for the year 1710. No other information is provided. There is also a "Corlaer," apparently living in the area of Lakeville, Connecticut, who appears in a daybook kept during a 1714 survey of the Livingston patent. What may be the earliest record of "Corlar" being attached to an Indian-language personal name was its use as the "alias" for the Mahican Kennanaquen (var.) found in a 1721 deed to lands about Wautaug, namely "Kennanaquen alias Corlar" and "Kenanaquin, alias Corlar." A "Metoukson" or "Metauxson," in the company of other Indians, sold land near Sharon, Connecticut, in 1726 and again in 1738. Next is "Corlair" in Stephen Williams's 1735 letter from Stockbridge. Then, in 1742, the names "Collonel" and "Corlow" are for the first time directly connected to a person called Metoxson. The following year, as mentioned before, the Moravians at Shekomeko spoke of a "Corlaar" at Freehold, absent any reference or tie to the name Metoxson. By 1748 a person named Metoxson was living at Stockbridge on seventy acres of land that had been laid out for him and his family.[61]

There is every appearance that the names Metoxson and Corlaer were carried by more than one person. There is "Kennanaquen alias Corlar," mentioned in the 1721 deed, whose Indian name, Kennanaquen, is linguistically unrelated to Metoxson.[62] However, Metoxson was linked to "Collonel" and "Corlow" by Connecticut authorities in 1742. There is the Metoxson and his wife at Stockbridge in 1748, where he is elected to the office of constable. The "Corlaar" at Freehold, who the Moravians learned of in 1743, was said to have been about seventy years old, making it unlikely that at seventy-five, assuming he was still alive and was now living with his wife in Stockbridge, he would have been assigned such a post.[63] What is more, given where this Corlaar resided in 1743, and from all indications earlier than that, on the west side of the Hudson Valley, it seems improbable that he was the Metoxson, the "Collonel" and "Corlow," identified as the headman who claimed all of the unsold lands about Sharon, Connecticut, in October 1742. What is probably the case is that certain Indians—and they seem to always be Mahicans—were recognized by, or presented themselves to, first Dutch and then English authorities and record keepers as headmen, and were so identified with the name "Corlaer" or one of its variants. The use of this word, then, suggests the meanings "governor," "king," or "captain," that is, a person holding leadership status.

The Indians at Stockbridge farmed. During the mission's early years they added oats and other grain crops to the usual corn and beans and began to raise cattle, pigs, and horses, not unlike what was done at nearby Indian towns. This intensification, in effort and kind, was sometimes made easier and more efficient with the use of horse-drawn plows, either hired by the Indians or driven by themselves, and the addition of fenced fields. None of this, however, promised successful or plentiful harvests. In spring 1741, for example, a killing frost ruined the Indians' corn, leaving them dangerously short of food. Hunting, and probably fishing, added to the Natives' larder. Nevertheless, as a result of decades of the fur trade and ever encroaching colonial farmers, game had become scarce, requiring considerable time and effort to procure.[64]

Hopkins reported that maple sugar represented an important food. However, Colee cautions that it is unclear whether the information on sugar making came from the records Sergeant left behind or from Hopkins, who may have gotten it secondhand. According to Hopkins, sugar making began about the middle of February and continued for the next six to eight weeks, furnishing enough of a supply to last well into the year. Sugar making was also reported at Wechquadnach and Shekomeko, but not at Pachgatgoch, farther down the Housatonic. There, on one occasion, Indian girls went into the woods in early March to collect birch sap from either black or sweet birch, perhaps for a treat.[65]

As noted before, Indians at Stockbridge hired themselves out to surrounding colonial farmers to work at the harvest. There are also references to Indians in the employ of the missionaries and others in the community, where they served as interpreters and housekeepers or received some form of recompense in exchange for goods and services they could provide, such as food, firewood, and the odd job. The most negotiable commodity available to the Indians, yet a disputed and ultimately fleeting commodity, was the land they had been granted, held for a time, and then would lose to avaricious colonials, now and again with the complicity of a few of their own people. Finally, for a short time beginning in the early 1750s, there was some involvement of the Indians at Stockbridge, along with the resident Mohawks, in the ginseng trade.[66]

There are three instances of what evidently were traditional ritual practices among the Mahicans, although those described were specific to the Indians at Stockbridge. All are found in Sergeant's journal as quoted by Hopkins. The first, which took place in early November 1734, describes what Sergeant reported to be a *"religious Ceremony, they had learn'd of their Fathers."*

He and his party entered Wnahktukook for the observance after first passing a "large Heap of Stones" that the Indians added to whenever they happened to pass by, a custom they said their ancestors had followed. At Konkapot's house they found several Indians in attendance. Soon two men appointed for the ceremony "took a Deer down that had been hung up in the Wigwam, which was to be offer'd, and laid the four Quarters upon a *Bark* in the Middle of the House (the Rest sitting round very serious)." The quarters were then placed together, and the skin and head, which had been removed, arranged on top, suggesting a reassembling of the animal, over which a man offered words of thanks. A string of wampum was then given to the orator, after which the deer pieces were boiled and eaten, and the skin, head, and some of the innards presented to "an Old Widow Woman, which is a Deed of Charity they always practice upon such Occasions."[67]

A second ceremony or ritual was one designed to discover who may have been responsible for the recent deaths of two men, where poisoning was suspected. Some forty Indians gathered in the evening at Umpachenee's wigwam for what Sergeant said was a "Pawwaw." There, it was hoped, "those who did the Fact would appear to their *Priests*," who were called "Pawwaws" (powwows).[68] Inside the wigwam, which had been swept clean and where fires had been built, each Indian present sat with two sticks, a foot and a half long, placed under him, one of which had a split end.

> They began with rapping their Sticks, and singing; their eldest *Priest* sitting, and talking, and acting a different Part from the Rest. *This continu'd about an Hour.* Then the *Priest* rose up, and threw off all his Cloaths, except the Flap that cover'd his Nakedness: And then, naked, pass'd from one End of the *Wigwam* to the other, with his Eyes fast shut, seeming to be in the utmost Agony; used all the frightful Motions and distorted Gestures imaginable. *This continu'd about another Hour.* Then the first *Priest*, being beat out, retir'd, and a second

rose, and acted the same Part; so a third, and a fourth. *This* continu'd all Night, without any Intermission, except some short Intervals, in which they smoak'd a Pipe, and some Times, for a short Space, they all got up and danc'd.[69]

There is no indication whether the culprit or culprits were revealed to the powwows, but none of this behavior pleased Sergeant, who informed the Indians of his displeasure.

Last is a ritual held for the *"Mourning for the Dead*, and is celebrated about twelve Months after the Decease, when the Guests invited make Presents to the Relations of the Deceas'd, to make up their Loss, and to end their Mourning."* The presents are delivered to a speaker appointed for the occasion, who then lays them "upon the Shoulders of some elderly Persons." After addressing the gathering, the speaker distributes the presents to the mourners, consoling them about their loss and asking them to set aside their sorrow. Afterward the Indians share food, "make Merry," and *"Keutekaw,* or *Dance,"* a word also found in Hopkins as *"Kentikaw."* This is one of several known phonetic spellings of the Munsee word *kundkaan* 'one dances', with closely related forms in Unami and Pidgin Delaware. It carries with it no other meaning. Indeed, Sergeant questioned the Indians about the Kentikaw, asking whether "there were any Religion in it?" No, was their answer, "it was only a civil Custom of their Nation."[70]

War: French and Indian

Of the wars that so indelibly marked the shared history of Native people and colonial Americans, two stand out in their impact on the Indians at Stockbridge — the French and Indian War and the American Revolution. The first has been written about by a number of historians, the most comprehensive and authoritative treatment by far being Patrick Frazier's *The Mohicans of Stockbridge*. Stockbridge warriors, often mistrusted by their colonial neighbors, as were most Indians, and their allegiance questioned, nonetheless fought on their side in the struggle against

New France. Recruited by Sir William Johnson and William Shirley, the governor of Massachusetts Bay Colony, and from 1755 to 1756, in command of North American forces, the Stockbridge formed their own company led by their headmen or by colonial militia captains. They initially saw little action but soon joined with Shirley's troops for what turned out to be an aborted campaign against Niagara. Later, following Johnson's advice to commander-in-chief James Abercromby, the company was reorganized into small scouting units assigned to Roger's Rangers, the storied guerrilla force of light infantry. Operating mostly in and around Lake Champlain and Lake George, it was with the rangers that Stockbridge warriors attained a rather uneven reputation in battle against the French and their Indian allies. Around this came frequent disputes over pay, often ill-treatment by their English superiors, and their own failings when it came to alcohol and the resultant drunken brawls. Along the way the Stockbridge suffered losses not only in combat but even more so to disease. At war's end there were probably just twenty able-bodied men of fighting age remaining at Stockbridge.[71]

It has been suggested that Stockbridge men, along with their Native neighbors, went to war to reaffirm both their status as warriors and their Indian identities, intangibles that are impossible to measure or confirm.[72] The documentary record, however, provides sufficient evidence to show that there were more immediate concerns confronting Indian people. Having left behind many of their former subsistence practices, the Indians at Stockbridge and neighboring communities had by midcentury entered into a cash economy. Foodstuffs, household items, clothing, and other forms of matériel were bartered or paid for in coin. But this shift in economic pursuits also brought with it debt. And it was debt, or the attempt to avoid debt obligations, that most often drew men to enlist—to fight, to work as laborers, or both.[73] Some Indians, however, benefitted in other ways from the war. At Pachgatgoch, for example, a colonial recruiter, a "captain from Westenhook," bribed the headman Gideon, who "immediately gave all the young people the liberty — indeed, he advised them to go to war; there, they would be able to get plenty of money."[74]

The French and Indian War wreaked havoc in the colony and especially among Native communities, Stockbridge included. Many Native groups in New England were beaten into submission and displaced, reduced to mere shadows of their former selves. The war gave rise to acts of belligerency and bigotry against Indian people throughout the region and opened even wider the door to indirect rule. The movement of Stockbridge men in and out of the community put a strain on families and disrupted village routine. Accompanying all of this were hunger, sickness, alcohol abuse, and destitution. No longer viewed as serving a useful military purpose, to be a buffer on the colony's frontier, the Indians at Stockbridge found themselves increasingly disadvantaged amid the growing disinterest of those who had allegedly been their comrades-in-arms and benefactors. Seriously undermining the Indians' ability to maintain their community was the acceleration of land loss as settlers flooded into western Massachusetts.[75]

Beginning early in the eighteenth century, through the years of King George's War and the French and Indian War, numbers of Indians made their way out of New England and eastern New York, south from Iroquoia, north from Pennsylvania and the broad area surrounding Chesapeake Bay, and elsewhere, to settle in the upper Susquehanna Valley. These and other conflicts, in combination with aggressive colonial expansion and landgrabs, had displaced hundreds, if not thousands, of Native people from their homelands and into what would turn out to be a culturally erosive and baneful exile. There were Tuscaroras from North Carolina; Conoys (Nanticokes and Piscataways) from Maryland, Delaware, and Virginia; Shawnees; and Tutelos out of the Roanoke River Valley. Additional arrivals came from Long Island and southern New England, while Munsee-Delawares moved west from their homes in the lower Hudson Valley.

Stockbridge and Its Companions

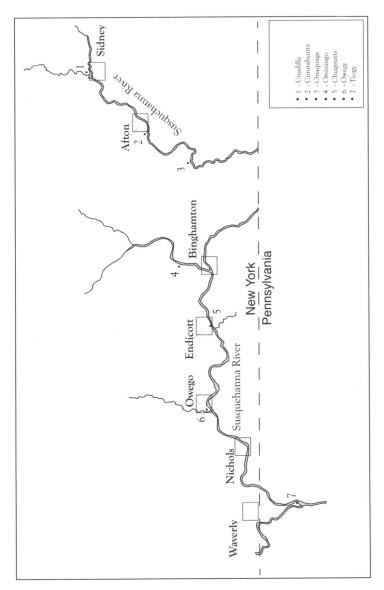

MAP 9. Susquehanna Valley Settlements. After Gillette and Funk, "Europeans Come to the Upper Susquehanna."

• 1 - Unadilla
• 2 - Cunnahunta
• 3 - Onaquaga
• 4 - Otsiningo
• 5 - Chugnutts
• 6 - Owegy
• 7 - Tiogy

Mahicans and River Indians were a significant part of the exodus — this resettling of Indian populations — coming out of the Hudson and upper Housatonic Valleys. Those Mahicans who in the 1750s had gone into Pennsylvania with the Moravians, however, appear to have remained where they were.[76] The main settlements in the upper valley, almost all of which were formed of small farmsteads and hamlets strung along the river, began at Unadilla, at the time located just west of what is to-day Sidney, New York, and continued downriver through Cunnahunta, Onaquaga, Otsiningo, Chugnutts, Owego, and then to Tioga, at Athens, Pennsylvania (map 9). Mingling with the residents of these communities were the six nation Iroquois, who themselves had become somewhat scattered, their once compact, fortified villages of longhouses replaced by smaller bark and hewn board-covered cabins placed along the waterways of their homelands.[77]

The earliest of these relocations followed efforts by the Iroquois to encourage Natives to settle in the Susquehanna Valley. Their intent was to impede further colonial intrusions on lands that they viewed as being under their supervision; to stabilize the trade coming out of the Chesapeake Bay area, critical to their economies; and to extend Iroquois claims of dominion, thus buttressing their military and political positions situated, as they were, between competing French and English forces.[78] Soon after, however, it also became the strategy of Sir William Johnson to put Indians on the frontier, drawing them out of the Hudson Valley and western New England, in this way removing them from around colonial towns and farmsteads where they were widely regarded to be a danger. More important, however, were Johnson's more immediate objectives: to reinforce his Indian allies, especially the Mohawks, and to have these Native forces on the Susquehanna where they might serve as a buffer in the war with New France.

Even so, in 1763 nearly fifty Stockbridge Indians met with Johnson in Albany. "As Many of the Mohicander Indians are gone from these parts Some years ago to live along the Susquahana & its Branches, wh. gives their friend here much concern," they told Johnson. "We therefore Father earnestly request You will call them all from thence."[79] Still, the Native settlement of the upper Susquehanna Valley would continue through the Revo-

Stockbridge and Its Companions

lution, much of it at the urging of missionaries and ministers, colonial and Indian alike.[80]

War: American Revolution

The story of Stockbridge and the American Revolution has been carefully reconstructed and told by historian Colin Calloway.[81] As they had during the French and Indian War, although unsure about the source of the conflict, the Indians at Stockbridge prepared to fight, but this time on the side of the Americans. "Wherever you go, we will be by your sides," intoned Solomon, the Stockbridge headman, to the Indian commissioners of the Northern Department at a 1775 meeting in Albany. "Our bones shall lie with yours. We are determined never to be at peace with the red coats, while they are at variance with you."[82] How sympathetic the Stockbridge might have been to the theme of liberty, or averse to the imposition of taxes and laws, or opposed to the highhanded actions taken in the colony by British General Gage, all or any of which might have pushed them to enlist, is unknown. But they did live in the midst of the Americans and had called Stockbridge home for several decades, perhaps reason enough to commit to the cause. Moreover, that their colonial neighbors and influential men such as John Sergeant Jr. had sided with the rebels may have been another factor in their decision. Finally, and perhaps a tipping point for the Indians, was their indebtedness, individually and collectively. It remained a constant and overwhelming problem, driving men to take a soldier's salary even as Stockbridge lands were being sold off.[83]

By 1774 the original Indian holdings at Stockbridge of just over 23,000 acres had been reduced through sales and other takings to just 1,200 acres. The same year, with war on the horizon, Indians from the New England praying towns of Farmington, Niantic, Mohegan, Groton, Stonington, Charlestown, and Montauk, received a grant to land in Oneida country. This conveyance was the result of negotiations between the Mohegan preacher Joseph Johnson, Sir William Johnson, who, upon his death that July was replaced by his nephew Guy Johnson, and Oneida headmen. Known collectively as the Brothertown (sometimes Brotherton) Indians, a membership composed primarily of Narragansetts, Mohegans, Eastern and Western (Mashantucket) Pequots, and Montauks, they had lost virtually all of their holdings in New England and on Long Island.[84] The Mohegan preacher Samson Occom (1723–1792) "served as an elder statesman, advocate, and spiritual advisor" in the founding of the Brothertown community, which he often visited, ministering to Indians and colonists alike and assisting his people in political matters. Occom also appears to have played a role in bestowing upon the community its name, which he spelled "Brotherton" and translated into Mohegan as "Eeyawquittoowauconnuck" in 1785.[85] Although they were determined to create a new place for themselves and distanced from their homelands, one that would be "united around principles of self-determination and Christian worship," the Indians' move into Oneida country was short-lived, thwarted by the onset of the Revolution. Instead, some forty Brothertowns dropped whatever they were doing there and retreated east to Stockbridge to wait out the war.[86]

The Stockbridge volunteered to form their own companies of "minutemen" even before hostilities had begun (fig. 3). In March 1775 the Continental Congress accepted their services, "assuring them they were fighting in the common cause." They initially performed diplomatic rather than military duties, sent out to recruit Indians from places such as the Mohawk community at Kahnawake, near Montreal, and from among the Delawares and Shawnees. But Stockbridge warriors also saw a good deal of action in New York, New Jersey, and also Canada, earning a "reputation for zealous service." And they suffered for their allegiance. In summer 1778 a Stockbridge unit was decimated in an engagement at Kingsbridge (Indian Field) in the Bronx, with casualties amounting to some twenty men killed, an equal number missing, and others gravely wounded. Despite these losses and continued difficulties at home, thirty Stockbridge vol-

Stockbridge and Its Companions

FIG. 3. A Stockbridge Indian, 1778 (watercolor). Courtesy of the
Bloomsburg University Archives, Bloomsburg, Pennsylvania.

unteered to take up arms in General John Sullivan's campaign
against the Cayugas in 1779.[87]

The participation of the Stockbridge in the war, amid the losses they sustained, which included several of their headmen, did
little to benefit them at home. Land holdings were further reduced as war widows struggled to pay off debts their husbands

had left behind. As the war came to an end, the Indians found themselves essentially without place or voice in the town's government, leaving them even more vulnerable to what had been a long history marked by the chicanery and avarice of its citizenry. With their lands reduced to such a point that they could no longer sustain themselves, the Stockbridge turned to the Americans.[88]

In February 1782 Stockbridge leaders, several of whom were the sons of headmen lost in the war, forwarded petitions to the governments of New York and Vermont. In stylized, metaphorical language reflecting a protocol long familiar to Indian-colonial discourse, they reminded each government of the lands they had lost and requested that they be granted lands for their service and sacrifice during the recent war. Unfortunately there is no record in New York legislative or administrative documents that the Stockbridge petition was ever received or acted upon, although it is possible that whatever documentation there was may not have survived the 1911 state library fire. The Stockbridge had also laid a claim to lands on the east side of the Hudson River, a portion of their original homeland. However, New York rejected the claim, first arguing that the Indians had been unable to prove their case when they had initially brought it before government officials in 1766, and then contending that the claim had been extinguished by the 1768 Treaty of Fort Stanwix, which established the Line of Property set by the 1763 Royal Proclamation. For its part Vermont first offered the Stockbridge a tract of land west of Ticonderoga, then another on the Canadian border, and then nothing at all.[89] But in the end it was the Oneidas, their allies in the Revolution, who would provide the Stockbridge relief by granting them, in 1783, a six-mile square tract of their land in central New York. It would be called New Stockbridge.

Ten

New Stockbridge and Beyond

In 1783 New York State took steps to settle its boundaries and assert its claims of jurisdiction over Indian lands west of the 1768 line of property. It first called for a council with the Iroquois nations to be held at Fort Stanwix in late summer 1784, the foremost object of which was to purchase lands occupied by the Oneidas and then move them west to live among the Senecas. However, much to the state's disappointment, the council accomplished little.[1] That October, over the strong objections of and attempts by New York to obstruct the negotiations, federal commissioners met with the Oneidas and the four so-called hostile nations, also at Fort Stanwix, where the "Treaty with the Six Nations" was concluded.[2] An immediate effect of this treaty was to spur New York to extinguish remaining Indian title as quickly as possible — in particular, that of the Oneidas — in order to secure its claim to a preemption right in the face of a counterclaim by Massachusetts. Its more lasting objectives included expanding its borders and, as a matter of self-interest, circumventing any further involvement by the United States.[3]

Establishing New Stockbridge

New York's efforts to acquire Oneida lands were complicated by the first arrivals of the Indians from Stockbridge in 1785. There is no dispute about the timing of this in-migration or to the fact that the community had responded positively to an invitation by the Oneidas to settle on their lands in central New York, a tract six miles square. The relocation of the Stockbridge was essentially completed by 1788.[4] There is no contemporary record describing the original grant of land, nor has the paper deed to the land, issued by the Oneidas to the Stockbridge, surfaced. However, other associated documentation demonstrates that the transfer from the Oneidas to the Stockbridge did take place and was made without any known conditions or negative covenants, as described below.

On February 5, 1785, appears the first entry in New York legislative documents relative to the grant to the Stockbridge Indians. It follows a senate committee report ordering that a bill be written to prevent the purchase of Indian lands outside the authority and consent of the state. This action was taken after John Harper, a trader and land speculator, had negotiated a cession of Oneida land on the Susquehanna River, south of Unadilla, with some of their headmen.[5] During the same legislative session a second bill was ordered brought in "for confirming a grant from the Oneida to the Stockbridge Indians, under proper restrictions."[6] No other information on this proposed bill is found in this or the surviving surrounding documentation.

Oneida headmen, along with Hendrick Aupaumut, the prominent Stockbridge headman, were in New York City on January 27, 1785, to personally deliver the complaint of Grasshopper, "the Chief Oneida Sachem," to Governor Clinton about Harper's efforts to buy Oneida land.[7] They also were in the city on February 5, when the bill to confirm the Oneidas' grant of land to the Stockbridge—the six-mile square—was ordered out of committee.[8] The bill would receive two readings, be sent back to committee where amendments were attached and agreed to by the senate, read a third time, and on March 1 passed. The bill was then sent to the assembly. However, there the issue of John Harper's interest in Oneida lands again surfaced, the outcome of which was the attachment by the assembly of additional amendments directed to authorize and license Harper to make the purchase. Once the senate reviewed the amendments, to which it did not agree, the bill was sent back to the assembly on April 9 and died there.[9]

To all appearances the senate bill to confirm the grant from the Oneidas to the Stockbridge Indians had been written at the joint request of the Oneida headmen and Aupaumut, all of whom were present for the legislative sessions being held in New York.[10] This was perhaps seen as a way to ensure the validity of the grant, at least in the state's eyes, through the enactment of a law. Nonetheless, from the perspective of the Oneida and Stockbridge Indians, there was no question as to the status and legality of the grant. Writing to Governor Clinton on April 11, 1785, shortly after his return from New York City, Aupaumut asked that "in order that I may make my Nation feel more easy I wish [letters or word illegible] you would see that we should have justice done us concerning our rights of Lands — and wish you would send up our Deed the Oneidas gave us which I left in your hands by our good friend Timothy Edward[s] who will carry this letter."[11]

The deed that Aupaumut had put in the hands of Governor Clinton seems to have remained there. It has not been seen since, nor is it mentioned in any of the surviving official documentation having to do with the original grant. Nonetheless neither the missing deed nor the death of the proposed bill "for confirming a grant from the Oneida to the Stockbridge Indians, under proper restrictions," altered in any way the status of the Stockbridge tract insofar as the Indian parties and the state were concerned. The Oneidas had ceded a six-mile square of their land to the Stockbridge Indians.

The matter of Stockbridge lands was next dealt with during the proceedings of the 1788 state treaty with the Oneidas held at Fort Schuyler (formerly, Fort Stanwix). There, Colonel Louis (also Lewis), the Oneida spokesperson, gave the following address to Governor Clinton and the commissioners in his company:

Brother! I must insist upon your considering well the Proposals we shall make, so that we come to a fixed Agreement, and there be no Altercation or further Dispute upon the Subject. There are three

Brothers of ours that must be established in their Settlements by you. The Tuscaroras in theirs, and the Stockbridge Indians in theirs. The third Brother, who lives beyond the Stockbridge Indians (alluding to the New England or Brotherton Indians), is like the White People; he has long Arms: we gave him a large Piece of Land, and he was not contented with it. We contracted it and he was not contented yet, and we then cut it off shorter and left him sufficient still. He has now a Tract three Miles by two. This let him enjoy, and secure it to him forever. We have Nothing further to do with him.[12]

Colonel Louis's speech to the governor, in the immediate context of the 1788 treaty and as it pertained to the Stockbridge, was a further acknowledgment—a reaffirmation—of the Oneidas' grant of the six-mile square to these Indians. Moreover Louis's request, representing the express wishes of the Oneidas that the Stockbridge "must be established" in their settlement "by you," was clearly aimed at confirming the original transfer of land in a manner identical to the failed 1785 act "for confirming a grant from the Oneida to the Stockbridge Indians, under proper restrictions." Furthermore, Louis's statement explicitly released or set aside the tract as separate and apart from lands the state would both purchase from and reserve to the Oneidas. Finally, article two of the treaty, quoted in part below, not only makes plain and faithfully reflects the original intent of the Oneidas as it concerned their grant of land to the Stockbridge, but it unambiguously spells out the state's understanding and full recognition of the transfer: "and further, notwithstanding any Reservations of Lands to the Oneidas for their own Use, the New England Indians (now settled at Brotherton under the Pastoral Care of the Revd. Samson Occom) and their Posterity forever, and the Stockbridge Indians and their Posterity forever, are to enjoy their Settlements on the Lands heretofore given to them by the Oneidas for that Purpose, that is to say, a Tract of two Miles in Breadth and three Miles in Length for the New England Indians, and a Tract of six Miles Square for the Stockbridge Indians."[13]

New Stockbridge and Beyond

On February 25, 1789, "A N A C T for the sale and disposition of lands, belonging to the people of this State" was passed by the New York State legislature.[14] Within its sections is a specific reference to the Stockbridge Indians, which in the main provided for the laying out and survey of lands purchased from the Oneidas in the 1788 treaty and the issuance of letters patent to certain non-Indians.

The 1789 act provided "that the tract of land, confirmed by the Oneida Indians to the Stockbridge Indians at the said [1788] treaty, shall be and remain to the said Stockbridge Indians and their posterity, under the restrictions and limitations aforesaid." That is, the 1789 act changed the status of the land conveyed to the Stockbridge by the Oneidas in 1785, leaving the Stockbridge "without any power of alienation or right of leasing the same lands, or any part thereof, for any longer term than ten years."[15] Although there is no extant documentation on the original cession of Oneida lands to the Stockbridge Indians, the stipulations on powers of alienation and the leasing of lands represent, for all intents and purposes, conditions not previously known or acknowledged by the Oneidas, the Stockbridge Indians, or New York State. There is, however, a proscription on alienation found in the 1774 deed to Oneida lands, drawn up by Guy Johnson, that were ceded to the New England (Brothertown) Indians: "that the said Oneidas do grant to the said New England Indians, & their Posterity, without power of Alienation the aforedescribed Tract with its Appurtenances in the amplest manner."[16] Still, there is nothing in the surrounding documentation that can be construed to place the same condition on the original grant of land from the Oneidas to the Stockbridge Indians.

The 1794 Treaty of Canandaigua

At Canandaigua, Seneca land was the central issue and Seneca neutrality the essential concern. The participation of the other Indian nations was more ceremonial and clearly incidental to the treaty's primary purpose.[17] What deserve emphasis, however, are the following facts: (1) the Stockbridge were a party and signatory to "A Treaty between the United States of America, and the Tribes of Indians called the Six Nations"; (2) they were the "Indian friends" of the Oneidas, their six-mile square grant of land located outside of the boundaries of the Oneida reservation established by the September 1788 treaty at Fort Schuyler; and (3) that by having been a party to the Canandaigua treaty, the Stockbridge received an annuity through to 1830, beginning again in 1836 and sporadically thereafter until the federal treaty of 1856, where "their portion of the annuities under the treaties of November the eleventh, one thousand seven hundred and ninety four" was set aside "for educational purposes exclusively."[18] On December 2, 1794, three weeks after the signing of the Canandaigua Treaty, "A Treaty between the United States of America and the Oneida, Tuscarora, and Stockbridge Indians, dwelling in the country of the Oneidas" was concluded. On two occasions in the treaty text, the Stockbridge and the other signatories were described as "residing in the country of the Oneidas."[19] There is no mention of the Oneida lands reserved in the 1788 treaty.

Timothy Pickering was the federal Indian commissioner appointed to negotiate and conclude the Canandaigua Treaty that "(like all other Indian treaties) was to remove complaints respecting lands." Although the tracts in question were those of immediate concern to the Senecas, "it was natural that an object so important to one should interest the whole." Thus, Pickering explained, "by the terms of the present treaty all the complaints of the Six which were the immediate occasion of it have been removed [and] I trust no heartburnings for past transactions will be felt nor reproaches used in future."[20] Pickering's account of the treaty negotiations at Canandaigua is silent on the lands granted by the Oneidas to the Stockbridge Indians.

Also present at Canandaigua was a delegation of four Quakers, whom the Senecas and the U.S. government had encouraged to attend as independent observers.[21] Three left accounts of the treaty negotiations. Two of these make brief mention of the Stockbridge Indians, those of William Savery and James Emlen. Savery reported that the Stockbridge and Brothertown Indians were on land that had been *"granted to them* by the Oneidas and *confirmed by government,* viz.: Stockbridge, twenty-three thousand and forty acres."[22] Emlen observed: "There are also a Remnant of those tribes ~~of Indians~~ which formerly inhabited New England, and now settled *near the Oneida's Country,* know[n] by the Name of the Stockbridge Indians in Number about 250. — & also about 20 or 30 families at a place called Brothertown."[23] Thus, if the Quakers were aware of the grant of land to the Stockbridge, and that the Stockbridge tract was near, and not within, the lands reserved to the Oneidas, then, it must be assumed, so was Pickering.

The 1811 Quit Claim

"A N A C T for the Benefit of the Onondaga Tribe of Indians, and for other Purposes" was passed by the New York State legislature on March 29, 1811.[24] Addressed in the statute is a claim alleged to have been brought by "the Oneida nation of Indians to the lands occupied by the Brothertown and Stockbridge Indians." Although there is no direct historical context for this claim, it nonetheless appears to represent a continuation of the process of selling lands either held by or, in this case claimed by, the Oneidas. These sales began in 1785 and proceeded apace in the years 1788, 1795, 1798, 1802 (two sales), 1807, 1809 (two sales), 1810, and 1811. And there would be further sales, all but the first in violation of the Indian Trade and Intercourse Act of 1790, which barred states or individuals from purchasing Indian lands absent federal authority.[25] According to the March 1811 statute, "several tracts of land occupied by the Brothertown and Stockbridge Indians, have been sold in fee simple under the authority of the state," conveyances that were "likely to create controversies and disputes between the said Indians, and will materially affect the interest of the state." Given these circumstances, the statute authorized the state to investigate the Oneidas' claim. In the event that the claim would be found "just, legal or equitable," it would "be purchased, or otherwise extinguished."

Governor Tompkins requested an opinion on the Oneida claim from the state's attorney general, Matthias Hildreth, in April 1811. His specific question was whether, acknowledging the previous grants of land, "the New-Stockbridge and Brothertown Indians have the right with Legislative sanction, to alienate those lands to the State, although not to individuals, or whether the cession merely grants a right of occupancy, with a reversion to the Oneida Indians whenever the grantees shall remove or cease to possess the lands described in the treaty of grant?" There is no known record of a reply to Tompkins's question.[26]

The governor's request for a legal opinion may have stemmed in part from an assembly select committee's report, dated March 14, 1809, in response to a petition from the Stockbridge Indians. There, member Richard van Horne reported that "with respect to the selling a part of their land, the committee can only say from the best information that they can obtain, it appears that the Oneida Indians gave the said tract of land to the Stockbridge Indians, on the following terms; the Stockbridge Indians were to occupy and enjoy the land, and that if at any time the said Stockbridge Indians should quit the said land, in that case it was to remain the property of the said Oneida Indians."[27]

This is the first declaration, coming a quarter century after the fact, that there had been a reversionary clause surrounding the original cession of Oneida land to the Stockbridge Indians. Even so, the committee's words cannot be accepted on their face, not without considering the motives of both New York State and the Oneidas at this time. Furthermore, the groping words of the committee do not suggest a high level of confidence in its findings. It is proposed here that what the committee had so tentatively concluded about the Stockbridge lands was very likely based on or projected from wording found in the 1774 deed to the transfer of Oneida lands to the New England (Brothertown) Indians, and also "AN ACT for the sale and disposition of lands, belonging to the people of this State," passed on February 25, 1789." The 1774 deed denies the New England Indians the power to alienate their lands. In the 1789 act land was granted to the Stockbridge Indians "without any power of alienation or right of leasing . . . for any longer term than ten years." Again, there is no extant documentation for the original cession of Oneida lands to the Stockbridge Indians, other than a statement by Hendrick Aupaumut, mentioned before, that there indeed was a deed and that it was in the hands of Governor Clinton.[28]

The record is clear that since 1784 the state had been unrelenting in its efforts to extinguish Oneida title. Moreover, the Oneidas, in most ways impoverished and unable or incapable of maintaining their former way of life, were fundamentally willing sellers. There is no evidence that there was opposition from within their communities to the sales. It is therefore likely that New York, perhaps with the tacit approval and support of some Oneidas, simply manufactured the claim of a reversionary clause, creating a convenient fiction primarily for its own benefit. The Oneidas, in turn, would also have stood to gain by having title revert to them in the event that the Stockbridge "quit the said land," for it would again be theirs to sell to the state.

On July 20, 1811, a treaty was concluded between the Oneidas and Governor Tompkins at Oneida Castle. For the sum of $200, the Oneidas quit claim to New York State all rights and title to the lands then occupied by the Stockbridge and Brothertown Indians, "which lands are described in the Certificate of Guy Johnson Esquire Superintendent of Indian Affairs for the Northern Department the fourth day of October one thousand seven hundred and Seventy four."[29] In a report to the chairman of the assembly committee on Indian affairs, dated February 12, 1812, Tompkins repeated the treaty's characterization of the Oneida claim, now extinguished, as "reversionary."[30] But this is of little import.

The July 1811 treaty was concluded in violation of the Indian Trade and Intercourse Act.[31] However, there is a much more serious, even fatal flaw regarding this treaty. It is not a quit claim by the Oneidas to the lands held by the Stockbridge Indians, the so-called six-mile square. The lands described in the treaty are unequivocally the lands laid out in Guy Johnson's 1774 deed to Oneida land, the lands conveyed to the New England or Brothertown Indians. And those lands were east of and entirely separate from those within the boundaries of the Stockbridge grant. Although the language of the treaty refers to the Stockbridge and Brothertown Indians, it is only the original land grant to the Brothertown (New England) Indians that deserves mention.

The starting point for the metes and bounds of the 1774 land grant to the Brothertown Indians was at the west end of "*Scaniadaris*, or the Long Lake."[32] This is present-day Madison Lake adjacent to the village of Madison, in the town and county of Madison. The west line of the grant runs northerly from Madison Lake to "the Road or Path leading from Old Oneida to the German Fflats, where the said Path crosses Scanandowa [Sconondoa] Creek." This point is at the northern limits of the village of Vernon, town of Vernon, Oneida County. It too lies east of the Stockbridge lands. From the points at Madison Lake and Sconondoa Creek, the remainder of the Brothertown lands trend east toward the 1768 property line, which forms the eastern boundary of the tract, roughly one hundred square miles in extent. No other lands, certainly not the six-mile square granted the Stockbridge, are mentioned (map 10).

Life at New Stockbridge

Stockbridge Settlements

Some of the first Stockbridge families to find their way to the six-mile square appear to have stopped for a short period of time at Old Oneida (map 11). This was the Oneida village that Samson Occom had first visited in July 1774, at about present-day Vernon

New Stockbridge and Beyond

MAP 10. New Stockbridge (detail). From Samuel W. Durant, *History of Oneida County, New York* (Philadelphia: Everts & Farris, 1878).

Center. It was seven miles from Brothertown, a settlement located astride the Oriskany Creek and the modern border of the towns of Kirkland and Marshall, Oneida County, around what is now Deansboro. Old Oneida was well known to the Indians in the area and also to a resident minister, the Reverend Samuel Kirkland (1741–1808), who by 1785 had spent two decades among the Oneidas and other Iroquois.[33]

Within the six-mile square granted to the Stockbridge Indians were two loosely amalgamated settlements—towns—New Stockbridge and Tuscarora. They and the surrounding area became home to Indians who, about 1750, much before the move

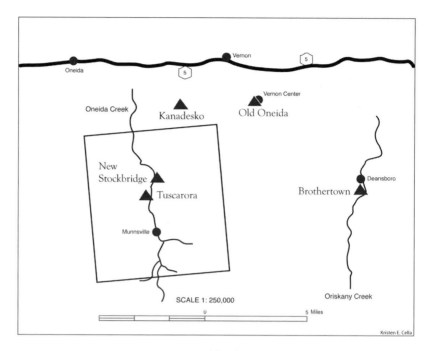

MAP 11. New Stockbridge Settlements.

from Massachusetts, were said to comprise "a hundred and fifty families." By 1763 this number was "reduced to two hundred and twenty one persons." In 1786, soon after the migration from Stockbridge to New York had begun, they were "about one third of that number." Two hundred eighty Indians were residing in the six-mile square or in the vicinity in 1791, not all of whom were Stockbridge.[34] There were about two hundred fifty Stockbridge Indians on the granted land in 1794. Three hundred Indians were reported there in 1796, well settled and ministered by the Reverend John Sergeant Jr. (1747–1824), who had followed them from their former home. In 1820 there were 438. To complete the circle, the last contingent of New Stockbridge Indians left New York for Wisconsin, a move discussed later, in 1829, putting the population there between 225 and 350. An October 1834 census has 320 Stockbridge Indians living on Lake Winnebago in Wisconsin.[35]

New Stockbridge and Beyond

In 1796 appears the first detailed description of New Stock-bridge, the center of which became Cook's Corners and after-ward, called by its present name, Valley Mills.[36] It was here in 1792 that Sergeant and the Indians built a meeting house, used also as a school, supported by funds from the federal govern-ment and Harvard College. Two years later a grist mill was erect-ed, and by fall 1795 a much needed saw mill. Planned for 1797 was a blacksmith shop, including the hiring of a smith, fund-ed by what would be the third annuity under the 1794 Treaty of Canandaigua.[37] It was not until 1800, however, that funds were appropriated by the state of New York to erect "a house of public worship" for the use of the Stockbridge Indians, who had been introduced to Christianity many decades before.[38]

The settlement of New Stockbridge stretched for three miles along the southwest side of Oneida Creek, where there were seen large numbers of deer, passenger pigeons, and fish in the streams. It was isolated from non-Indians, except "there is a good road thro' their village, on which there is frequent pass-ing of white people, and too often on the Lord's Day." The In-dians' lands were described at the time as well fenced around good corn, their pastures kept separate, reflecting farming meth-ods that had been practiced at Stockbridge. The Oneidas, on the other hand, built their homes within large fenced areas that also served as common pastures for their cows, horses, and pigs. There are no descriptions of the homes of New Stockbridge In-dians. However, neighboring Oneidas in 1796 lived mostly in log "huts" and a few in frame houses, several of which were outfit-ted with "covered stoops or piazzas in the Dutch style."[39]

The second settlement within the six-mile square was called Tuscarora. In late March 1790 Samuel Kirkland described it as "at the centre of the tract of Land granted by the *Oneida's* to the Stockbridge Indians, and where a majority of the Tribe have set-tled and built the winter past." Forty years earlier the Tuscaro-ras, southern Iroquoian-speakers who had been displaced from their homeland in North Carolina in the second decade of the eighteenth century, occupied this place, giving it the name Tuscarora. They had since removed to Kanadesko, a second village of Tuscaroras located one-half mile north of the northeast corner of the six-mile square in the town of Vernon. Tuscarora village was located at the northern limits of present-day Stockbridge, formerly Knoxville, just east of Route 33.[40]

Economy

At New Stockbridge in 1796 it was reported that "two-thirds of the men and nine-tenths of the women are industrious." Farming, corn being the main crop, and raising cattle and pigs provided the bulk of foodstuffs for the Indians. There were but a few sheep to provide meat or wool, and little flax, from which linen could be woven, although there was an interest in expending more effort toward these ends as soon as funds became available. Headman Hendrick Aupaumut was singled out as having "a good field of wheat, Indian corn, potatoes, and grass," and owning a yoke of oxen. In general enough food was produced so that the Stockbridge Indians could bring their surpluses to market, the proceeds from which were used to purchase clothing and other goods. Their Oneida neighbors, who evidently paid much less attention to farming, were often "obliged to buy their corn and meat of them." At about this time a handful of Stockbridge Indians attempted to lease their lands for income, a scheme that was opposed by the headmen.[41]

An important sidebar to events at Stockbridge, and certainly elsewhere in Indian country, was the malignant and disruptive effects of alcohol abuse. Both resident ministers, Sergeant and Kirkland, the headman Aupaumut, and most contemporary visitors had something to say about the consequences of drink on members of the community. Thus, one month after the state legislature had made funds available to build a church at Stockbridge, it passed "An act for the relief of the Oneida, Stockbridge, Brothertown, and Shinnecock." Said to have been promulgated at the request of the Stockbridge and Oneidas, along with surrounding non-Indians, the statute prohibited "the evil practice of selling strong or spiritous liquor to Indians, which is destructive to the health[,] morals[,] and civilization of other Indian tribes as well as their own." The law's reach was extended to Long Island's Shinnecock Indians. It did little, however, to staunch the supply of alcohol or to mitigate the damage it caused, and would continue to bring, to these Indian communities.[42]

Governing at New Stockbridge

In 1791 the state, by statute, installed elective governments at New Stockbridge and Brothertown.[43] All males "above the age of twenty-one years" were to meet annually and by a plurality of votes elect a clerk to preside over and keep a record of the meeting.[44] Also to be elected were three trustees, two of whom formed a quorum, whose primary duties were to lay out and allot parcels of their lands to resident Indians. These lands were held in fee simple, with the restriction that they could not be sold to "white people." In addition the trustees were authorized "to lease out to any person or persons such quantity of the undivided lands in Brothertown or New Stockbridge," that is, lands not otherwise assigned to tribal members, following a majority vote to do so.[45] Lastly, the trustees were empowered to bring actions against "any white persons" who trespassed on any of the lands not allotted and to adjudicate complaints between Indians that in other circumstances would be brought before a justice of the peace. Orders of the trustees would be carried out by a person elected "marshall." Even so, several headmen, other than the elected trustees, continued to exert considerable influence in the community.[46]

The 1791 statute was repealed in 1792, although the bulk of its content was retained, with several sections added, by "An Act for the relief of the Indians residing in New Stockbridge and Brothertown." It was made lawful, reads one of the amendments, "for the said inhabitants at any of their said public meetings by a majority of votes, to admit any Indian or Indians of any other tribe or nation to become an inhabitant or inhabitants of the said town, to enjoy equal privileges with the other Indians of the same town, the votes respecting the admission of such person or persons, to be first entered into the clerk's book."[47]

The addition of this particular section, which may have come at the request of the Stockbridge Indians, seems aimed at the anticipated arrival of Delawares from New Jersey. One of the earliest indications of their impending move is a November 1792 diary entry of the Moravian David Zeisberger, who had spent considerable time in Iroquois country. Having discovered "that the Indians have all left Stockbridge (Massachusetts), and now live with the Oneidas, who have given them land," it had been reported to Zeisberger that "the Indians from the Jerseys will also move thither."[48] These were Delaware Indians, primarily Unami-speakers, who had been the subject of the ministerial efforts of David Brainerd, late of Kaunaumeek in the Hudson Valley. His mission at Crosswicks, a place known to the Indians as "Crossweeksung," near present-day Bordentown, was established in 1745. However, the surrounding fields did not produce sufficient crops to feed a population that stood near 130, forcing a move to Cranbury, Middlesex County, some fifteen miles distant. Brainerd died in 1747 and was replaced by his brother John. Nonetheless, from the dispossessed Indians who had been drawn by Brainerd's teachings to Crosswicks and then Cranbury, renamed Bethel, soon emerged the community that would be called Brotherton.[49]

Following the French and Indian War, small groups of Delaware Indians had remained in the colony. In 1758 a series of treaties was entered into between New Jersey and the Delawares, the purpose of which was to extinguish Indians' claims to land, to address their grievances, and to ensure that they would not present a problem to surrounding colonists in the future. An important outcome of these negotiations was the establishment of the Brotherton Indian Reservation in Evesham Township, Burlington County, New Jersey, in August of that year. John Brainerd

New Stockbridge and Beyond

was appointed reservation superintendent and guardian in 1762. According to historian C. A. Weslager, "the place-name Brotherton," bestowed on the reservation in 1759, "apparently was selected by Governor Bernard to connote brotherliness, although he gave no reason for his choice." Although Brotherton initially was home for between two hundred and three hundred Delawares, by 1774 there were only fifty or sixty persons remaining.[50]

To continue for the moment the story of the New Jersey Brothertons, in 1801 they petitioned New Jersey to sell their lands, intending to use the proceeds to relocate to New Stockbridge. Eight years earlier, in October 1793, headman Hendrick Aupaumut, writing from New Stockbridge, formally invited the Brothertons to join his people there. This followed from a meeting of members from both groups in Philadelphia the previous year. In their response the Brothertons alluded to a lack of means to make the journey so that they "could see your fire place." Aupaumut repeated his offer in 1794: "Near two years ago I have take hold of your hand and from h[e]art gave you Strong invitation that you and your nation Should rise up And remove to Our Country where we have a good Dish in which we could Eat together As truly Grand Father and Grand Children wherein we Could be Satisfied And where we Could help one another." He assured the Brothertons that "your Nation shall have Equal Privelege with us which you may be Depend on."[51]

A delegation from Brotherton made its way to New Stockbridge in late 1796, where Aupaumut again urged them to move. On this occasion their reply, couched in solemn ritual language, was in the affirmative. "Be it known unto you that I have deeply considered your Invitation & finding it heartily sincere & your dish so durable & your Paths straight, I accept of your Invitation & lay hold of it with both of My hands, hoping that the great good Spirits may enable & protect us in promoting each others welfare & happiness & that we may live & die together by the side of this fire place."[52]

Unfortunately, there is little in the record that would shed light on the reasons behind Aupaumut's invitation, that is, the Stockbridge Indians' invitation, to the Brothertons to join them. Perhaps Aupaumut, whose plans early on included leaving New York and finding his people a place for themselves farther west, away from ever encroaching settlers, simply wished to augment the numbers of Stockbridge with other awakened Indians, increasing their chances for federal or even state assistance, or for aid from a religious society. There is also, of course, the likelihood of a religious connection between these communities. John Brainerd, who ministered to the Brotherton Delawares until his death in 1781, had followed in the footsteps of his brother David, who, as just mentioned, had served the Mahicans at Kaunaumeek. The Reverend David Simon, an ordained Indian, preached briefly at Brotherton in 1783, but neither the Scottish Society for Propagating Christian Knowledge nor the synod appointed anyone to succeed him, leaving the Indians without a preacher.[53]

Commenting on the fact that the Brothertons had not accepted a long-standing invitation to join their brethren in the Ohio country, Weslager suggests that a schism among the Delawares during the Revolution forestalled such a move. Much more of a stretch is his guess that there may have been ethnic Mahicans within the Brotherton community who preferred to rejoin their own people in central New York, thus influencing the others.[54]

In November 1802 commissioners appointed by the New Jersey legislature reported that the "property of the Delaware Tribe of Indians" had been disposed of, and that eighty-three of their members "were ready and desirous of going" to New York. "They likewise request leave to present a number of speeches together with five Strings of Wampum delivered in full council of the Moheahunnuk or New Stockbridge Indians to the Said Commissioners as a pledge of Friendship and as a security for the Lands and Privileges given by the Said New Stockbridge Tribe of Indians to the Delaware Tribe."[55]

In a journal entry dated October 1804, John Sergeant sketched out the relationship that prevailed between these Indians once the Brotherton had taken up residence at New Stockbridge. At the end of a speech by an unnamed Delaware headman, where he pointed to his now being at a place where the gospel was preached and there was a school, and where his people would have "all the privileges you enjoy equal with you," a wampum belt was brought out and presented. Portrayed in the beads were two persons with a tree standing between them "to represent the council fire place established by the Mahhukunnuk tribe," suggesting that each people would remain autonomous and governed by their own councils.[56]

The imposition by New York of governments at Stockbridge and Brothertown was repeated with the Shinnecocks of Long Island in 1792 and then with the St. Regis (Akwesasne) Mohawks in 1802 and 1812. These statutes were part of a pattern of action taken by the state legislature to institute elective governments in certain Native communities, designed to formalize its claims of jurisdiction and administrative control over these Indians and their lands. Insofar as New Stockbridge and Brothertown were concerned, these initiatives would serve the state well, determined as it was to extinguish Indian title wherever it could and move Native people beyond its borders.[57] For the Indians of New Stockbridge in 1796, however, there were pressing political concerns that required attention, for "the principal division now among them is between those who are in favor of leaving their lands to the white people and those who prefer cultivating them with their own hands."[58]

Stockbridge Removal

By the turn of the century the Stockbridge found themselves under increasing pressure to sell their lands. So it was that in 1803 Hendrick Aupaumut led a delegation of Stockbridge Indians to the Delaware, Munsee, Shawnee, and Miami communities on and about the environs of the White River, Indiana Territory. His activities there stemmed partly from previous diplomatic missions he had undertaken in the Ohio country and the southern Great Lakes region on behalf of the United States, primarily through the offices of Indian commissioner Timothy Pickering. On this occasion, however, Aupaumut intended to deliver a message aimed at renewing ties from the past, to counsel for the adoption of settled farming and Christianity, and, perhaps most important, to confirm a long ago Miami promise of land to the Mahicans, now the Stockbridge Indians.[59]

Beginning in 1807 Aupaumut lived among the Indians on White River with an eye toward acquiring a tract of land upon which the Stockbridge might permanently settle. His efforts seem to have been rewarded late the next year by President Thomas Jefferson, who confirmed that the Miami had granted "to the Dellawares Mohiccaners and Muncies and their descendants forever a certain portion of their Lands on the White River."[60] It was these actions that marked the first stage of the migration of the Stockbridge out of New York and into the West.

Aupaumut returned home in 1815 and with others in the community began to organize efforts to move his people west. In July 1818 the Stockbridge Indians conveyed nearly six thousand acres of the six-mile square to New York State.[61] Soon afterward "one quarter part of the tribes," that is, "sixty or seventy persons," began their journey toward the White River and the lands they believed were theirs, apparently funded by a portion of the payment that had been received from the state.[62] Their plans, however, were thwarted by treaties that the Delawares and Miamis had just concluded with the United States, whereby all rights to lands on the White and Wabash Rivers were extinguished, including those promised to the Stockbridge.[63] Finding themselves landless, with no hope of returning to New York, the party of Stockbridge became refugees, living here and there among the various mixed Indian communities in Ohio. By 1819 they were at Piqua, Ohio, penniless. Moving on to Shawneetown, the Stockbridge were reported to be "in a starving condition."[64]

The majority of the Stockbridge continued to reside in New York, even as the state bore down hard on them to sell more of their holdings. The state's efforts were aided by the encroachment of settlers on the Indians' remaining land, which drew frequent complaints from Stockbridge leaders. In 1801 the state legislature passed "An act relative to Indians," which contained language that would ostensibly protect Stockbridge lands from further loss, in addition to confirming the agreement embodied in the 1788 treaty between New York and the Oneidas respecting the grant of the six-mile square.[65] However, the state's actions to secure Stockbridge holdings were taken primarily to ensure that its own acquisition of land could continue unimpeded, and it did.

Between 1818 and 1847 the state made fifteen purchases of Stockbridge land, amounting to over twenty thousand acres, virtually the entire six-mile square.[66] With the piecemeal sale of their lands, small parties of Stockbridge Indians left New York, making their way to Wisconsin. They first settled on the Fox River, near Green Bay, but in 1833 they were forced to move to land on the east side of Lake Winnebago. Soon afterward they were joined by some two hundred Munsee refugees from Munseetown (also Muncy Town, Muncey Town) and Moraviantown, southwestern Ontario, who in 1792 had come there from Moravian mission communities in Pennsylvania. Together with the Indians from New Stockbridge, they formed the Stockbridge-Munsee tribe.[67] Then came a series of attempts to relocate the Stockbridge west of the Mississippi, which were successfully resisted. Through time, however, their lands were divided in severalty, and they were made citizens of the United States. Yet in the face of decades of legal and political upheaval, intratribal divisions, and appeals to Congress for redress, the Stockbridge persevered, continuing to govern their own affairs.

In 1938 the Stockbridge-Munsees restructured their community under the Indian Reorganization Act of 1934, and the Bureau of Indian Affairs returned to them a tract of land in Shawano County, Wisconsin.[68] Today, home for the federally recognized Stockbridge-Munsee Community is a reservation of over sixteen thousand acres in the rural northeastern part of the state.

Afterword

The system of removing the Indians west of the Mississippi, commenced by Mr. Jefferson in 1804, has been steadily persevered in by every succeeding President, and may be considered the settled policy of the country.

Stipulations have been made with all the Indian tribes to remove them beyond the Mississippi, except with the bands of the Wyandots, the Six Nations in New York, the Menomonees, Munsees, and Stockbridges in Wisconsin, and Miamies in Indiana.

—President MARTIN VAN BUREN
State of the Union Address,
December 5, 1837

In the 1630s Martin van Buren's ancestors arrived from Holland, settling and flourishing on Mahican lands in the Hudson Valley. Yet as president, Van Buren had a direct hand in the relocation of Native people from New York State and the thousands of Indians from America's south—the ignominious Trail of Tears—following the Indian Removal Act of 1830. Although the Indians of New Stockbridge were ultimately permitted to remain in Wisconsin, it was the federal and state policies that Van Buren supported and enforced while holding political office in New York and then as president that sealed their fate.

Van Buren's tenure in government, both at the state and national levels, was lengthy and his influence considerable. From 1812 to 1820 he was a member of the New York State Senate, serving simultaneously from 1815 to 1819 as the state's attorney general. He became a U.S. senator in 1821 and was reelected in 1827. Van Buren returned to the state in January 1829 for a three-month stint as governor, but he was drawn back to Washington to be President Jackson's secretary of state (1829–1831). Van Buren was vice president during Jackson's last term, and with Jackson's encouragement and support he ran for president, holding this office from 1837 to 1841. At the end of his term Van Buren retired to Lindenwald, his estate at Kinderhook, but remained active in national politics. Although he failed in his bid to be nominated for the presidency in 1844, success came four years later. However, Van Buren's party did not win the electoral vote.

President Van Buren inherited the removal policy from the administration of Andrew Jackson, whose harsh and intolerant views of American Indians were then and are still today well known. Van Buren would ensure the policy's seamless implementation. Moreover, it was on Van Buren's watch that the Buffalo Creek Treaty of 1838, regarded as so rife with fraud that the Senate refused to ratify it until it was amended, was negotiated through the offices of Ransom H. Gillet, a New York democrat and former congressman Van Buren had appointed U.S. commissioner. The impact of the treaty was especially great on the Senecas in western New York, who as a result lost a large portion of their lands.[1] By this time, however, the Indians of New Stockbridge, the immediate successors of the Mahicans, were no longer in their homeland, whether in the Hudson and Housatonic Valleys or, after the Revolution, in central New York. Home was now in northeastern Wisconsin, where they would begin their lives anew.

NOTES

Abbreviations Used in the Notes

BA   James W. Bradley, *Before Albany: An Archaeology of Native-Dutch Relations in the Capital Region, 1600–1664* (Albany: University of the State of New York, 2007).

DNN   Adriaen van der Donck, *A Description of New Netherland, by Adriaen van der Donck*, ed. Charles T. Gehring and William A. Starna, trans. Diederik Willem Goedhuys (Lincoln: University of Nebraska Press, 2008).

IACNY   Allen W. Trelease, *Indian Affairs in Colonial New York: The Seventeenth Century* (Ithaca: Cornell University Press, 1960).

NNN   J. Franklin Jameson, ed., *Narratives of New Netherland, 1609–1654* (New York: Scribner's, 1909).

NYCD   E. B. O'Callaghan and Berthold Fernow, eds., *Documents Relative to the Colonial History of New York; Procured in Holland, England, and France by John R. Brodhead* (Albany: Weed, Parsons, 1853–1887).

VRBM   Kiliaen van Rensselaer, *Van Rensselaer Bowier Manuscripts: Being the Letters of Kiliaen van Rensselaer, 1630–1643, and Other Documents Relating to the Colony of Rensselaerswyck*, trans. and ed. A. J. F. van Laer (Albany: University of the State of New York, 1908).

Introduction

1. Jennings, *Empire of Fortune*, xxii, 483.

2. Indian Entities Recognized and Eligible to Receive Services from the United States Bureau of Indian Affairs, 67 Fed. Reg. 46331 (July 12, 2002).

3. It is widely acknowledged that *tribe* is difficult to define in ethnological or historical terms. This is especially so when relevant sociopolitical information is missing, as it is for seventeenth- and eighteenth-century Mahicans.

4. See synonymy in Brasser, "Mahican," 211.

5. Richter, *Ordeal of the Longhouse*, 5–7.

6. Wheeler, *To Live upon Hope*.

Prologue

1. *VRBM*, 180n56, 807; Huey and Luscier, "Early Rensselaerswijck Farms," 64–65.

2. *VRBM*, 307, 809.

3. Pearson, *Early Records*, 1:74, 161–62; Albany County Deeds, 5:161–62.

4. Pearson, *Early Records*, 4:151–52.

5. For the genealogy of the Van Buren family, see Peckham, *History of Cornelis Maessen van Buren*.

1. Landscape and Environment

1. See O'Toole, *Different Views*; Howat, *American Paradise*.

2. [Aupaumut] " Indian History."

3. U.S.G.S., National Water Quality Assessment Program—The Hudson River Basin, http://ny.water.usgs.gov/projects/hdsn/fctsht/su.html, accessed Dec. 1, 2010. It was the tidal quality of the river that was said to explain its attraction to the ancient ancestors of the Mahicans who, it was claimed, had migrated east from a place of "great waters or sea, which are constantly in motion, either flowing or ebbing." [Aupaumut] " Indian History," 100.

4. For a comprehensive treatise on the river see Levinton and Waldman, *Hudson River Estuary*.

5. R. Smith, *Tour of the Hudson*, 80.

6. Purchas, *Purchas His Pilgrimes*, 369.

7. *NNN*, 46–47; Adams, *Hudson River Guidebook*, 10. The best history of these islands and their importance to the Mahicans and the Dutch is Huey, "Mahicans, the Dutch, and the Schodack Islands." *Beer* can denote either a bear or a boar in Dutch. Misguided by the pronunciation, the English mistakenly renamed it Barren Island. *DNN*, 153n40.

8. *NNN*, 48.

9. *Morgen*, a Dutch land measure of about two acres.

10. *NNN*, 171.

11. *NNN*, 170. An editor's note on this page identifies the farmer as Brant Peelen, whose fields were on Castle Island, the former site of Fort Nassau.

12. Danckaerts, *Journal of Jasper Danckaerts*, 198.

13. Benson, *Peter Kalm's Travels*, 331–32.

14. R. Smith, *Tour of the Hudson*, 69.

15. Quotes from R. Smith, *Tour of the Hudson*, 76–81, 80n2.

16. *DNN*, 58–60. Van der Donck sometimes applied European species names to the Hudson River, New York Bay, and Long Island Sound fishes that he listed. He also made a few mistaken identifications. For example, he reported the presence of carp, a fish that was not found in New York State waters until the 1830s and later still in New England. R. Smith, *Tour of the Hudson*,

162n103. Also, it is now understood that the Hudson did not support a salmon population. Those that were captured were most likely strays from the nearby Connecticut River system. Limburg et al., "Fisheries of the Hudson Valley," 191. As an important aside, and in preparation for writing his book, it is likely that Van der Donck read the earlier reports of Megapolensis (1644), David de Vries (1655), and perhaps others, who described to differing degrees the flora and fauna of New Netherland. See NNN, 168–71, 220–23. In turn, De Vries may have read Megapolensis before he set pen to paper. See, generally, the endnotes in DNN.

17. Purchas, *Purchas His Pilgrimes*, 366, 370. "Breames," probably perch or perch-like fish. "Barbils," barbels, here catfishes.

18. New York State Department of Health, Hudson River Fish Advisories, http://www.health.ny.gov/environmental/outdoors/fish/health_advisories/docs/advisory_booklet.pdf, accessed July 17, 2012.

19. NNN, 242. This mention in 1643 of Mohawks fishing the Hudson in July and using snares suggests that their quarry was sturgeon. Although he was writing chiefly about the Mohawks, Megapolensis did describe fish and fishing in the Hudson, where he noted the presence of sturgeon and shad, neither of which were found in the Mohawk River. NNN, 171.

20. Funk, *Hudson Valley Prehistory*, 6.

21. See Starna, "Checklist of Higher Edible Plants"; Brooks, *Catskill Flora and Economic Botany*, vol. 4, pts. 1 and 2; McVaugh, *Flora of the Columbia County Area*; Waugh, *Iroquois Food and Food Preparation*; Parker, *Iroquois Uses of Maize*; Herrick, *Iroquois Medical Botany*.

22. See NNN, 177.

23. Funk, *Hudson Valley Prehistory*, 6–7.

24. See DNN, 47–52; NNN, 169–70.

25. NNN, 48. "Wild cats" suggests lynx, bobcats, or perhaps mountain lions.

26. DNN, 116–26.

27. See Funk, *Hudson Valley Prehistory*, 7; Grayson, "Riverhaven No. 2 Vertebrate Fauna."

28. DNN, 52–58. For a discussion of the fauna of the proximate Upper Susquehanna Valley, which provides broad comparative data for the region, see Starna and Funk, "Floral and Faunal Resource Potential."

29. Shorto, foreword.

30. The quoted passages that follow, along with the general description offered on the seasons and weather in New Netherland, are from Van der Donck. See DNN, 64–71.

31. Megapolensis wrote that "the summers are pretty hot, so that for the most of the time we are obliged to go in just our shirts." NNN, 171.

2. Natives on the Land

1. Two works that early on demonstrated attempts to write history from an Indian perspective include Jaenen, "Amerindian Views," and Ronda, "Indian Critique." Axtell's later "Through Another Glass Darkly" and "Imagining the Other" are important theoretical and historiographical contributions. Of more recent vintage is Richter's geographically and culturally expansive *Facing East from Indian Country*. This methodological approach, it must be said, is not novel, having first been proposed in 1922 by the anthropologist Bronislaw Malinowski in his *Argonauts of the Western Pacific*, 25. However, in Malinowski's telling, and in his phrase "from a native's point of view," the reference was to the practice of living ethnography, not to the study of an historical past.

2. See Carmack, "Ethnohistory"; Axtell, "Ethnohistory."

3. Juet's complete journal of Hudson's third voyage is filled with navigational information such as wind and weather observations, records of soundings and star and sun sightings that he took himself, and daily notations of compass variations. Purchas, *Purchas His Pilgrimes*, 13:333–74.

4. *NNN*, 7.

5. See Campisi, "Hudson Valley Indians," 169; Gehring and Starna, "Dutch and Indians," 8.

6. Purchas, *Purchas His Pilgrimes*, 13:363–64.

7. Purchas, *Purchas His Pilgrimes*, 348. Juet was probably influenced by Dutch in the crew who referred to a second boat as a "scute." The long vowel diphthongizes in most dialects to /ui/ as in *schuyt*, a boat. Charles Gehring, personal communication, 2009. "Murderer," a small cannon or mortar (OED).

8. Purchas, *Purchas His Pilgrimes*, 13:372.

9. Purchas, *Purchas His Pilgrimes*, 367. Assuming that he had read Juet's journal, Van Meteren's "friendly and polite people" might well have been a paraphrase of Juet's "loving people."

10. Purchas, *Purchas His Pilgrimes*, 363–66.

11. Purchas, *Purchas His Pilgrimes*, 347. The "red Cassockes" here were long or loose coats (OED). All indications are that a small stock of "red Coates" was carried on the *Halve Maen*, two of which were given to the Indians Hudson's crew had tried to take hostage while anchored in Sandy Hook Bay. Purchas, *Purchas His Pilgrimes*, 365. The color red carried with it special significance to Indians throughout the Eastern Woodlands, finding symbolic and ritual expression in many realms. See Miller and Hamell, "New Perspective," 325–26. That the French had been trading red coats, and that Hudson had aboard his ship similar items, was in all likelihood no coincidence. Also in Sandy Hook Bay, Juet reported that the Indians who had come to trade "desire Cloathes," suggesting that none of this was new to them. Purchas, *Purchas His Pilgrimes*, 13:363.

12. *BA*, 49–50.

13. Purchas, *Purchas His Pilgrimes*, 13:351. See Hamell, "Trading in Metaphors."

14. *NNN*, 6; Stokes, *Iconography of Manhattan Island*, 2:49–51.

15. *BA*, 23.

16. See De Laet, "Extracts from the New World," 299–300.

17. *NNN*, 47.

18. *NNN*, 50.

19. *NNN*, 58.

20. *NNN*, 105, 126–27. It is tempting to blame Michaëlius's rancor on the loss of his wife to an unstated condition seven weeks after the family had landed in New Amsterdam, leaving him with their three children and finding himself "very much discommoded, without her society and assistance." *NNN*, 122. Still, the bigotry he expressed may simply have come from who he was.

21. *NNN*, 72–73, 80.

22. *DNN*, 74, 95–96.

23. Purchas, *Purchas His Pilgrimes*, 13:346, 363.

24. De Laet, "Extracts from the New World," 299.

25. *DNN*, 3–4.

26. Wood, *New England's Prospect*, 87; Thwaites, *Jesuit Relations*, 5:119–21.

27. See Miller, "Doctrine of Discovery," 15–16, 20–21.

28. See Shannon, *Indians and Colonists*; Day, "Missisquoi"; *NYCD*, 6:864.

29. *NYCD*, 6:881.

30. *NYCD*, 881–82. "The[se]" in the original. For an earlier example of the refrain about the Mahicans being few and the Dutch many, see Leder, *Livingston Indian Records*, 37.

31. Quinney, "Interesting Speech," 317.

32. Oberly, *Nation of Statesmen*, 52–53.

33. Quinney, "Interesting Speech," 314–15.

34. Quinney, "Interesting Speech," 318–19. There is no historical, archaeological, or demographic evidence that would confirm the numbers of Mahicans that Quinney recounted.

35. Heckewelder, *History, Manners, and Customs*, 71.

36. Heckewelder, "Indian Tradition," [71].

37. Heckewelder, "Indian Tradition," [70] citing a letter from Heckewelder.

38. Heckewelder, "Indian Tradition," [71]-73.

39. Purchas, *Purchas His Pilgrimes*, 13:365, 368.

40. Hoes were not a part of trade assemblages until about 1640. Moreover, archaeological data demonstrate that heavy iron axes, while frequently modified by Native people, were used as tools, not as cumbersome pendants

(subjectively considered) weighing three pounds and more. Smaller, lighter axes do not appear until after 1650. BA; James Bradley, personal communication, 2009.

41. Heckewelder, *History, Manners, and Customs*, 75n1. The commentary in this note does not appear in Heckewelder's "Indian Tradition."

42. Dorson, "Comic Indian Anecdotes," 121.

43. The reference here is to Haefeli, "First Contact and Apotheosis," where, building primarily on the work of Bruce Trigger and others, the attempt is made to cast Heckewelder's narrative of first contact in the same light as Marshall Sahlins's sophisticated work on Captain Cook. Marred by factual errors and theoretical misunderstandings, in addition to a lack of critical insight, Haefeli's analysis is wide of the mark.

44. Stokes, *Iconography of Manhattan*, 2:63–72, C.PL.23, following page 75.

45. Stokes, *Iconography of Manhattan*, 2:C.PL.44, following page 129. See also Hart, *New Netherland Company*, 17, 63–64.

46. Hart, *New Netherland Company*, 25–31, 48–51; Jacobs, *New Netherland*, 32–33.

47. Hart, *New Netherland Company*, 27.

48. Translation by Charles Gehring.

49. Stokes, *Iconography of Manhattan*, 2:C.PL.24, following page 75.

50. Stokes, *Iconography of Manhattan*, 2:72.

51. See Huey, "Mahicans, the Dutch, and the Schodack Islands."

52. Stokes, *Iconography of Manhattan*, 2:C.PL.32, 2:C.PL.31, following page 90.

53. White, *America 1585*, 62 pl. 32. See also 66 pl. 36. See BA, 9, 37.

54. *Beschrijvinghe van Virginia*, 42. Translation by Charles Gehring.

3. Mahican Places

1. BA. A largely theoretical work on Mahican archaeology, one that places some reliance on questionable secondary histories, is Brumbach and Bender, "Woodland Period Settlement."

2. BA, 37.

3. Unless otherwise noted, the general discussion that follows is drawn from BA. Bradley and others, however, are cited in support of specific statements or interpretations.

4. See Brumbach, "'Iroquoian' Ceramics," and "Algonquian and Iroquoian Ceramics."

5. BA, 17–18. Snow, *Iroquois*, 50–51, maintains that, for the immediate pre-contact period and perhaps beyond, ceramics are a good indicator of the ethnic boundary that separated the Mohawks and the Mahicans.

6. James Bradley, personal communication, 2011, explains that linking the sites in the northern cluster to the Mahicans—aside from his examination of site assemblages that are admittedly difficult to assign to any one specific group—relies on their chronological alignment (late precontact to about 1676), their position in a physiographic locale distinct from that of Mohawk sites, and their distance from the Mohawk homeland. However, when considered in the context of the ambiguous ceramic data, this is insufficient evidence upon which to base a determination of whether these sites are affiliated with either Mahicans *or* Mohawks, leaving the question of an exclusive Mahican presence in the area moot. See chapter 7.

7. Lavin, et al., "Goldkrest Site."

8. On wigwams and Iroquois longhouses, see Sturtevant, "Wigwams at Niantic"; Snow, "Architecture of Iroquois Longhouses."

9. Dally-Starna and Starna, "Picturing Pachgatgoch," 9–10; Dally-Starna and Starna, *Gideon's People*, 1:33–34.

10. The time periods discussed are those defined and used in BA.

11. NNN, 49. The new translation was provided by Janny Venema and Charles Gehring, personal communication, 2009.

12. VRBM, 33; O'Callaghan, *History of New Netherland*, 1:123–25, map following 203. Original map reproduced in Venema, *Kiliaen van Rensselaer*, [236–37].

13. BA, 65.

14. The published Minuit map is a 1660 copy of the 1630 original. See Stokes, *Iconography of Manhattan*, 2:C.PL.40, following page 120.

15. Van der Donck (1655) describes palisaded Mohawk villages, information that, in large part, was based on Van den Bogaert's 1634–35 journal, painting only a thumbnail sketch of what may have been Hudson Valley settlements. DNN, 81–84; Gehring and Starna, trans. and eds., *Journey into Mohawk and Oneida Country*, 3–4, 12–13.

16. James Bradley, personal communication, 2011.

17. BA, 106, 155.

18. See chapter 9.

19. The literature on the subject of Native demography is vast, controversial, and often contentious. See, for example, Dobyns, *Their Number Become Thinned*; Thornton, *American Indian Holocaust*; Ubelaker, "American Indian Population Size"; Henige, *Numbers from Nowhere*; Snow, "Microchronology and Demographic Evidence"; Snow, "Setting Demographic Limits."

20. Snow, "Setting Demographic Limits," 259.

21. BA, 8–9.

22. Snow, *Archaeology of New England*, 33–34; Snow and Lanphear, "European Contact and Indian Depopulation," 24.

23. *BA*, 12.

24. *VRBM*, 307. Van Laer's phrase "in their time" has been construed as meaning at contact, which may or may not be the case. Dunn, *Mohicans and Their Land*, 257. Hendrick Aupaumut, in his 1791 "An Indian History," wrote that "before they began to decay," the Mahicans could raise 1,000 warriors" (102). See also [Aupaumut], "History of the Muhheakunnuk," 42. In his July 4, 1854, speech, another leading Mahican, John Quinney, claimed that in 1604 there were 25,000 of his people, 4,000 of whom were warriors. These numbers, offered in the context of political appeals and as part of revitalist histories, cannot be verified, nor are they credible. See chapter 2.

25. See Brasser, *Riding on the Frontier's Crest*, 9; Dunn, *Mohicans and Their Land*, 257; Jennings, *Ambiguous Iroquois Empire*, 48n2.

26. Van Rensselaer never visited his patroonship or the colony of New Netherland.

27. *VRBM*, 158–61.

28. *VRBM*, 166–69, 306; *NYCD*, 14:1–2. On the island holdings of the Mahicans, see Huey, "Mahicans, the Dutch, and the Schodack Islands," 97–100.

29. Ruttenber, *Indian Tribes of Hudson's River*, 95, links the Catskill Indians to the "Esopus chieftaincies." Following Ruttenber, Trelease, in *IACNY*, 7, refers to these Natives as Munsees. In *BA*, 106, Bradley asserts, absent supporting documentation, that by the mid-seventeenth century the Mahicans had split into two groups, one of which became known as the Catskills. The Catskill or Katskill Indians are known solely from their being named in documents reporting on midcentury political intrigues and hostilities in the Hudson Valley, in addition to the sale of their lands. Van Wassenaer (1626) makes brief mention of a "captain of the Maykans [also Maikans, that is, Mahicans], who is named Cat," which may suggest the etymology of "Catskill." *NNN*, 86; Charles Gehring, personal communication, 2009. The names recorded of certain Catskill headmen appear to be Mahican. *NYCD*, 13:308, 309, 379, 545; Ives Goddard, personal communication, 2009. The Catskill Indians, or a descendant group, remained in the area through at least the 1740s. Their community at the time, at Freehold, a short distance up Catskill Creek, had been home to a Moravian missionary and his wife for about one year. Dally-Starna and Starna, *Gideon's People*, 1:5, 13–14. See chapter 9 for further discussion on this question.

30. Starna, "Biological Encounter," 511–12; Newman, "New World Epidemiology"; Baker and Armelagos, "Origin and Antiquity of Syphilis"; Elting and Starna, "Pre-Columbian Treponematosis"; Alchon, *Pest in the Land*; Cook, *Born to Die*; Thornton, *American Indian Holocaust*.

31. Snow and Lanphear, "European Contact and Indian Depopulation,"

22; Spiess and Spiess, "New England Pandemic"; Marr and Cathey, "New Hypothesis for Cause of Epidemic."

32. *NNN*, 105. "Wappenos," the Eastern Abenakis. Snow, "Eastern Abenaki," 147.

33. Thornton, *American Indian Holocaust*, 44–45; Newman, "New World Epidemiology." See also Starna, "Biological Encounter," 513.

34. Snow and Lanphear, "European Contact and Indian Depopulation," 23; Snow, "Mohawk Demography," 174. See also Van den Bogaert, *Journey into Mohawk and Oneida Country*, 4.

35. *DNN*, 69. Interestingly, the "one for every ten" comment appears again nearly a century later. In 1735, an Indian among the Housatonic Mahicans reported that his people had been "greatly diminished; so that (says he) since my remembrance, there were Ten Indians, where there is now One." Appleton, *Gospel Ministers*, v.

36. Brasser, *Riding on the Frontier's Crest*, 29.

37. These estimates are based on assuming a conservative 3:1 ratio of total persons to warriors. *NYCD* 4:337.

38. See *IACNY*, 235; Jennings, *Ambiguous Iroquois Empire*, 148–49; Day, "Missisquoi." There are two unsupported claims that Schaghticoke had been a Mahican village prior to 1677. See Brasser, *Riding on the Frontier's Crest*, 24; Dunn, *Mohicans and Their Land*, 150; cf. *BA*, 13 fig. 1.4, 106 fig. 4.19, 157 fig. and 5.21.

39. See Thornton, *American Indian Holocaust*; Dobyns, *Their Number Become Thinned*; Newman, "New World Epidemiology"; Trigger, *Children of Aataentsic*, 1:250; Lanphear, "Biocultural Interactions"; Morton, *New English Canaan*, 23. See also Starna, "Biological Encounter," 514–15, and the sources cited therein.

4. Native Neighbors

1. Fenton and Tooker, "Mohawk," 466.

2. Van den Bogaert, *Journey into Mohawk and Oneida Country*. See also Snow, *Mohawk Valley Archaeology*; Grumet, *Historic Contact*, 353–76.

3. Snow, "Mohawk Demography," 164, 174.

4. Campisi, "Oneida," 481. For a detailed discussion of Iroquois settlements, see Engelbrecht, *Iroquoia*, 88–110. See also, Pratt, *Archaeology of the Oneida*; Grumet, *Historic Contact*, 377–86.

5. See Van den Bogaert's description of the Oneida village in *Journey into Mohawk and Oneida Country*, 12–13. On Sinnekens, see Ives Goddard's synonomy in Abler and Tooker, "Seneca," 515.

6. Blau, Campisi, and Tooker, "Onondaga," 491. See also Bradley, *Evolution of the Onondaga*; Grumet, *Historic Contact*, 387–95.

7. White, Engelbrecht, and Tooker, "Cayuga," 500. See also Niemczycki, *Origin and Development*; Grumet, *Historic Contact*, 396–402.

8. Abler and Tooker, "Seneca," 505. See also Niemczycki, *Origin and Development*; Grumet, *Historic Contact*, 403–15.

9. Goddard, "Ethnohistorical Implications"; Goddard, "Delaware," 213–14. See also Grumet, *Munsee Indians*. A commonplace work on the Munsees is Otto, *Dutch-Munsee Encounter*.

10. Goddard, "Delaware," 214–15; Grumet, *Munsee Indians*.

11. The portrait entitled *Unus Americanus ex Virginia*, by Wenceslaus Hollar (1607–1677), shown in fig. 1, is likely that of a Munsee Indian. See Hamell, "Jaques: A Munsee."

12. See Diamond, "Terminal Late Woodland."

13. Grumet, *Historic Contact*, 215; Snow, *Archaeology of New England*, 33–34, 42; Grumet, *Munsee Indians*, 15–16.

14. See Rudes, "Indian Land Deeds," 20–23.

15. Dally-Starna and Starna, *Gideon's People*, 1:4–5, 653n7. See chapter 9.

16. Dally-Starna and Starna, *Gideon's People*, 1:4–5; Wojciechowski, *Paugussett Tribes*; Salwen, "Indians of Southern New England."

17. Salwen, "Indians of Southern New England," 160–66.

18. Day, "Western Abenaki," 148–49. See also Peterson, et al., "St. Lawrence Iroquoians"; Day, *In Search of New England's Native Past*; Calloway, *Western Abenakis*.

19. Day, "English-Indian Contacts," 28.

20. Snow, *Archaeology of New England*, 71–73; Calloway, *Western Abenakis*, 10–11.

21. Snow, *Archaeology of New England*, 33–34.

22. Day and Trigger, "Algonquin," 792–93. "Algonquin" refers to a people, distinct from "Algonquian" languages, here Eastern Algonquian, all of the Algic language family.

23. Day and Trigger, "Algonquin," 795–96.

24. Jennings, "Susquehannock," 362–63; Grumet, *Historic Contact*, 307–8, 424–25.

25. Grumet, *Historic Contact*, 305; Jennings, "Susquehannock," 363–66; Kent, *Susquehanna's Indians*.

5. The Ethnographic Past

1. See Aupaumut, quoted in Jones, *Stockbridge, Past and Present*, 14–23; [Aupaumut], "Indian History." As with most oral traditions, Aupaumut's history is infused with the influences of his transcultural experiences, including his Christian education, and must be read as such. See Ronda and Ronda, "Chief Hendrick Aupaumut," 44–47.

2. *IACNY*, 4; Starna, "Assessing American Indian-Dutch Studies," 13–14.

3. Enthusiastic statements by Dutch men of the cloth of their good intentions to minister to the Indians remained just that. See *IACNY*, 38–40; Burke, *Mohawk Frontier*, 151–55; Jacobs, *New Netherland*, 318–23. See also G. L. Smith, *Religion and Trade*. Axtell, *Invasion Within*, provides a detailed and useful history of Protestant missionary activity in New England and the efforts of their Roman Catholic counterparts in New France.

4. Jacobs, *New Netherland*, 271.

5. Rink, *Holland on the Hudson*, 18, 206–7; Jacobs, *New Netherland* 2.

6. See *IACNY*; Jacobs, *New Netherland*.

7. Brasser, *Riding on the Frontier's Crest*. This 1974 monograph is a later—that is, a succeeding—version of Brasser's essay "Mahican," submitted for inclusion in *Handbook of North American Indians*, vol. 15. "Mahican," however, was not published until 1978. See Goddard, Review of *Riding on the Frontier's Crest*, 185–86. The monograph, unlike the essay, contains an extensive set of endnotes that, for better or worse, lists the many sources that Brasser tells us he employed.

8. Dunn, *Mohicans and Their Land*; Dunn, *Mohican World*, 13–35.

9. See Starna, "Assessing American Indian-Dutch Studies," 13–14; Gehring and Starna, "Dutch and Indians," 9.

10. See, for example, Snow, *Archaeology of New England*, 88–90; Grumet, *Historic Contact*, 164–68; A. Taylor, "Captain Hendrick Aupaumut," 437–39; Brumbach and Bender, "Woodland Period Settlement"; Wheeler, *To Live upon Hope*.

11. *NNN*, 68, 73, 86–87. Ives Goddard, personal communication, 2009.

12. *NNN*, 49, 57. "Savages in the north" is likely a reference to Indians residing in the Connecticut Valley.

13. *NNN*, 217.

14. See *DNN*, 162n102, n105; 163n9, n11; 164n15; 166n27; 167n34, n37. In 1649 Van der Donck drew up what was essentially a lengthy and detailed protest by aggrieved citizens about conditions in the colony, which was submitted to the States General, the governing body of the United Provinces of the Netherlands. For the complete text see *NYCD*, 1:271–318. Referred to as the *Representation*, it is essentially a first draft of Van der Donck's *Description of New Netherland*, in particular the sections on physical geography, natural history, and also Indian lifeways.

15. Gehring and Grumet, "Observations of the Indians." Danckaert's manuscript did not see the light of day until it was purchased from a bookseller in Amsterdam in 1864 and published three years later.

16. See, generally, Cronon, *Changes in the Land*; Snow, *Archaeology of New England*, 42–99; Bragdon, *Native People*; Starna, "Pequots in the Early Seventeenth Century"; Salwen, "Indians of Southern New England," 160–64.

17. *NNN*, 49.

18. *VRBM*, 306–8.

19. Charles Gehring, personal communication, 2009.

20. *DNN*, 98. See also *NNN*, 218–20.

21. See *BA*, 9, 12; Brumbach and Bender, "Woodland Period Settlement," 229–30.

22. Chilton, "'Towns They Have None,'" discusses farming among southern New England Native people, a region within which she includes eastern New York, suggesting that the evidence thus far does not appear to indicate the same level of involvement as was the case among the Iroquois, in particular the nearby Mohawks.

23. *VRBM*, 159.

24. See Dunn, *Mohicans and Their Land*, 279–309; Starna, "American Indian Villages to Dutch Farms."

25. Van Laer, *Documents Relating to New Netherland*, 5.

26. Rink, *Holland on the Hudson*, 78.

27. Purchas, *Purchas His Pilgrimes*, 13:367–68.

28. *NNN*, 50, 57–58.

29. *NNN*, 69–70, 80. While in the vicinity of Cape Cod in 1606, Champlain reported of the Indians there: "They have chiefs whom they obey in regard to matters of warfare but not in anything else. These chiefs work, and assume no higher rank than their companions. Each possesses only sufficient land for his own support." Champlain, *Works of Samuel de Champlain*, 1:413. It is possible that, as had Van der Donck and perhaps others, Van Wassenaer and also De Laet, neither of whom had ever set foot in New Netherland, had read Champlain.

30. *NNN*, 127.

31. Goddard, "Eastern Algonquian Languages," 75; Goddard, "Ethnohistorical Implications," 17; Goddard, "Pidgin Delaware." See also Bragdon, *Native People*, 20, 249n3.

32. Wampum, from "wampumpeag" (various spellings), soon shortened in English to "wampum" and "peag," was borrowed directly from Massachusett. It means 'white wampum beads' (pl.). Ives Goddard, personal communication, 2012. Manufactured primarily from Busycon whelk and quahog shells, wampum is small (ca. 1/4 inch in length by ca. 1/8 inch in diameter) white and purple tubular beads worn as a part of dress, strung into strings, or woven into belts. The Dutch, however, knew wampum as "sewan" or "zeewant," from Pidgin Delaware "<sewan> 'wampum', presumably from a Northern Unami word for 'loose wampum'; cf. Munsee *sé·wan* 'it is scattered, all over the place'." Goddard, "Linguistic Variation," 43n27. See also Bradley, "Re-visiting

Wampum." Throughout this work, where English translations of the original Dutch are cited, readers should assume that "sewan" was written where "wampum" appears in the quote. Also, because wampum is the more familiar term, I have used it in all other cases.

33. NNN, 109. Given the nature of such small-scale, egalitarian societies, the word "election" should be read as choosing or making a selection, and not as casting a vote. The editor of NNN notes that at least four pages are missing from De Rasière's original manuscript, which continued his discussion on Native government and may also have touched on religion or other topics.

34. See DNN, xviii, 167n37.

35. DNN, 105.

36. NNN, 230–31.

37. Although the ethnographic record on Iroquoian sociopolitical organization for the seventeenth century is thin, the literature suggests transitional egalitarian- to-ranked societies. The positions of war chiefs and "civil chiefs" or sachems were believed to have been achieved, but also, in part, ascribed. See Fenton, "Iroquoian Culture Patterns," 309–15; Fenton, Great Law.

38. NNN, 68.

39. NNN, 69.

40. Christopher Vecsey, personal communication, 2011.

41. Hopkins, Historical Memoirs, 23–24; NNN, 72.

42. NNN, 68.

43. NNN, 126–27.

44. NNN, 57. De Laet, writing in 1633, analogized Menutto (var.), a word, he said, "the Canadians" used, with oqui (oki), a Huron word. His information, however, was drawn from Champlain, the only known source for the spelling oqui. See Tooker, Ethnography of the Huron Indians, 78, 92; Champlain, Works of Samuel de Champlain, 3:143.

45. See Bragdon, Native People, 184–85; Goddard, "Pidgin Delaware," 68, 73.

46. DNN, 106–7.

47. The green corn ceremony mentioned by Brasser, absent a citation to the source of his information, is not derived from any of the literature on the Mahicans. It does exist among Iroquoians, although its antiquity among these people is unknown.

48. See chapter 9.

49. Hopkins, Historical Memoirs, 11–12; Brasser, Riding on the Frontier's Crest, 4; Frazier, Mohicans of Stockbridge, 21; Wheeler, To Live upon Hope, 119. Lafitau describes a similar ceremony, not only among the Iroquois, but among "all the Indians in general," whose purposes were to "give them victory over their enemies; to make the wheat [corn] grow in their fields, to cause them

to have good hunting or fishing." Fenton and Moore, *Customs of the American Indians*, 1:208.

50. See chapter 9.

51. But see Jeffries, "Denying Religion."

52. Fogelson, "Native North Americans," 147. On the topics of secularism and nonbelief in "traditional" societies, see Douglas, "Primitive Religion." Suggestions of nonbelief in the sources just examined are when the Indians are said not to be concerned with the spiritual or when they are said not to have superstitions. A religious indifference is expressed when an Indian is said to have offered food to Menetto without ceremony.

53. NNN, 70, 106, 218.

54. NNN, 77, bracketed comment in the original. De Rasière wrote that should a man and woman part, and "if there are children, they remain with her, for they are fond of them beyond measure." NNN, 108.

55. DNN, 85.

56. Brasser, *Riding on the Frontier's Crest*, 8; NNN, 70, 218; DNN, 84; Goddard, "Delaware," 219.

57. Aupaumut, quoted in Jones, *Stockbridge, Past and Present*, 22.

58. Salwen, "Indians of Southern New England," 166–67; Day, "Western Abenaki," 156; Bragdon, *Native People*, 156–61; Newcomb, *Delaware Indians*, 48; Goddard, "Delaware."

59. See chapter 10.

60. Unless otherwise noted, the following discussion is based on Goddard, "Notes on Mahican."

61. Although the majority of Shekomeko's inhabitants were Mahicans, this was a mixed community formed also of Hudson Valley Esopus, Wappinger, and Minisink Indians, in addition to Wompanoos from Connecticut's Housatonic Valley. Goddard, "Delaware," 213–14. Dally-Starna and Starna, *Gideon's People*, 1:6. See also Goddard, "Ethnohistorical Implications"; Salwen, "Indians of Southern New England," 175.

62. See also Goddard, "Eastern Algonquian Languages," 71–72.

63. Brasser, *Riding on the Frontier's Crest*, 2; Brasser, "Mahican," 198; Dunn, *Mohicans and Their Land*, 39.

64. On "Wompona," see Dally-Starna and Starna, *Gideon's People*, 1:664n18.

65. Goddard, "Eastern Algonquian Languages," 72. See Costa, "Southern New England Algonquian."

66. Goddard, "Eastern Algonquian Languages," 71–72.

67. Frazier, *Mohicans of Stockbridge*, 11; Dunn, *Mohicans and Their Land*, 232–33; Brasser, *Riding on the Frontier's Crest*, 30. But see Colee, "Housatonic-Stockbridge Indians," 87–110.

68. *NYCD*, 13:345.

69. Pynchon, *Pynchon Papers*, 1:65.

6. The Mahicans and the Dutch

1. S. Hart, *New Netherland Company*, 18–22, 27, 54. See also Jacobs, *New Netherland*, 30–37; *NNN*, 47–48. For a contrarian view on the building of Fort Nassau, see Bachman, *Peltries or Plantations*, 11–12. Castle Island, in the heart of Mahican country, has been known at various times as Martin Gerritsz's Island, Patroon's Island, and Westerlo Island.

2. Pendergast, "Introduction of European Goods."

3. See Gehring and Starna, "Dutch and Indians," 14–16; Hart, *New Netherland Company*, 52–53.

4. Rink, *Holland on the Hudson*, 80.

5. Rink, *Holland on the Hudson*, 83–93.

6. The discussion of the Mohawk-Mahican war that follows is drawn from Starna and Brandão, "Mohawk-Mahican War." Portions of the essay included here are by permission of the publisher, Duke University Press.

7. The possibility that the Mohawk-Mahican war of the mid-1620s led to the Beaver Wars was tentatively introduced over sixty years ago. More than twenty years passed before the notion appeared again in print, and then another decade before a full and detailed exposition was published. See Murray, "Early Fur Trade"; *IACNY*, 46–48; Trigger, "Mohawk-Mahican War." See also Richter, *Ordeal of the Longhouse*, 56. Brandão, *Iroquois Policy*, offers an extended critique of the Beaver Wars interpretation, focusing on Iroquois-French and Iroquois-Huron relations.

8. Snow, *Mohawk Valley Archaeology*, 29–30, 197; Lenig, "Dutchmen, Beaver Hats and Iroquois"; Trigger, *Natives and Newcomers*, 148; see Trigger, "Mohawk-Mahican War," 277, where it is stated that before 1610 iron goods, specifically axes, were acquired through war; O'Callaghan, *History of New Netherland*, frontispiece map; *NYCD*, 1: map facing page 13. Translation provided by Charles Gehring.

9. Hart, *New Netherland Company*, 17–21; *NNN*, 47; *NYCD*, 1:14.

10. Jennings, *Ambiguous Iroquois Empire*, 78 (1st quotation). See also Lenig, "Dutchmen, Beaver Hats and Iroquois," 80; Trigger, "Mohawk-Mahican War," 277; *NNN*, 68 (2d quotation); Brasser, *Riding on the Frontier's Crest*, 12 (3d quotation); Richter, *Ordeal of the Longhouse*, 54 (4th quotation).

11. Innis, *Fur Trade in Canada*, 3. See, for example, Murray, "Early Fur Trade," 367; Trigger, "Mohawk-Mahican War," 278; Trigger, *Children of Aataentsic*, 1:229; Jennings, *Invasion of America*, 100; Salisbury, *Manitou and Providence*, 82; Richter, *Ordeal of the Longhouse*, 57; Delâge, *Bitter Feast*, 94; Fenton, *Great Law*, 244.

12. Richter, *Ordeal of the Longhouse*, 57. See Brandão, *Iroquois Policy*, 83–89, for a critical discussion on the depleted beaver hypothesis.

13. Lenig, "Dutchmen, Beaver Hats and Iroquois," 77, 80.

14. Boucher, *Histoire véritable et naturelle*, 63, in describing *all* of New France, states: "beavers which are from the northern parts are worth much more and their hair [fur] is much better than of those from the southern parts." In drawing a similar comparison, however, Nicholas Perrot is clear about where "south" is: "In that region the heat is as great as in the islands of the south or in Provence; and it is a country abounding in parroquets." Perrot, "Manners, Customs, and Religion," 1:114–15.

15. Furs were graded on the basis of whether they had been worn as garments by Indians before they found their way into European hands. For example, in differentiating beaver pelts, *castor gras*, pelts whose guard hairs had been worn away through use, were considered more valuable than *castor sec*, which retained the guard hairs. Norton, *Fur Trade in Colonial New York*, 104–5.

16. Obbard, "Fur Grading and Pelt Identification," 722, 724.

17. Van Laer, *Documents Relating to New Netherland*, 172–251.

18. N N N, 84–85. According to Van Wassenaer, the Mahicans had "requested to be assisted by the commander of Fort Orange and six others." Van Laer, *Documents Relating to New Netherland*, 84. The Mohawks may have been forewarned about the attack. It is doubtful that what must have been a sizeable party of Mohawk warriors would have been wandering around the area for no apparent reason. There is no indication why Van Crieckenbeeck chose to violate company policy to remain neutral and assist the Mahicans. See "Instructions for Willem Verhulst" in Van Laer, *Documents Relating to New Netherland*, 52–55. In early 1627 Samuel de Champlain's Indian allies were told that the Mohawks had killed twenty-four Mahicans and five Dutchmen, but it is unclear if these deaths were an outcome of the single reported fight involving Van Crieckenbeeck or whether there had been other skirmishes. Champlain, *Works of Champlain*, 5:214.

19. Murray, "Early Fur Trade," 370. Murray was the first historian to write about the early Dutch-French-Indian fur trade, employing in large part what was available of the primary Dutch and French sources. Trigger, *Children of Aataentsic*, 2:463, expands the discussion, alleging that Dutch traders knew that the Mohawks were intent on gaining control of the territory around Fort Orange and, by doing so, could block trade with the French Indians. Moreover, these traders had "commissioned" Van Crieckenbeeck to assist the Mahicans. No evidence was found to support these allegations.

20. Van Laer, *Documents Relating to New Netherland*, 175–76 (1st quotation); Murray, "Early Fur Trade," 370 (2d quotation).

21. See, for example, *IACNY*, 46–47; Trigger, "Mohawk-Mahican War," 279–80; Trigger, *Children of Aataentsic*, 2:463–64 Trigger, *Natives and Newcomers*, 310–11; Lenig, "Dutch, Beaver Hats and Iroquois," 80; Jennings, *Ambiguous Iroquois Empire*, 49; Richter, *Ordeal of the Longhouse*, 56–57; Dennis, *Cultivating a Landscape of Peace*, 130–31. George Hunt, in his influential *Wars of the Iroquois*, did not cite Murray's article, nor did he have much to say about either the Van Crieckenbeeck disaster or De Rasière's 1626 letter.

22. Champlain, *Works of Champlain*, 5:208–9, 214. Misled by the translator's note on this page, most historians have read "Wolves" to mean the Mahicans. This, however, results in the logical fallacy of the Mohawks going to war against the Mahicans because the Mahicans would not let the Mohawks attack them.

23. Day, "Identity of the Sokokis." The French called the Sokokis, as well as a number of other New England groups, and at times, the Mahicans, "Loups." Day, Mots loups *of Father Mathevet*, 44–62. But see the caveat in Day, "English-Indian Contacts in New England," 26. Champlain, however, knew the Mahicans as "Maganathicois," in one instance remarking that their name "signifies 'nation of wolves.'" Champlain, ed., *Works of Champlain*, 5:308, 209, 217.

24. Day, "Identity of the Sokokis," 239; *NYCD*, 13:379–81.

25. Van Laer, *Documents Relating to New Netherland*, 212. De Rasière mistakenly wrote "Minquaes" (Susquehannocks) instead of "Maquas" (Mohawks) in this passage, an obvious error to which others have previously pointed. *IACNY*, 48n60.

26. Van Laer, *Documents Relating to New Netherland*, 212–15. The word "discovering," translated from the Dutch, should more precisely be read "exploring" or "investigating." Van Laer's translation of this passage from De Rasière's letter is accurate. Charles Gehring, personal communication, 2009.

27. Murray, "Early Fur Trade," 370; *IACNY*, 46–47; Trigger, "Mohawk-Mahican War," 279.

28. Van Laer, *Documents Relating to New Netherland*, 223–24. Trigger, "Mohawk-Mahican War," 278, claims that the French Indians traded with the Mahicans for wampum. No evidence was found to support this contention. "North" for the Dutch was the Connecticut River Valley.

29. *NNN*, 47.

30. Bachman, *Peltries or Plantations*, 81–83.

31. *NNN*, 86. The two Indian groups named in this passage are probably Algonquins from the Ottawa Valley. Day and Trigger, "Algonquin."

32. Champlain, *Works of Champlain*, 5:73. Although the Dutch had abandoned Fort Nassau in 1617, trade continued on the Hudson River. In 1622 Fort Orange was still two years in the future.

33. Champlain, *Works of Champlain*, 5:74.

34. Champlain, *Works of Champlain*, 5:77.

35. Champlain, *Works of Champlain*, 5:79.

36. Le Clercq, *Premier Établissement de la Foy*, 1:258–60.

37. Trigger, "Mohawk-Mahican War," 276, 279. Desrosiers, *Iroquoisie*, 87, also gives a start date of 1624, but supplies no supporting authority. To back his claim for an early start of the Mohawk-Mahican war, Trigger, "Mohawk-Mahican War," 276, citing Hodge, states: "We are informed that in 1623 the Mahican fort that stood opposite Castle Island in the Hudson River was 'built against their enemies, the Mohawks.'" Hodge, however, had incorrectly reported the date of a passage from Van Wassenaer as 1623, instead of November 1626. *NNN*, 84. Compare Hodge, ed., *Handbook of American Indians*, 1:922.

38. *NNN*, 47; *VRBM*, 306. Trelease, in *IACNY*, 32, 46, writes that early in the seventeenth century the Mahicans "were engaged in nearly constant warfare with the not-too-distant Mohawks," which, by the time Fort Orange was up and running, had persisted for "a generation or more." Other than De Laet's statement that they were enemies, there is no evidence for a previous history of warfare between these two Indian groups.

39. *NNN*, 84–85. Trigger, "Mohawk-Mahican War," 279, has the Mohawks attacking the Mahicans, an action for which no evidence was found. Also in 1626, either prior to or following the July clash, a Mahican force drove Mohawks out of their easternmost village. Although nothing further is known about this attack, it must be considered a part of ongoing hostilities between these Native people. Van den Bogaert, *Journey into Mohawk and Oneida Country*, 23.

40. Champlain, *Works of Champlain*, 5:208–9, 214.

41. Champlain, *Works of Champlain*, 5:78.

42. Champlain, *Works of Champlain*, 5:77.

43. Trigger, "Mohawk-Mahican War," 279, citing Desrosiers, writes: "It is noteworthy that 1624, the year in which the Dutch founded Fort Orange . . . appears to have also been the year when the Dutch began to make more intensive efforts to lure the northern Algonkians to trade on the Hudson." He also maintains that the "efforts to expand trade northward" were made by Van Crieckenbeeck. Trigger, "Mohawk-Mahican War," 280. No documentary evidence was found to support either of these statements.

44. Van Laer, *Documents Relating to New Netherland*, 227.

45. *VRBM*, 483–84.

46. Champlain, *Works of Champlain*, 5:221–31.

47. Van Laer, *Documents Relating to New Netherland*, 203 (quotation, emphasis added), 212.

48. Brasser, *Riding on the Frontier's Crest*, 12–15.

49. Jennings, *Ambiguous Iroquois Empire*, 31 (1st quotation, emphasis added), 48 (2d quotation), map 3 facing page 33.

50. Champlain, *Works of Champlain*, 5:214; NYCD, 13: 378–81; Day, "English-Indian Contacts," 69, and "Identity of the Sokokis," 242–43. Murray, "Early Fur Trade," 369, claims that "the Mahican were on friendly terms with their northern neighbours." This view is echoed by Trigger, "Mohawk-Mahican War," 278, who writes that "at various times in the past" the French Indians and the Mahicans "seem to have been allies against the Mohawk." No supporting evidence was found for this allegation. However, the difficulty with Murray's and Trigger's interpretations here may be traceable to confusion over what De Rasière, whose letter they both cite, meant when he used the term "north."

51. Champlain, *Works of Champlain*, 5:214.

52. Champlain, *Works of Champlain*, 5:215.

53. Van Laer, *Documents Relating to New Netherland*, 176, 243–48; VRBM, 306.

54. Immediately following the Van Crieckenbeeck incident, Minuit ordered the Dutch settlements on the Delaware and Connecticut Rivers evacuated. The families living at Fort Orange were moved to Manhattan, leaving behind a detail of just sixteen men, probably a mix of traders and soldiers. NNN, 85; Rink, *Holland on the Hudson*, 83. The Mohawk population at this time is estimated to have been about 7,700. Snow, "Mohawk Demography," 164. By 1630 there were only 300 Europeans in New Netherland, 270 of whom were on Manhattan Island. Rink, *Holland on the Hudson*, 144.

55. NNN, 85, 87.

56. NNN, 87.

57. Van Laer, *Documents Relating to New Netherland*, 192–95.

58. Van Laer, *Documents Relating to New Netherland*, 223–31.

59. Van Laer, *Documents Relating to New Netherland*, 227–28. For the Dutch, "north" was the Connecticut River Valley and environs, while "south" was the Delaware, all bearings made from the reference point of Fort Amsterdam on Manhattan Island. To complete this picture, "upwards" was up the Hudson River and to Fort Orange. See NNN, 84. Charles Gehring, personal communication, 2009.

60. This is not to say that the Mahicans did not have some successes in their war with the Mohawks. Sometime in 1626, possibly following the Van Crieckenbeeck business, they attacked the eastern-most Mohawk village and drove out its residents. Van den Bogaert, *Journey into Mohawk and Oneida Country*, 22. This village was one of four on the north side of the Mohawk River in the 1620s. Snow, *Mohawk Valley Archaeology*, 242.

61. Champlain, *Works of Champlain*, 5:216–17.

62. Van Laer, *Documents Relating to New Netherland*, 215, bracketed word in the translation. Murray, "Early Fur Trade," 370, writes that West India Company policy did not allow De Rasière to carry out his threat. Trelease, *IACNY*, 47, maintains that the Amsterdam directors "refused to endanger what they had already had in order to grasp at more." If there was a response to De Rasière's letter and specifically to his request to attack the Indians, it has not been discovered. Trigger, "Mohawk-Mahican War," 279–80, links De Rasière's request to the allegation that the Dutch had sent belts to the French Indians to encourage them to join with the Mahicans and attack the Mohawks. Those who appear responsible, Trigger continues, were the associates of Van Crieckenbeeck. No evidence was found that supports either the link that Trigger suggests or implicates unknown and unnamed Van Crieckenbeeck associates.

63. Day, "Eastern Boundary of Iroquoia, 7–13. It is generally accepted that the presence of Abenakis on the east side of Lake Champlain and environs cannot be firmly documented until the 1670s. However, this does not mean that these Natives were not in the area prior to this date, as suggested by ongoing archaeological research. Peterson et al., "St. Lawrence Iroquoians"; John G. Crock, personal communication, 2011.

64. *NNN*, 86.

65. Champlain, *Works of Champlain*, 5:222.

66. Champlain, *Works of Champlain*, 5:224–25.

67. Champlain, *Works of Champlain*, 5: 229. Champlain states that the killings were carried out, not by the Mohawks, but by "Ouentouoronons," probably Onondagas, who "had come in all haste to avenge themselves." Just before they killed the French Indians, the Onondagas reportedly announced to them: "While you come here to arrange a peace, your companions kill and massacre our people." Champlain, *Works of Champlain*, 5: 230.

68. *NNN*, 89. Jonas Michaëlius, the first Dutch minister in New Netherland, also mentioned that the war ended in 1628. *NNN*, 131. Dennis, *Cultivating a Landscape of Peace*, 132, misreporting the literature he cites as evidence, asserts that "epidemic disease, rather than a crushing military campaign by the Mohawks was responsible for the displacement of the Mahicans." However, there is no evidence that European-introduced disease reached the upper Hudson and Mohawk Valleys until 1633–34. Snow and Lanphear, "European Contact and Indian Depopulation," 23; Snow, *Iroquois*, 82, 94–97.

69. *VRBM*, 306; Champlain, *Works of Champlain*, 6:3–4.

70. Brasser, *Riding on the Frontier's Crest*, 15, claims that the translation of the Dutch words it is assumed he examined in Van Wassenaer's original manuscript as "fresh river" is incorrect. According to Brasser, this alleged

error caused later historians to mistakenly place the retreating Mahicans in the Connecticut Valley instead of on the Hoosic River near Troy, New York. However, there is nothing wrong with the original translation, and although Brasser was technically right in his statement that the Connecticut is not, by compass direction, "towards the north" from Fort Orange, the statement "towards the north" to a Dutchman of the period was a clear reference to this river. Charles Gehring, personal communication, 2009.

71. Trigger, "Mohawk-Mahican War," 281–82. This assertion is repeated in the most recent literature on the Iroquois, although Richter notes: "there is virtually no evidence that, before about 1670, peoples of the Five Nations systematically pursued an intermediary's role." Richter, *Ordeal of the Longhouse*, 56, 57. See Fenton, *Great Law*, 270. In addition, Trigger, "Mohawk-Mahican War," 286, maintains that, once the Mohawks had closed the doors of Fort Orange to the French Indians, "the best chance that the Dutch traders had of obtaining furs from the north was to arm their Mohawk allies so that they could better pirate these furs from among the tribes allied to the French." The business of Mohawks plundering furs has also been restated by historians. Nevertheless, there is no evidence that the Dutch sold firearms to the Mohawks to be used in such a manner; indeed, the Mohawks were not able to obtain guns in any number until the late 1630s, more than a decade after they had defeated the Mahicans. Hunt, *Wars of the Iroquois*, 166–69. The question of whether the Mohawks went to war with the express aim to pirate furs is examined by Brandão in *Iroquois Policy*, who concluded that, for all intents and purposes, they did not.

72. VRBM, 248, bracketed words are in the translation.

73. Nissenson, *Patroon's Domain*, 173.

74. Brandão, *Iroquois Policy*, 84–85.

75. It is important to note that the annual Dutch fur take for the years 1624 to 1635 was remarkably consistent, averaging about 6,600 pelts per year. This fits well with Van Rensselaer's own estimate that 5,000 to 6,000 pelts were taken every year in the Fort Orange area from 1625 to 1640. Brandão, *Iroquois Policy*, 86–87. "There is no lack of furs," Van Rensselaer reported in 1640. VRBM, 483.

76. VRBM, 306.

77. VRBM, 166, 182, 307.

78. Jacobs, *New Netherland*, 112–14.

79. See chapter 7.

80. Dunn, *Mohicans and Their Land*, 279–86.

81. This discussion on Eelckens is based on Starna, "Retrospecting the League of the Iroquois," 302–4.

82. Information on this episode is in *NYCD*, 71–81, 91–95; *NNN*, 186–89. See also Eekhof, *Bastiaen Jansz. Krol*, xxv–xxxi. I thank Charles Gehring for translating for me Krol's June 30, 1634, interrogatory in Eekhof. The depositions cited from *Documents Relative* were taken as part of a claim for damages brought by Eelckens against the Dutch West India Company for the losses he allegedly suffered. The large number of furs that he apparently arranged to be delivered by the Mohawks and Mahicans, however, would have been unrelated to any settlement; thus, these figures should be taken at their face value.

7. The Mahican Homeland

1. *NNN*, 67.

2. See Boxer, *Dutch Seaborne Empire*, 342.

3. Ruttenber, *Indian Tribes of Hudson's River*, 34–35.

4. *IACNY*, 4.

5. Brasser, *Riding on the Frontier's Crest*, 2. See Dunn, *Mohicans and Their Land*, 50.

6. [Aupaumut], "Extract from an Indian History," 99, 101.

7. *BA*, 12. See chapter 3.

8. Dunn, *Mohicans and Their Land*, 48–49.

9. Jeremy Hurst, New York State Department of Environmental Conservation, personal communication, 2009. See also Starna and Relethford, "Deer Densities."

10. *NNN*, 47.

11. See Dineen, Huey, and Reilly, *Geology and Land Uses*; Newman, et al., "Late Quaternary Geology"; Connolly, Krinsley, and Sirkin, "Late Pleistocene Erg," 1538–39. Schenectady is derived from the Mohawk *skahnéhtati* 'it is beyond the pines'.

12. Pearson, *Early Records of the City*, 2:197.

13. See Fenton, *Great Law*, 259–60; Richter, "War and Culture."

14. Starna and Brandão, "Mohawk-Mahican War"; *IACNY*, 128–30. See chapter 6.

15. Nammack, *Dispossession of the Indians*, 53–69.

16. See *BA*; Huey, "Mahicans, the Dutch, and the Schodack Islands."

17. Goddard, "Eastern Algonquian Languages," 72–73; Dally-Starna and Starna, *Gideon's People*, 1:46, 625n47.

18. Goddard, "Notes on Mahican," 246–47; Dally-Starna and Starna, *Gideon's People*, 1:426.

19. Ruttenber, *Indian Tribes of Hudson's River*, 83–84; Goddard, "Delaware," 214.

20. "Map of Livingston Manor Anno 1714," O'Callaghan, *Documentary*

History, 3: map facing 414. Ives Goddard, personal communication, 2009. See also Goddard, "Review of *Indian Names*." On the deed these place-names are Sankhenak, Wachanekassik, Saaskahampka, and Mahaskakook. Pearson, *Early Records of the City*, 2:189–92. The text accompanying the 1714 map lists Mawanagwassik, Ahashawahkik, Wichguapakkatt, Sakahka, Acawaisik, and Sackahampa.

21. Ives Goddard, personal communication, 2009. See Series A0272, Applications for Land Grants 44:31, and Series 12943, Letters Patent, Book 6:325, New York State Archives, Albany; J. H. Smith, *History of Dutchess County*, 173; E. M. Smith, *Documentary History*, 22. Deed recorded on June 25, 1787. See O'Callaghan, *Calendar of NY*, 747. Pearson, *Early Records of the City*, 2:85, lists Pakakeincq. See also the Munsee place-names Korenagkoyosink, Wimpeting, and Aquasing, in J. M. Smith, "Highland King Nimhammaw," 79, 82–83.

22. See *NNN*, 86.

23. Canasenix, Pesquanachqua, and Quachanock. Pearson, *Early Records of the City*, 2:303–4. Ives Goddard, personal communication, 2009.

24. Dunn, *Mohicans and Their Land*, 45–62.

25. Portions of this discussion are drawn from Starna, "American Indian Villages to Dutch Farms."

26. See Cronon, *Changes in the Land*, 58–65.

27. *DNN*, 74.

28. Grotius, *De Iure Praedae Commentarius*, 227; Grotius, *Freedom of the Seas*, 20–25.

29. See Sahlins, *Stone Age Economics*, 93; Sahlins, *Tribesmen*, 76.

30. Grotius, *De Iure Praedae Commentarius*, 221.

31. Grotius, *De Iure Praedae Commentarius*, 221. For a thorough discussion on the Doctrine of Discovery and its legacies, see R. A. Williams, *American Indian*.

32. See Miller, "Doctrine of Discovery," 15–16.

33. R. J. Miller, "Doctrine of Discovery," 6–7. The land tenure system of the Dutch West India Company, along with the concomitant recognition of Indian land rights, is discussed in Rife, "Land Tenure in New Netherland," 41–73.

34. Insofar as Iroquoian relocations or removals are concerned, see Starna, Hamell, and Butts, "Northern Iroquoian Horticulture"; Starna, "Aboriginal Title."

35. See Gramly, "Deerskins and Hunting Territories"; Starna and Relethford, "Deer Densities." For a discussion of the range of factors leading to the shifts in settlement locations, see Engelbrecht, *Iroquoia*, 101–4.

36. See Brandão, *Iroquois Policy*.

37. The earliest firsthand account suggestive of an epidemic among the Munsees of the lower Hudson Valley is from Isaack de Rasière writing about 1628. *NNN*, 105. See Snow and Lanphear, "European Contact," 15–33.

38. Starna, "Biological Encounter," 513–14.

39. *NYCD*, 13:20; Versteg, *Kingston Papers*, 1:ix.

40. *VRBM*, 149.

41. Van Laer, *Documents Relating to New Netherland*, 105–6.

42. Grumet, "'We Are Not So Great Fools,'" 256.

43. Grumet, "'We Are Not So Great Fools,'" 256–62. See also E. W. Baker, "'A Scratch with a Bear's Paw,'" 237–39; Silverman, "'Natural Inhabitants,'" 1–10. The argument made by several historians that deeds and other forms of land conveyances are useful devices for providing insight into Native sociopolitical organization or territorial boundaries receives a much needed critical examination in Rudes, "Indian Land Deeds," 19–48.

44. The question of Native literacy was directly addressed in the 1660 treaty between the Dutch and Indian communities that occupied far western Long Island, northern New Jersey, Staten Island, and the lower Hudson Valley: "Whereas our [Dutch] descendants for many years can see and know what we now talk over with them and conclude, which their [the Indians'] descendants cannot do, because they [the Indians] can neither read nor write, it would be good and necessary, that they leave some of their children with us to be educated." *NYCD*, 13:148–49.

45. Jennings, *Invasion of America*, 128–45.

46. Grumet, "Selling of Lenapehoking," 20.

47. In a wide-ranging discussion on the alienation and purchase of Native lands, Stuart Banner, who has little to say about the Dutch and New Netherland, presents Indians as primarily victims in these transactions. Banner, *How the Indians Lost Their Land*, especially 49–84.

48. Dunn, *Mohicans and Their Land*, 280.

49. *Schout*, a law enforcement officer who served as both sheriff and prosecutor.

50. Gehring, "Encountering Native Americans"; Jacobs, *New Netherland*, 124–26.

51. Gehring, "Encountering Native Americans."

52. The following discussion is from Gehring, "Translation of Mahican Passages." The quoted text is that translated from Slictenhorst's court submissions, that is, his written testimony.

53. See, for example, Cronon, *Changes in the Land*, 66–69.

54. This is a good example of a kind of usufructuary privilege believed to have been practiced by Native people.

55. "Melyn Papers," 125.

56. "Hoges" is Anthony de Hooges, secretary of Rensselaerswijck.

57. See Dunn, *Mohicans and Their Land*, 279–309.

58. In 1734 an Indian named "Ompamet" and "Ompawmet" (Aupaumut?), who may have been a Housatonic Mahican, laid claim to lands on "each Side Connecticutt River, about two Miles up and down the River," in the vicinity of present-day East Putney VT. Asking a price of 300 pounds, he settled for 100. *Acts and Resolves*, 12:58–59.

59. Dunn, *Mohicans and Their Land*, 279–309.

60. Starna, "American Indian Villages to Dutch Farms," 82–83. Although the numbers of fur-bearing animals had been sharply reduced in much of the Hudson Valley and coastal New England by 1625–30, thousands of furs nevertheless found their way to Fort Orange, carried in by Indians residing to the west and north of Fort Orange.

8. A Century Of Mahican History

1. Starna and Brandão, "Mohawk-Mahican War." See chapter 6.

2. See Day, "Indian as an Ecological Factor," 331–32; Crockett, *Vermont*, 1:47.

3. Huey, "Mahicans, the Dutch, and the Schodack Islands," 97–99.

4. Until the late 1740s, although by this time their numbers had greatly diminished, Mahicans maintained a steady presence in what is generally regarded as their core territory, "two leagues below Fort Orange," that is, in the broad environs of the Schodack Islands. See VRBM, 483–84; NNN, 206; BA, 106. The best discussion on the Mahicans living in this area, including their land holdings and sales of lands, is Huey, "Mahicans, the Dutch, and the Schodack Islands."

5. See Brandão, *Iroquois Policy*, 81–90.

6. Day, "Ouragie War," 37.

7. NYCD, 13:6. Trelease, in IACNY, 65, raises the reasonable question as to what degree Kieft sought to enforce the levy ordinance. Even so, in 1640, De Vries, in NNN, 209, reported that near Tappan in the lower Hudson, he found "the Company's sloop there for the purpose of levying a contribution from the Indian Christians, of a quantity of corn." The phrase "Indian Christians" in the original is *"vande Wilde Christenen."* Charles Gehring, personal communication, 2009. However, in spite of some initial enthusiasm for doing so, there is no evidence that the Dutch converted a single Native to Christianity anytime before 1640, and perhaps not until the end of the century. Thus, De Vries's report of "Indian Christians" is puzzling. See Jacobs, *New Netherland*, 318–23.

8. *IACNY*, 60–84; Jacobs, *New Netherland*, 133–35; J. H. Williams, "Great Doggs," 245–64.

9. See *NYCD*, 1:150; *NNN*, 213, 274–75. De Vries says that it was the murderer, not a headman, who told Dutch authorities that he was exacting revenge, this for the killing of his uncle.

10. *IACNY*, 69.

11. *NNN*, 225.

12. See discussions in Jennings, *Invasion of America*, 155–57; Salisbury, *Manitou and Providence*, 48; Bragdon, *Native People*, 147–48.

13. *NNN*, 225. The patroonship of Pavonia was on the east shore of New Jersey at about present-day Hoboken and Jersey City.

14. *NYCD*, 1:150–51.

15. Winthrop, *Winthrop's Journal*, 2:95.

16. *NNN*, 225.

17. *NYCD*, 1:196, 198, 200, 412.

18. See *VRBM*, 817. Commissary, "a position appointed by the council at Manhattan to oversee the WIC [West India Company] trading operations at posts such as Fort Orange and to serve as commander of the garrison." Gehring, *Fort Orange Court Minutes*, xxxv.

19. *IACNY*, 116–17.

20. De Vries reported that after the fleeing Wiechquaeskecks had arrived at Vriesendael, his home on the Hudson River about Tappan, he paddled an Indian canoe "between the cakes of ice" downriver to Fort Amsterdam to get help. *NNN*, 226. Venema, *Beverwijck*, 176, explains that the upper Hudson was usually not free of ice or fully navigable until April.

21. Dunn, *Mohicans and Their Land*, 111, cites a statement by Brant van Slichtenhorst, a former director of Rensselaerswijck, to support her assertion that the Mahicans who had moved against the Wiechquaeskecks had "been summoned to fight in the service of the Mohawks against the Mohawk's enemies, *i.e.*, the tribes from whom the Mohawks collected tribute." Van Slichtenhorst, however, said no such thing. In specific regard to the Mohawks, he wrote that they summoned Indians from whom they received tribute "to go fight with them against their enemies the French Christians and Indians who live in Canada." Van Slichtenhorst was not talking about a war against the Wiechquaeskecks, nor was he referring to events in 1643 when these Indians were attacked. The time frame of his remarks is between the years 1648 and 1651. See Gehring, "Encountering Native Americans," 286. See also Venema, *Beverwijck*, 30. Indeed, there is nothing in the record to suggest that the Mohawks had summoned the Mahicans or any other Algonquians in the region to join them in their military campaigns at this or any other time.

Brasser, *Riding on the Frontier's Crest*, 17, contends that by about 1640, "existing evidence suggests that they [Mahicans] forced all Indian groups along the east side of the Hudson River to acknowledge Mahican rule," which, if true, may in some way explain their assault on the Wiechquaeskecks. Still, Brasser cites nothing of the "existing evidence" to support his claim.

22. O'Callaghan, ed., *Documentary History*, 4:66.

23. *NYCD*, 13:14, 17–18, 14:44–45.

24. *DNN*, 39. See also *IACNY*, 74–84; O'Callaghan, *History of New Netherland*, 1:355–56.

25. *NYCD*, 13:18. This may be Cornelis Anthonisz van Schlick, "appointed the patroon's *voorspraecke*, or representative, May 12, 1639." *VRBM*, 809.

26. *NYCD*, 13:18. See a slightly revised translation in Scott and Stryker-Rodda, *New York Historical Manuscripts*, 279–80.

27. Dunn, *Mohicans and Their Land*, 167, 280. See Gehring, "Translation of Mahican Passages."

28. Although there are a few exceptions, Aepjen's alleged political activities, as Dunn describes them in *Mohicans and Their Land*, especially 185–90, are left undocumented.

29. See chapter 7.

30. Dunn, *Mohicans and Their Land*, 173, says that Aepjen was involved in "at least seven major land sales between 1648 and 1665."

31. Dunn, in *Mohicans and Their Land*, 171–73, writes imaginatively that Aepjen's "generous land policies, had resulted in an informal but effective alliance between officials of Rensselaerswyck and the Mohicans," and that he "seemed anxious to enjoy interaction with the Dutch. . . . Through his position as chief sachem and because of his outgoing personality, he was suited for the role of broker." Equally inventive, Grumet, *Munsee Indians*, 62, sees Aepjen, along with the other headmen at the treaty, as representing "three Munsee coalitions gathered at high levels of sociopolitical organization," the meaning of which is unclear.

32. *IACNY*, 110.

33. *NYCD*, 13:72.

34. Day, "Ouragie War," 41.

35. *NYCD*, 9:6–7.

36. See Salisbury, "Toward the Covenant Chain," 64; Brandão, *Iroquois Policy*.

37. Day, "Ouragie War," 40; Day, "Western Abenaki," 151; Shea, "Journal of Father Druillet[t]es," 309–14, 317. See Salisbury, "Indians and Colonists," 88.

38. *NYCD*, 9:5.

39. Shea, "Journal of Father Druillet[t]es," 317; Day, "Ouragie War," 40.

40. Day, "Ouragie War," 41; Salisbury, "Indians and Colonists."

41. *NYCD*, 13:83.

42. *NYCD*, 13:90.

43. *NYCD*, 13:113.

44. For the best treatment of the Esopus wars, see *IACNY*, 138–68.

45. *NYCD*, 13:123.

46. *NYCD*, 13:127, 131.

47. *NYCD*, 13:132.

48. *NYCD*, 13:152.

49. *NYCD*, 13:162.

50. *NYCD*, 13:168–69.

51. *NYCD*, 13:169, 178–79.

52. *NYCD*, 13:171–73.

53. *NYCD*, 13:179–83.

54. *NYCD*, 13:191, 204, 223, 227–29.

55. *NYCD*, 13:245–47.

56. *NYCD*, 13:261, 264.

57. *NYCD*, 13:275.

58. *NYCD*, 13:292, 300.

59. *IACNY*, 160–68; *NYCD*, 13:308, 310.

60. *NYCD*, 13:375–77.

61. *NYCD*, 27, 33, 35, 224–27. See Day, "Ouragie War," 41; *IACNY*, 128–29.

62. Day, "Ouragie War," 42–45.

63. *NYCD*, 13:302.

64. *NYCD*, 303–4, 308.

65. *NYCD*, 308. "Wissatinnewag" is not a reference to or a linguistic/phonetic variant of Housatonic, as Bruchac and Thomas, "Locating 'Wissatinnewag,'" have claimed. Ives Goddard, personal communication, 2009.

66. See *NYCD*, 13:297–98, 308–9; Van Rensselaer, *Correspondence*, 413; Starna and Brandão, "Mohawk-Mahican War." Jeremias van Rensselaer (1632–1674), a son of Kiliaen, assumed the position of director of the patroonship from his brother, Jan Baptist, in 1658.

67. *NYCD*, 13:355, 356; Day, "Ouragie War," 42.

68. *NYCD*, 13:378–80, 2:371–72; Day, "Ouragie War," 42. During their meeting with English authorities at Fort Albany, on September 24, 1664, the Iroquois charged the Pocumtucks with having killed the members of their peace delegation. *NYCD*, 3:68.

69. *IACNY*, 130.

70. Van Rensselaer, *Correspondence*, 358.

71. Rink, *Holland on the Hudson*, 260–63; Jacobs, *New Netherland*, 178–80.

72. *NYCD*, 3:67–68.

73. *NYCD*, 3:67–68; *IACNY*, 228; Richter, *Ordeal of the Longhouse*, 98; Jennings, "Susquehannock," 365–66. In February 1668/69, the South Indians (Susquehannocks), Navesinks, and Esopus Indians proposed a peace with the Mohawks and other Iroquois, which seems to confirm Munsee participation in the war as allies of the Susquehannocks. Similarly, the following July New York colony's governor Francis Lovelace sought a general peace among the Indians, naming the Mohawks, on one side, and the Esopus, Catskills, and Wappingers, on the other. In neither case are the Mahicans mentioned. At the same time, Connecticut's governor, John Winthrop ("The Younger," 1606–1676), was attempting to quiet the Indians in the western part of that colony, probably the Wiechquaeskecks. *NYCD*, 13:423, 427.

74. Kerhonkson, Sullivan County, New York.

75. *NYCD*, 13:399–400.

76. See Day, "Ouragie War"; Salisbury, "Indians and Colonists."

77. Snow, *Iroquois*, 110.

78. *BA*, 106.

79. Day, "Ouragie War," 43–44; Richter, *Ordeal of the Longhouse*, 102–4.

80. Richter, *Ordeal of the Longhouse*, 103–4; Leder, *Livingston Indian Records*, 29–30.

81. Leder, *Livingston Indian Records*, 31–32.

82. Leder, *Livingston Indian Records*, 34–35.

83. In a letter to King Louis XIV dated October 1669, Jean Talon, intendant of New France, reported that the "Mohegans (*Loups*) and the other the Socoquis" lived near the English. However, calling the Mahicans "Loups" is uncommon in the literature. Given the relatively small number of these Indians in the Hudson Valley at this time, it is unlikely that, by themselves, they "infested" any roads in Iroquois country, not without the more numerous Northern Indians by their side. *NYCD*, 9:66.

84. The fullest account of this battle is in Gookin, *Historical Collections*, 26–27. Despite the movement of warring Indians back and forth across the Hudson River, there are no reports on the attack by English authorities sitting in Albany. See Day, "Ouragie War," 44; *IACNY*, 229–30; Jennings, *Ambiguous Iroquois Empire*, 133–35. The conclusion by both Trelease and Jennings that it had been Mahicans who had attacked the Mohawk village is based on the mistaken connection they drew between the Mahicans and Indians identified as Loups. Although the Mahicans were infrequently called Loups, it was the Northern Indians, specifically the Sokokis, to whom that name properly belonged. See Starna and Brandão, "Mohawk-Mahican War," 731, 746n55 and n56. In his account, cited above, Gookin has the Northern Indians traveling some two hundred miles to launch their assault against the Mohawks, a

distance that, while an exaggeration, nonetheless represents an obvious counter to the claim that it was carried out by Mahicans.

85. *NYCD*, 13:439–40, 458. In his letter to Governor Winthrop, Lovelace clarified "what is meant by ye *Highland* Indians amongst us, ye *Wappingoes & Wickersheck* [Wiechquaeskecks] &c have alwayes beene reckoned so."

86. Jennings, *Ambiguous Iroquois Empire*, 134–35; Leder, *Livingston Indian Records*, 35–37.

87. Day, "Ouragie War," 44–45; *NYCD*, 13:491, 494. This peace accord was reached just as King Philip's War, begun the previous summer, spread through New England from its point of origin in Plymouth Colony. See Leach, *Flintlock and Tomahawk*; Lapore, *Name of War*; Drake, *King Philip's War*; Jennings, *Invasion of America*, 298–326; Pulsipher, *Subjects unto the Same King*; Mandell, *King Philip's War*.

88. *NYCD*, 13:495–96.

89. Leder, *Livingston Indian Records*, 39–40. Emphasis added.

90. *IACNY*, 230.

91. *NYCD*, 9:117.

92. *NYCD*, 13:497.

93. Van Laer, *Minutes of the Court*, 2:48–49, 56–58. *NYCD*, 3:255, 265.

94. Trumball and Hoadley, *Colony of Connecticut*, 2:460–62; Leach, *Flintlock and Tomahawk*, 142, 163, 232–36.

95. Jennings, *Invasion of America*, 301.

96. *BA*, 179; *NYCD*, 3:254. Schaghticoke signifies "the confluence of two streams." Dally-Starna and Starna, trans. and eds., *Gideon's People*, 1:4. The best history of Schaghticoke, from its founding to its abandonment, is in Calloway, *Western Abenakis*.

97. Leder, *Livingston Indian Records*, 77–78; *NYCD*, 4:744, 902, 991. See Calloway, *Western Abenakis*, 82; Pulsipher, *Subjects unto the Same King*, 131; Richter, *Before the Revolution*, 287–88. The metaphor of a tree of peace or tree of welfare was a commonly used diplomatic phrase for the period. Although a few Mahicans may have resided at Schaghticoke, the overwhelming numbers of Indians there were Sokokis, Pocumtucks, Nonotucks, Agawams, and others. See Day, "Missisquoi," 51–57.

98. See *IACNY*, 230–33; Jennings, *Invasion of America*, 307–8; Richter, *Ordeal of the Longhouse*, 135.

99. *NYCD*, 4:337, 902, 991. In 1735 secondhand information has three or four hundred River Indians under arms, suggesting a total population of between 1,200 and 1,600. Appleton, *Gospel Ministers*, iii.

100. Goddard, "Ethnohistorical Implications," 20; Grumet, *Native American Place Names*, 57–58. For a treatment of the alleged Wappinger confederacy, see Grumet, *Munsee Indians*, 14, 296n16.

101. Wheeler, *To Live upon Hope*, 25, 37; Oberly, *Nation of Statesmen*, 6; Brasser, *Riding on the Frontier's Crest*, 23; Brasser, "Mahican," 204.

102. Ruttenber, *Indian Tribes of Hudson's River*, 41, 85.

103. Grumet, *Munsee Indians*, 296n16.

104. See Jones, *Stockbridge, Past and Present*, 20–23.

105. Brasser, *Riding on the Frontier's Crest*, 23.

106. Leder, *Livingston Indian Records*, 37.

107. Brasser, *Riding on the Frontier's Crest*, 23.

108. Quinney, "Speech of John W. Quinney," 316.

109. Beauchamp, *Aboriginal Place Names*, 20.

110. Brasser, *Riding on the Frontier's Crest*, 23.

111. O'Callaghan, *Documentary History*, 2:90.

112. *NYCD*, 4:123.

113. See *IACNY*, 215, 323n51, 326; Fenton, *Great Law*, 6; Richter, *Ordeal of the Longhouse*, 15, 292n13. Grumet, *Munsee Indians*, 205, offers: "Acting in concert with Schaghticokes and Mahicans as River Indians, more independently as Lower River Indians, or individually as residents of particular places or members of particular kin groups, Indians in Munsee country continued to represent themselves with English authorities at all political levels for a long time after 1701"; "Unlike most Iroquoians, River Indians and many other Eastern Algonquians traditionally tended to avoid living close to one another for any extended period of time." See also Dunn, *Mohican and Their Land*, 202.

114. See Brasser, *Riding on the Frontier's Crest*, 24; Jennings, *Invasion of America*, 322–23; Jennings, *Ambiguous Iroquois Empire*, 148; Richter, *Ordeal of the Longhouse*, 136; Colden, *History of the Five Indian Nations*, 95; Day, "Missisquoi," 51–57. For Soquans's remark, see *NYCD*, 4:744.

115. Andros, *Andros Papers*, 2:72–73.

116. *NYCD*, 13:508. This is the prominent trader Philip Pietersz Schuyler (d. 1683). See Venema, *Beverwijck*, 254–63.

117. *NYCD* 13:510; Richter, *Ordeal of the Longhouse*, 124.

118. *NYCD*, 13:523.

119. *IACNY*, 326.

120. *NYCD*, 9:259. See Richter, *Ordeal of the Longhouse*, 149–55, on La Barre's thwarted plans to attack the Iroquois.

121. *IACNY*, 326.

122. *NYCD*, 13:531–32.

123. *NYCD* 3:439.

124. *NYCD*, 3:444.

125. *NYCD*, 3:521, 533.

126. Brandão and Starna, "Treaties of 1701," 213–14. See also Richter, *Ordeal of the Longhouse*, 156–61; Jennings, *Ambiguous Iroquois Empire*, 195–96.

127. Richter, *Ordeal of the Longhouse*, 165–66; O'Callaghan, *Documentary History*, 2:161–62. French sources refer to the participation of the "Mohegans," a translation of "Loups." Nonetheless, one account, describing the impact of the smallpox epidemic, has it that "in the great Mohegan town where they had been, only sixteen men had been spared by the disease." This town is Schaghticoke. See *NYCD*, 9:490.

128. One of the listed River Indians' headmen carried a Mahican-language name: Eetowacamo 'on both sides of the water'. A second, Eetewapo, may also have been a Mahican. Ives Goddard, personal communication, 2010. *NYCD*, 3:802.

129. *NYCD*, 3:800–805, 840. Pieter (Peter) Schuyler (1657–1724), soldier, Indian commissioner, and member of the provincial council, became Albany's first mayor in 1686.

130. *IACNY*, 282–83. See *NYCD*, 3:439, 9:569.

131. Leder, *Livingston Indian Records*, 64–68; Grumet, *Munsee Indians*, 153.

132. For an overview of these Indians, see Callender, "Shawnee."

133. Arent Schuyler (1662–1730), Pieter Schuyler's brother, was a prominent Albany trader and city alderman.

134. Arnout Viele (1640–1704), a merchant and translator, resided in Beverwijck (Albany).

135. *IACNY*, 324–26; Jennings, *Ambiguous Iroquois Empire*, 205–7; Grumet, *Munsee Indians*, 191–93; *NYCD*, 4:90, 99. A seminal source cited by historians on the Shawnee episode is Hanna, *Wilderness Trail*, 1:137–43.

136. See Jones, *Stockbridge, Past and Present*, 16–18; Jennings, *Ambiguous Iroquois Empire*, 196–99.

137. Day, "Western Abenaki," 151.

138. Richter, *Ordeal of the Longhouse*, 6.

139. *NYCD*, 4:123.

140. *NYCD*, 193–96. Fitz-John Winthrop (1637–1707), soon to be governor of Connecticut, was the son of John Winthrop (the Younger) and Elizabeth Reade Winthrop.

141. Huey, "Mahicans, the Dutch, and the Schodack Islands," 101–3.

142. *NYCD*, 4:248.

143. See Brandão and Starna, "Treaties of 1701," 219.

144. *NYCD*, 4:743–44.

145. *NYCD*, 744.

146. Leder, *Livingston Indian Records*, 95.

147. *NYCD*, 4:745.

148.On the treaty in Montreal, see Havard, *Great Peace of Montreal*; Brandão and Starna, "Treaties of 1701," 229–32.

149.Brandão and Starna, "Treaties of 1701," 223.

150.*NYCD*, 4:902–3.

151.*NYCD*, 903–4.

152.Calloway, *Western Abenakis*, 116, 167; Day, "Oral Tradition," 105; Day, "Missisquoi."

153.Leder, *Livingston Indian Records*, 189–90; *NYCD*, 9:763.

154.See Wallace, *Conrad Weiser*.

155.*NYCD*, 5:562–63.

9. Stockbridge and Its Companions

1.Huey, "Mahicans, the Dutch, and the Schodack Islands," 103–4; Bridenbaugh, *Gentleman's Progress*, 60.

2. Secondary works on Shekomeko, in addition to Moravian activities in eastern New York and western Connecticut, include Loskiel, *History of the Mission*; Reichel, *Dedication of Monuments*; De Cost Smith's romantic although historically approximate *Martyrs of the Oblong*; Westmeier's eccentric and often faulty *Evacuation of Shekomeko*; and Dunn's *Mohican World* and "Adapting a Culture." Dunn's writings on the Moravians are undercited, unoriginal, and often mistaken. Moreover, she does not avail herself of the extensive and essential German-language primary record on the missions. For Indian and Moravian religious life at Shekomeko, see, generally, Wheeler, *To Live upon Hope*.

3. Useful English-language sources on the origins and history of the Moravian Church and its North American missions are Hamilton and Hamilton, *History of the Moravian Church*; Loskiel, *History of the Mission*; Reichel, *Memorials of the Moravian Church*; [Neisser], *History of Moravian Work*; Heckewelder, *Narrative of the Mission*.

4. *Records of the Moravian Mission* (cited by reel, box, folder, item number, and date, where available), 3/113/5/2, Sept. 1743. See also 3/113/5/6, Oct. 16, 1743; 3/113/5/11, n.d. The German-language records of the Moravians, cited here and elsewhere in this chapter, were translated by Corinna Dally-Starna.

5. "Hay barrack" is written *Schut Scheur* on the sketch and *Schutt [Schütte] Scheune* in the "Master Diary" kept by the Moravians at Shekomeko. See *Records of the Moravian Mission*, 1/111/1/1, Sept. 6 and 8, 1744. "Barn" in German is *Scheune* and in Dutch is *Schuur*. The origin of the hay barrack, *Hooiberg* in Dutch, is Zuid Holland and Utrecht. See Noble, "Hay Barrack."

6. Dally-Starna and Starna, *Gideon's People*, 1:6, 33–36, 77, fig. 1; Elliot, "Otsiningo," 94–100. See *Records of the Moravian Mission*, 1/111/1/1, June 28, July 1, 1745.

7. Information on the subsistence and economy of Shekomeko is drawn primarily from the "Master Diary," *Records of the Moravian Mission*, 1/111/1/1, *passim*.

8. *Records of the Moravian Mission*, 1/111/1/1, Jan. 25, June 28, 1743.

9. See, generally, Wheeler, *To Live upon Hope*.

10. Dally-Starna and Starna, *Gideon's People*, 1:15–18, 627n68.

11. Dally-Starna and Starna, *Gideon's People*, 1:18, 23–24; *Colonial Laws of New York*, 3:424, 428; O'Callaghan, *Documentary History*, 3:617.

12. Dally-Starna and Starna, *Gideon's People*, 1:13–14. The Mohawk language does not contain the consonant cluster "rl" found in a word like Corlaer. Thus, in Mohawk Corlaer becomes *kó:ra*, with the augmentative suffix *kowa*, translated as "the Great King," hence "governor." "Corlaer" has since been used by Iroquois people as the name, the honorific, for New York's governors. See Fenton, *Great Law*, 200.

13. Colee, "Housatonic-Stockbridge Indians," 114; Frazier, *Mohicans of Stockbridge*, 45; Dunn, *Mohican World*, 214. See Sherwood, *Memoirs of Rev. David Brainerd*, 60, 77, 96, 99, 123.

14. Colee, "Housatonic-Stockbridge Indians," 143 and 185, citing Sergeant's journal; Frazier, *Mohicans of Stockbridge*, 45; Hopkins, *Historical Memoirs*, 61, 74.

15. Goddard, "Notes on Mahican," 247.

16. Dally-Starna and Starna, *Gideon's People*, 1:686n12.

17. Dally-Starna and Starna, *Gideon's People*, 1:637n8.

18. Dally-Starna and Starna, *Gideon's People*, 1:85–104, 412, 420.

19. Colee, "Housatonic-Stockbridge Indians," 93; Talcott, *Talcott Papers*, 2:402.

20. There is no documentary or archaeological evidence that would precisely locate Weataug village, nor establish the time of its founding. All that has been postulated in various sources is from unsubstantiated local histories and folklore.

21. Trumbull, *History of Connecticut*, 2:109.

22. Appleton, *Gospel Ministers*, iii.

23. A tract called "Weataok" is first mentioned in a handwritten copy of a deed dated August 22, 1719, entered January 1, 1759. Book of Deeds, Town of Salisbury, Connecticut, 3:504. Binzen, "Mohican Lands and Colonial Corners," 26, citing Trumbull, *History of Connecticut*, 2:83, puts what is apparently Weataug village in alliance with several others, including "Piscatacook (Kent)," that is, Pachgatgoch or Schaghticoke (CT), in 1704. However, Trumbull was mistaken. Pachgatgoch was not founded until 1736. See Dally-Starna and Starna, *Gideon's People*, 1:2.

24. In most recent histories the Indians at Stockbridge are identified as Mohicans rather than Mahicans. The name "Mohican," which actually stems

from an English rendering of the earlier Dutch "Mahican" or "Mahikander" (var.), was carried into New York and thence to Wisconsin and the reservation of the federally recognized tribe that, until 2002, was known as the Stockbridge-Munsee Community, Band of Mohican Indians, and today is the Stockbridge-Munsee Community. Alan Taylor, "Captain Hendrick Aupaumut," 432, explains that "Mohican" conveys the idea of "a partially reinvented, culturally synthetic, and ethnically and geographically diverse people that was not identical to its Mahican predecessor." While this portrayal of the Indians at Stockbridge, then New Stockbridge, is partially accurate, the same characterizations could easily be applied to most of the Indian communities in the Northeast at the time, including the six Iroquois nations.

25. A selection of the strongest works, in the order of the subject areas listed in the text, includes Frazier, *Mohicans of Stockbridge*; Colee, "Housatonic-Stockbridge Indians"; Calloway, "Stockbridge"; Axtell, "Scholastic Frontier"; Miles, "Red Man Dispossessed"; Ronda and Ronda, "Chief Hendrick Aupaumut'"; Taylor, "Captain Hendrick Aupaumut." Wheeler, *To Live upon Hope*, provides a thorough examination of the workings of Christianity at Stockbridge.

26. In addition is the contemporary evidence that Appleton supplied, which includes letters from Hopkins and Sergeant. Appleton, *Gospel Ministers*, iii–xiv.

27. Colee, "Housatonic-Stockbridge Indians," 40–41.

28. Colee, "Housatonic-Stockbridge Indians," 18–20. See Hopkins, *Historical Memoirs*, 6–7.

29. Trumball and Hoadley, *Colony of Connecticut*, 2:472.

30. Pearson, *Early Records of the City*, 2:19.

31. Appleton, *Gospel Ministers*, iii; Hopkins, *Historical Memoirs*, 1.

32. Hopkins, *Historical Memoirs*, 2; Miles, "Red Man Dispossessed," 47; Wright, *Indian Deeds*, 116–19; Goddard, "Notes on Mahican," 247. "Westonook" is Westenhook, the English spelling of the Dutch *Westenhoeck* 'western corner'. This name has historically had different applications, including as a locale on the New York–Connecticut boundary; as a name for the Housatonic River; as the area between Copake Falls N Y and South Egremont M A; and as an alternative name for Stockbridge, among others. See Dally-Starna and Starna, *Gideon's People*, 1:653n7.

33. Colee, "Housatonic-Stockbridge Indians," 4.

34. Goddard, "Notes on Mahican," 246–47.

35. Hopkins, *Historical Memoirs*, 9–10.

36. Hopkins, *Historical Memoirs*, 21–22.

37. Hopkins, *Historical Memoirs*, 27–28, 31,

38. Hopkins, *Historical Memoirs*, 43.

39. Hopkins, *Historical Memoirs*, 44.

40. Hopkins, *Historical Memoirs*, 44–51; Miles, "Red Man Dispossessed," 48–49.

41. Appleton, *Gospel Ministers*, xi.

42. Hopkins, *Historical Memoirs*, 54; Colee, "Housatonic-Stockbridge Indians," 199, citing Sergeant's journal.

43. These houses were most likely simple, rectangular frame structures, sided with hewn planks, with bark- or board-covered pitched roofs.

44. Hopkins, *Historical Memoirs*, 127; Dally-Starna and Starna, *Gideon's People*, 36.

45. Hopkins, *Historical Memoirs*, 143.

46. Colee, "Housatonic-Stockbridge Indians," 199, citing Sergeant's journal.

47. Colee, "Housatonic-Stockbridge Indians," 140, 187–88, citing Sergeant's journal.

48. Frazier, *Mohicans of Stockbridge*, 98–103; Axtell, "Scholastic Frontier," 69–70.

49. NYCD, 7:94; Ruttenber, *Indian Tribes of Hudson's River*, 230. See also Dally-Starna and Starna, *Gideon's People*, 2:551n69.

50. NYCD, 7:96, 99–100, 111, 113.

51. Dally-Starna and Starna, *Gideon's People*, 2:558n218, citing W. Johnson, *Papers of Sir William Johnson*, 2:477–78; NYCD, 7:152.

52. Grumet, "Nimhans of the Colonial Hudson Valley," 80–99.

53. Handlin and Mark, "Chief Daniel Nimham," 196–97. See also Nimham, "Petition of Daniel Nimham."

54. See generally Dally-Starna and Starna, *Gideon's People*; Wheeler, *To Live upon Hope*.

55. Axtell, *Invasion Within*, 131–37.

56. Hopkins, *Historical Memoirs*, 23–24.

57. See Frazier, *Mohicans of Stockbridge*, 175; Dally-Starna and Starna, *Gideon's People*, 1:221–22, 661n24; Bodley, *Victims of Progress*, 71–74.

58. Dally-Starna and Starna, *Gideon's People*, 1:71.

59. Colee, "Housatonic-Stockbridge Indians," 128–29; Hopkins, *Historical Memoirs*, 2; Frazier, *Mohicans of Stockbridge*, 112.

60. See Brasser, *Riding on the Frontier's Crest*, 33–34; Dunn, *Mohican World*, 128. Compare, however, Colee, "Housatonic-Stockbridge Indians," 167–70.

61. Dally-Starna and Starna, *Gideon's People*, 1:13–14, 625n52. On the names Metoxson and Corlaer, see Waterman, *Evert Wendell's Account Book*, 207; Livingston Family Papers, box 18, folder 5, page 5; Towns and Lands, Connecticut

State Archives, 7:245a; *The Law Papers*, 1:62; *Records of the Moravian Mission*, 1/111/2/1, Feb. 21, 1743. For Metoxson at Stockbridge, see Colee, "Housatonic-Stockbridge Indians," 169.

62. Ives Goddard, personal communication, 2010.

63. *Records of the Moravian Mission*, 1/111/2/1, Feb. 21, 1743.

64. Colee, "Housatonic-Stockbridge Indians," 144–47, 149–51; Barber, *Historical Collections*, 99; Dally-Starna and Starna, *Gideon's People*, vols. 1 and 2; Frazier, *Mohicans of Stockbridge*, 9–11.

65. Colee, "Housatonic-Stockbridge Indians," 147–48; Dally-Starna and Starna, *Gideon's People*, 1:83, 638n5, 465, 679n3.

66. Colee, "Housatonic-Stockbridge Indians," 152–55; Frazier, *Mohicans of Stockbridge*, 12–13, 105. For a detailed discussion of land loss at Stockbridge, see Miles, "Red Man Dispossessed."

67. Hopkins, *Historic Memoirs*, 11–12.

68. For a discussion on powwows, see Bragdon, *Native People*, 201–8; Simmons, "Southern New England Shamanism."

69. Hopkins, *Historic Memoirs*, 23–24.

70. Hopkins, *Historic Memoirs*, 37–38, 58, see also 22–23; Ives Goddard, personal communication, 2009.

71. Frazier, *Mohicans of Stockbridge*, 105–45 (145 for numbers of survivors). See generally Miles, "Red Man Dispossessed."

72. Frazier, *Mohicans of Stockbridge*, 111; Wheeler, *To Live upon Hope*, 106–8.

73. See Dally-Starna and Starna, *Gideon's People*, 2:224, 225; Miles, "Red Man Dispossessed," 64–72; Frazier, *Mohicans of Stockbridge*, 111–12.

74. Dally-Starna and Starna, *Gideon's People*, 2:277.

75. Frazier, *Mohicans of Stockbridge*; Dally-Starna and Starna, *Gideon's People*, 1:69, 71; Miles, "Red Man Dispossessed," 56–57, 74–76.

76. See Huey, "Mahicans, the Dutch, and the Schodack Islands," 109; Schutt, "Tribal Identity," 388.

77. See Gillette and Funk, "Upper Susquehanna"; Hauptman, "Dispersal of the River Indians"; Hauptman, "Refugee Havens"; Elliott, "Otsiningo"; Richter, *Ordeal of the Longhouse*, 256–62.

78. Mancall, *Valley of Opportunity*, 29–39.

79. W. Johnson, *Papers of Sir William Johnson*, 10:932.

80. Hauptman, "Refugee Havens," 131–33.

81. See Calloway, "Stockbridge."

82. NYCD 8:626.

83. Frazier, *Mohicans of Stockbridge*, 194–95.

84. Miles, "Red Man Dispossessed," 72. On the establishment of Brothertown, see Love, *Samson Occom*, 207–25. For general perspectives on

Brothertown, which favor certain alleged, although unsubstantiated, Oneida traditions regarding foreign peoples, see Wonderley, "Brothertown, New York" and Venables, "Brotherton History." See also Silverman, *Red Brethren*. The conveyance of Oneida lands to the Brothertown is discussed in chapter 10.

85. Occom, *Collected Writings*, 24, 308. "Eeyawquittoowauconnuck" is Occom's translation of "'Brotherhood Town,' literally 'brotherhood' [plus] the locative suffix ('in', 'at', common in place-names)." Ives Goddard, personal communication, 2010.

86. Love, *Samson Occom*, 231–32; Occom, *Collected Writings*, 24–25; Calloway, "Stockbridge," 91–92.

87. Calloway, "Stockbridge," 92–100; Frazier, *Mohicans of Stockbridge*, 221–26.

88. Calloway, "Stockbridge," 100–101.

89. Calloway, "Stockbridge," 101; Frazier, *Mohicans of Stockbridge*, 234–37. These petitions also found their way to the Continental Congress, where they were referred back to the states.

10. New Stockbridge and Beyond

1. Campisi, "From Stanwix to Canandaigua," 53. Thus began a decades-long jurisdictional struggle between the federal government and New York State over Indian lands, the consequence of which was the wholesale reduction of Indian holdings accompanied by an assault on sovereignty. See Vecsey and Starna, *Iroquois Land Claims*; Campisi, "Oneida Treaty Period" and "From Stanwix to Canandaigua"; Campisi and Starna, "Road to Canandaigua"; Starna, "'United States Will Protect You.'"

2. 7 Stat., 15. Kappler, *Indian Affairs*, 2:5–6.

3. See Manley, *Treaty of Fort Stanwix*; Campisi, "Oneida Treaty Period"; Campisi, "From Stanwix to Canandaigua," 49–60; Lehman, "Iroquois Mystique."

4. As late as 1794 "some families of the Stockbridge Indians" had remained living "upon a swamp near Clermont" in Dutchess County, New York. They would leave in December of that year to "join the Chiugas [Cayugas]." Strickland, *Journal of a Tour*, 116. I thank Ruth Piwonka for pointing me to Strickland's journal.

5. See discussion in A. Taylor, *Divided Ground*, 162–63.

6. *Journal of the Senate*, 10–11.

7. Aupaumut's life and noteworthy diplomatic career are best described in Ronda and Ronda, "Chief Hendrick Aupaumut," and A. Taylor, "Captain Hendrick Aupaumut." Wheeler, "Chief Hendrick Aupaumut," reiterates much of what can be found in Taylor, adding a discussion on Stockbridge experiences on the White River, Indiana Territory.

8. *Journal of the Senate*, 10–11, 16–17. The bill was brought out of committee by state senator Ezra L'Hommedieu (1734–1811), who would be among New York's appointed Indian commissioners at the 1788 Fort Stanwix Treaty. See Hough, *Proceedings of the Commissioners*, 1:117 (on L'Hommedieu), and 1:44, 58, 73 (on Harper).

9. *Journal of the Senate*, 16–17, 28–29, 80–81. The assembly's amendments may have been inspired by one of its members, William Harper, John Harper's brother.

10. *Journal of the Senate*, 10–11.

11. Hendrick Aupaumut to Governor George Clinton, Apr. 11, 1785. Gunther Collection. Timothy Edwards (1738–1813), judge probate of Berkshire Country, Massachusetts, and a leading merchant at Stockbridge, was the eldest son of Jonathan Edwards.

12. Hough, *Proceedings of the Commissioners*, 1:230. Colonel Louis (Lewis), of Abenaki and black ancestry, spent much of his life in the Mohawk community of Kahnawake, just south of Montreal, settling at Oneida after the Revolution, where he assumed headman status. A. Taylor, *Divided Ground*, 172–73.

13. Hough, *Proceedings of the Commissioners*, 1:243–44. Oberly, *Nation of Statesmen*, 20, restated by Geherin, "New Guinea," 149n27, mistakenly claims that upon their arrival the Stockbridge had "no landownership rights among the Oneidas," and that it was "an intertribal agreement between the Oneidas and Stockbridge," signed at Fort Schuyler in 1788, that granted them the six-mile square.

14. *Laws of the State of New York*, 3:65–71.

15. *Laws of the State of New York*, 70.

16. For versions of the text of the deed, see W. Johnson, *Papers of Sir William Johnson*, 13:683–84; J. Johnson, *To Do Good*, 242; Love, *Samson Occum*, 222–23. It has been erroneously asserted that a final covenant in the deed, "that Same shall not be possessed by any persons, deemed of the said Tribes, who are descended from, or have intermixed with Negroes, or Mulattoes," applied also to the Stockbridge grant. See Geherin, "New Guinea," 151n34. On this covenant, see Silverman, "Curse of God," 519–20.

17. Campisi and Starna, "Road to Canandiagua," 486.

18. Campisi and Starna, "Road to Canandiagua," 484; *American State Papers*, 1:545; Campisi, "History of the Stockbridge Munsee Tribe," 9. See 11 Stat., 663, article 7. Kappler, *Indian Affairs*, 2:742–55.

19. *American State Papers*, 1:546.

20. Pickering, Papers, 62:108.

21. F. R. Taylor, *Life of William Savery*, 122.

22. Savery, *Labours of William Savery*, 75, emphases added. Twenty-three thousand and forty acres is thirty-six square miles, the precise area of land (six-mile square) granted by the Oneidas to the Stockbridge Indians.

23. Fenton, "Journal of James Emlen," 326, emphasis added.

24. See *Report of Special Committee*, 278–79.

25. *Report of Special Committee*, 234–59, 263–78. Section 4 of the Indian Trade and Intercourse Act states: "That no sale of lands made by any Indians, or any nation or tribe of Indians within the United States, shall be valid to any person or persons, or to any state, whether having the right of preemption to such lands or not, unless the same shall be made and duly executed at some public treaty, held under the authority of the United States." Act of July 22, 1790, ch. 33, 1 Stat. 138. See also Act of Mar. 1, 1793, ch. 19, §8, 1 Stat. 330. The Trade and Intercourse Act was reenacted several times after 1790 and codified in 1834. 25 U.S.C. §177. It is noteworthy that the 1795 transaction specifically excepted "the Lands granted to the Stockbridge Indians." *Report of Special Committee*, 245. Starna, "'United States Will Protect You.'" See also Campisi, "Trade and Intercourse Acts."

26. Tompkins, *Public Papers of Daniel D. Tompkins*, 342–43.

27. *Journal of the Assembly*, 316.

28. Hendrick Aupaumut to Governor George Clinton, Apr. 11, 1785. Gunther Collection.

29. *Report of Special Committee*, 278–80.

30. Tompkins, *Papers of Daniel D. Tompkins*, 480.

31. See note 24.

32. See the text of the deed in Love, *Samson Occum*, 222–23, and J. Johnson, *To Do Good*, 242. For "*Scaniadaris* [Scaniadoris], or the Long Lake," see Beauchamp, *Aboriginal Place Names*, 114.

33. Occom, *Collected Writings*, 276, 308; Kirkland, *Journals of Samuel Kirkland*, 132. Kirkland sometimes spoke of "Old Oneida or New Stockbridge," suggesting that he was referring to an area rather than a specific settlement. By 1800 Old Oneida had become a place "formerly called Old Oneida." Kirkland, *Journals of Samuel Kirkland*, 144, 159, 350.

34. *Collections of the Massachusetts Historical Society, 1795*, 4:67. John Kirkland (1770–1840), who would serve as president of Harvard from 1810 to 1828, provided the figure of 280 Stockbridge Indians, which he said was from a census taken by his father, Samuel, in 1791. However, John misread the document, which says that the Oneidas' "dependants & Allies-Viz Tuscaroras Stockbridge & Mohegan Indians," numbered together 287 people. Census of the Six Nations, Oct. 15, 1791, 140a, in Kirkland, Papers.

35. *Collections of the Massachusetts Historical Society, 1792*, 1:195; Fenton,

"Journal of James Emlen," 326; Belknap and Morse, "Oneida, Stockbridge, and Brotherton," 6, 24; Morse, *Report to the Secretary*, appendix 77, 361. In 1837, several years after the Indians of New Stockbridge had presumably completed their move to Wisconsin, a census counted 217 of their people remaining in New York. *Report of Special Committee*, 158; Kappler, *Indian Affairs*, 2:508. The source of this number and its validity are unknowns. One possible explanation is that it was meant to refer to Indians in Wisconsin. On unspecified Indians remaining in New York and Stockbridge populations in Wisconsin, see Oberly, *Nation of Statesmen*, 44, 64. Sergeant, whose tenure as a salaried missionary at Stockbridge had been uneven, was recruited by the Scottish Society for Propagating Christian Knowledge to serve at New Stockbridge in 1787. Wigglesworth to Kirkland, Oct. 26, 1787, 102a. Kirkland, Papers.

36. Archaeological investigations conducted in the 1980s by Daniel Weiskotten revealed that much of the core site of New Stockbridge had been destroyed by development. In 1990 and 1991, while I was under contract with the Native American Rights Fund preparing a report for *Stockbridge-Munsee Community v. State of New York*, Weiskotten granted me full access to his archaeological field notes on the New Stockbridge, Oneida, and Brothertown sites. Information on these sites reported here is from Weiskotten.

37. New York State Surveyor-General's Maps & Field Books, Series No. 10424, #70. New York State Archives, Albany, New York; Belknap, "Oneida Journal," 410; Hammond, *History of Madison County*, 739. The annuity due the Indians of New Stockbridge, stipulated in two treaties signed at Canandaigua, New York, in 1794 was $350. 7 Stat., 44 and 7 Stat., 47. Kappler, *Indian Affairs*, 2:34–37, 37–39; Pickering, Papers, 60:250. See also Campisi and Starna, "Road to Canandaigua." The New Stockbridge Indians received no funds from New York State.

38. Act of Mar. 21, 1800, ch. 42, 1800 N.Y. Laws 486.

39. Belknap and Morse, "Oneida, Stockbridge, and Brotherton," 18; Belknap, "Oneida Journal," 410, 412, 413.

40. Kirkland, *Journals of Samuel Kirkland*, 160; Hammond, *History of Madison County*, 748. Kanadesko had been a Tuscarora village for many years, occupied well before 1770.

41. Belknap and Morse, "Oneida, Stockbridge, and Brotherton," 21–25.

42. Act of Apr. 7, 1800, ch. 115, 1800 N.Y. Laws 573.

43. Act of Feb. 21, 1791, ch. 13, 1791 N.Y. Laws 212.

44. The record books that, under this statute, the clerk was required to keep have never surfaced.

45. The amount of land to be leased to each non-Indian was limited to 640 acres, for a period not to exceed twenty-one years, the rents to be used for the

benefit of the Indians of New Stockbridge or Brothertown. See also Belknap and Morse, "Oneida, Stockbridge, and Brotherton," 29.

46. Act of Feb. 21, 1791, ch. 13, 1791 N.Y. Laws 212.

47. Act of Apr. 12, 1792, ch. 73, 1792 N.Y. Laws 379. There also were a few changes made in the wording. For example, "trustees" in the original statute was changed to "peacemakers," the purpose of which is unknown.

48. Zeisberger, *Diary of David Zeisberger*, 2:289.

49. Weslager, *Delaware Indians*, 262–63.

50. Weslager, *Delaware Indians*, 266–71; Goddard, "Delaware," 222.

51. Hendrick Aupaumut to Jacob Shohett, Oct. 20, 1793; Hendrick Aupaumut to Brotherton Delaware, Nov. 12, 1794. Foster-Clement Collection.

52. Speech of Brotherton Delaware at New Stockbridge, Oct. 18, 1796. Foster-Clement Collection.

53. A. Taylor, "Captain Hendrick Aupaumut," 443–44, 450–51; Brainerd, *Life of John Brainerd*, 417. See also Silverman, *Red Brethren*, 159–60.

54. Weslager, *Delaware Indians*, 274.

55. *Votes and Proceedings*, 25.

56. [Sergeant], "Journal of John Sergeant." In 1823, absent discernable historical context, articles of agreement were entered into between headmen of the New Jersey Delawares (Brotherton) and New Stockbridge Indians in respect to lands in Wisconsin. Of interest is that the agreement stipulates that the Brotherton were to be considered a "component part of the Muhheconnuck or Stockbridge nation to all lands comprehended within and described in the two treaties made at Green Bay with the six nations & the St. Regis Stockbridge Munsee nations of Indians the eighteenth day of August in the year one thousand eight hundred and twenty one." Thwaites, *Historical Society of Wisconsin*, 15:6–8. However, the suggestion that there was some sort of merger of the Stockbridge and Brotherton tribes is not borne out by subsequent events. These Indians went into Wisconsin and settled in areas separate from each other as distinct sociopolitical entities. And they have remained so.

57. Act of Feb. 4, 1792, ch. 15, 1792 N.Y. Laws 280; Act of Mar. 26, 1802, ch. 50, 1802 N.Y. Laws 62; 1 N.Y. Rev. Stat. at 272, 274–75 (1882)(§§ 13–14 of Act of Apr. 10, 1813, 1813 N.Y. Laws Rev. ch. 29). See Starna, "Repeal of Article 8," 297–302.

58. Belknap and Morse, "Oneida, Stockbridge, and Brotherton," 8.

59. Wheeler, "Chief Hendrick Aupaumut," 208–10; Oberly, *Nation of Statesmen*, 25–26. Aupaumut's diplomatic missions are discussed in A. Taylor, "Captain Hendrick Aupaumut."

60. Quoted in Weslager, *Delaware Indians*, 333. See also Oberly, *Nation of Statesmen*, 26; Wheeler, "Chief Hendrick Aupaumut," 211; Morse, *Report to the*

Secretary, appendix 110–11. The basis for what was a considered a joint claim to land was described in a memorial to Congress submitted by Stockbridge leaders in January 1839. See Campisi, "History of the Stockbridge Munsee Tribe," 9.

61. Recorded Indian Deeds and Treaties, 3:23.

62. Morse, *Report to the Secretary*, appendix 116, 119.

63. 7 Stat., 188 and 7 Stat., 189. Kappler, *Indian Affairs*, 2:170–71, 171–74.

64. Morse, *Report to the Secretary*, appendix 116–17; Oberly, *Nation of Statesmen*, 27, citing John Gregg to John Taylor; Wheeler, "Chief Hendrick Aupaumut," 211.

65. Act of Apr. 4, 1801, ch. 147, 1801 N.Y. Laws 364–67.

66. Campisi, "History of the Stockbridge Munsee Tribe," 10–11, citing Arvid E. Miller and Fred L. Robinson, "The Stockbridge Munsee Community, The Stockbridge Tribe of Indians and Munsee Tribe of Indians." Indian Claims Commission Docket 300-A:295–99.

67. Oberly, *Nation of Statesmen*, 55; Weslager, *Delaware Indians*, 20–25.

68. See, generally, Campisi, "History of the Stockbridge Munsee Tribe"; Oberly, *Nation of Statesmen*.

Afterword

1. Campisi, "Oneida Treaty Period," 61; Prucha, *American Indian Treaties*, 202–7.

BIBLIOGRAPHY

Unpublished Works

Albany County Deeds (1654–1895). Albany County Hall of Records, Albany.

Binzen, Timothy. "Mohican Lands and Colonial Corners: Weataug, Wechquadnach and the Connecticut Colony, 1675–1750." Master's thesis, University of Connecticut, 1988.

Book of Deeds, vol. 5. Town of Salisbury CT. n.d.

Campisi, Jack. "History of the Stockbridge Munsee Tribe." Draft report prepared for the Native American Rights Fund. 1990. Manuscript in author's possession.

Colee, Philip Sauve. "The Housatonic-Stockbridge Indians: 1734–1749." PhD diss., State University of New York at Albany, 1977.

Diamond, Joseph E. "The Terminal Late Woodland/Contact Period in the Mid-Hudson Valley." PhD diss., State University of New York at Albany, 1999.

Foster-Clement Collection. Historical Society of Pennsylvania, Philadelphia.

Gehring, Charles T. "Translation of Mahican Passages from Slichtenhorst Court Proceedings." 1999. Manuscript in author's possession and on file, New Netherland Project, New York State Library, Albany.

Grumet, Robert S. "'We Are Not So Great Fools': Changes in Upper Delawaran Socio-Political Life, 1630–1758." PhD diss., Rutgers University, 1979.

Gunther, Charles F. Gunther Collection. Research Center, Chicago Historical Society.

Hamell, George R. "Jaques: A Munsee from New Netherland, 1644." 1996. Manuscript in author's possession.

Kirkland, Samuel. Papers. Hamilton College, Clinton, New York.

Lanphear, Kim M. "Biocultural Interactions: Smallpox and the Mohawk Iroquois." Master's thesis, State University of New York at Albany, 1983.

Livingston, Philip. Livingston Family Papers. Clermont State Historic Site. Clermont NY.

Nimham, Daniel. "Petition of Daniel Nimham, et al."; "Brief to Accompany Petition." A0272 Application for Land Grants ("Land Papers"), vol. 18:127, 128. New York State Archives, Albany.

Pickering, Timothy. Papers. Microfilm, 69 reels. Massachusetts Historical Society.

Recorded Indian Deeds and Treaties, 1703–1871. 3 vols. A0448. New York State Archives. Albany.

Records of the Moravian Mission among the Indians of North America. Microfilm, 40 reels. Moravian Archives, Bethlehem PA.

[Sergeant, John]. "Journal of John Sergeant, Missionary to the Stockbridge Indians from the Society in Scotland for Propagating Christian Knowledge from January [1804] to July, 1805." Baker Library Special Collections, Dartmouth College.

Published Works

Abler, Thomas S. and Elisabeth Tooker. "Seneca." In *Handbook of North American Indians*, vol. 15, *Northeast*, edited by Bruce G. Trigger, 505–17. Washington DC: Smithsonian Institution, 1978.

Acts and Resolves, Public and Private, of the Province of the Massachusetts Bay . . . Volume 12 . . . 1734–1741. Boston: Wright and Potter Printing, 1904.

Adams, Arthur G. *The Hudson River Guidebook*. New York: Fordham University Press, 1996.

Alchon, Suzanne Austin. *A Pest in the Land: New World Epidemics in Global Perspective*. Albuquerque: University of New Mexico Press, 2003.

American State Papers: Indian Affairs. Washington DC: Gales and Seaton, 1832.

Andros, Edmund. *The Andros Papers: Files of the Provincial Secretary of New York during the Administration of Governor Sir Edmund Andros, 1674–1680*, edited by Peter R. Christoph and Florence A. Christoph. 3 vols. Syracuse: Syracuse University Press, 1989–1991.

Appleton, Nathanael. *Gospel Ministers . . . Illustrated in a Sermon Preached at Deerfield, August 31, 1735, at the Ordination of Mr. John Sergeant. . . .* Boston: S. Kneeland and T. Green, 1735.

[Aupaumut, Hendrick]. "Extract from an Indian History." Massachusetts Historical Society, *Collections*, 1st ser., 9 (1804):99–102.

———. "History of the Muhheakunnuk Indians." In *The First Annual Report of the American Society for Promoting the Civilization and General Improvement of the Indian Tribes of the United States. . . .*, 42–45. New Haven: S. Converse, 1824.

Axtell, James. *After Columbus: Essays in the Ethnohistory of Colonial North America*. New York: Oxford University Press, 1988.

———. "Ethnohistory: A Historian's Viewpoint." *Ethnohistory* 26, no. 1 (1979): 1–13.

———. "Imagining the Other: First Encounters in North America." In *Beyond 1492: Encounters in Colonial North America*, 25–74. New York: Oxford University Press, 1992.

————. *The Invasion Within: The Contest of Cultures in Colonial America*. New York: Oxford University Press, 1985.

————. "The Scholastic Frontier in Western Massachusetts." In Axtell, *After Columbus*, 58–85.

————. "Through Another Glass Darkly: Early Indian Views of Europeans." In Axtell, *After Columbus*, 125–43.

Bachman, Van Cleaf. *Peltries or Plantations: The Economic Policies of the Dutch West India Company in New Netherland, 1623–1639*. Baltimore: Johns Hopkins University Press, 1969.

Baker, Brenda J., and George J. Armelagos. "The Origin and Antiquity of Syphilis: Paleopathological Diagnosis and Interpretation." *Current Anthropology* 29, no. 5 (1988): 703–37.

Baker, Emerson W. "'A Scratch with a Bear's Paw': Anglo-Indian Land Deeds in Early Maine." *Ethnohistory* 36, no. 3 (1989): 237–39.

Banner, Stuart. *How the Indians Lost Their Land: Law and Power on the Frontier*. Cambridge M A: Belnap Press of Harvard University Press, 2005.

Barber, John W. *Historical Collections, Being a General Collection of Interesting Facts, Traditions, Biographical Sketches, Anecdotes, &c., Relating to the History and Antiquities of every Town in Massachusetts, with Geographical Descriptions*. Worcester: Dorr, Howland, and Co., 1839.

Beauchamp, William M. *Aboriginal Places Names of New York*. New York State Museum Bulletin 108. Albany: New York State Education Department, 1907.

Belknap, Jeremy. "Oneida Journal, 1796." *Massachusetts Historical Society Proceedings* 19 (1881–82): 393–423.

Belknap, Jeremy, and Jedidiah Morse. "Report on the Oneida, Stockbridge and Brotherton Indians, 1796." *Indian Notes and Monographs* 54 (1955): 1–39.

Benson, Adolph B., rev. and ed. *Peter Kalm's Travels in North America: The English Version of 1770*. New York: Dover, 1987.

Beschrijvinghe van Virginia, Nieuw Nederlandt, Nieuw Engelandt, en d'eylanden Bermudes, Berbados, en S. Christoffel. Dienstelijck voor elck een derwaerts handelende, en alle voort-planters van nieuw colonien. T'Amsterdam: Joost Hartgers, 1651.

Blau, Harold, Jack Campisi, and Elisabeth Tooker. "Onondaga." In Trigger, *Handbook of North American Indians*, vol. 15, *Northeast*, 491–99.

Bodley, John H. *Victims of Progress*. 3d ed. Mountain View C A: Mayfield, 1990.

Boucher, Pierre. *Histoire véritable et naturelle des moeurs et productions du pays de la Nouvelle France, vulgairement dite le Canada*. 1664. Reprint, Quebec: Société Historique de Boucherville, 1964.

Boxer, C. R. [Charles Ralph]. *The Dutch Seaborne Empire, 1600–1800*. London: Hutchinson, 1965. Reprint, New York: Penguin, 1990.

Bradley, James W. *Before Albany: An Archaeology of Native-Dutch Relations in the Capital Region, 1600–1664.* New York State Museum Bulletin 509. Albany: University of the State of New York, State Education Dept., 2007.

———. *Evolution of the Onondaga Iroquois: Accommodating Change, 1500–1655.* Syracuse: University of Syracuse Press, 1987.

———. "Re-visiting Wampum and Other Seventeenth-Century Shell Games." *Archaeology of Eastern North America* 39 (2011): 25–51.

Bragdon, Kathleen J. *Native People of Southern New England, 1500–1650.* Norman: University of Oklahoma Press, 1996.

Brainerd, Thomas. *The Life of John Brainerd, the Brother of David Brainerd, and His Successor as Missionary to the Indians of New Jersey.* New York: A. D. F. Randolph, 1865.

Brandão, José António, *"Your Fyre Shall Burn No More": Iroquois Policy toward New France and Its Native Allies to 1701.* Lincoln: University of Nebraska Press, 1997.

Brandão, José António, and William A. Starna. "The Treaties of 1701: A Triumph of Iroquois Diplomacy." *Ethnohistory* 43, no. 2 (1996): 209–44.

Brasser, Ted J. "Mahican." In Trigger, *Handbook of North American Indians*, vol. 15, *Northeast*, 198–212.

———. *Riding on the Frontier's Crest: Mahican Indian Culture and Culture Change.* National Museum of Man Mercury series; Ethnology Division Paper 13. Ottawa: National Museums of Canada, 1974.

Bridenbaugh, Carl, ed. *Gentlemen's Progress: The Itinerarium of Dr. Alexander Hamilton, 1744.* Chapel Hill: University of North Carolina Press, 1948.

Brooks, Karl W. *A Catskill Flora and Economic Botany.* Vol. 4, pt. 1. New York State Museum Bulletin 453. Albany: New York State Museum, 1983.

———, *A Catskill Flora and Economic Botany.* Vol. 4, pt. 2. New York State Museum Bulletin 454. Albany: New York State Museum, 1984.

Bruchac, Margaret, and Peter Thomas. "Locating 'Wissatinnewag' in John Pynchon's Letter of 1663." *Historical Journal of Massachusetts* 34, no, 1 (2006): 56–82.

Brumbach, Hetty Jo. "Algonquian and Iroquoian Ceramics in the Upper Hudson River Drainage." *Northeast Anthropology* 49 (1995): 55–66.

———. "'Iroquoian' Ceramics in 'Algonquian' Territory." *Man in the Northeast* 10 (1975): 17–28.

Brumbach, Hetty Jo, and Susan Bender. "Woodland Period Settlement and Subsistence in the Upper Hudson River Valley." In Hart and Rieth, *Northeast Subsistence-Settlement Change*, 227–39.

Burke, Thomas E., Jr. *Mohawk Frontier: The Dutch Community of Schenectady, New York, 1661–1710.* 2d ed. Albany: State University of New York Press, 2009.

Callender, Charles, "Shawnee." In Trigger, *Handbook of North American Indians,* vol. 15, *Northeast,* 622–35.

Calloway, Colin G. *The Western Abenakis of Vermont: 1600–1800: War, Migration, and the Survival of an Indian People.* Norman: University of Oklahoma Press, 1990.

————. "Stockbridge: The New England Patriots." In *The American Revolution in Indian Country: Crisis and Diversity in Native American Communities.* Cambridge: Cambridge University Press, 1995, 85–107.

Campisi, Jack. "From Stanwix to Canandaigua: National Policy, States' Rights and Indian Land." In *Iroquois Land Claims,* edited by Christopher Vecsey and William A. Starna, 49–65. Syracuse: Syracuse University Press, 1988.

————. "The Hudson Valley Indians through Dutch Eyes." In *Neighbors and Intruders: An Ethnohistorical Exploration of the Indians of Hudson's River,* edited by Laurence M. Hauptman and Jack Campisi, 158–80. Canadian Ethnological Services, Paper 39. Ottawa: National Museum of Man, 1978.

————. "Oneida." In Trigger, *Handbook of North American Indians,* vol. 15, *Northeast,* 481–90.

————. "The Oneida Treaty Period, 1783–1838." In *The Oneida Indian Experience: Two Perspectives,* edited by Jack Campisi and Laurence M. Hauptman, 48–64. Syracuse: Syracuse University Press, 1988.

————, "The Trade and Intercourse Acts: Land Claims on the Eastern Seaboard." In *Irredeemable America: The Indians' Estate and Land Claims,* edited by Imre Sutton, 337–62. Albuquerque: University of New Mexico Press, 1985.

Campisi, Jack, and William A. Starna. "On the Road to Canandiagua: The Treaty of 1794." *American Indian Quarterly* 19, no. 4 (1995): 467–90.

Carmack, Robert M. "Ethnohistory: A Review of Its Development, Definitions, Methods, and Aims." *Annual Review of Anthropology* 1 (1972): 227–46.

Champlain, Samuel de. *The Works of Samuel de Champlain.* Edited by H. P. [Henry Percival] Biggar. 6 vols. Toronto: Champlain Society, 1922–36.

Chilton, Elizabeth S. "'Towns They Have None': Diverse Subsistence and Settlement Strategies in Native New England." In Hart and Rieth, *Northeast Subsistence-Settlement Change,* 289–300.

Colden, Cadwallader. *The History of the Five Indian Nations of Canada, Which Are Dependent on the Province of New-York in America . . .* London: T. Osborne, 1747.

Collections of the Massachusetts Historical Society for the Year 1792. Vol. 1. 1792. Reprint, Boston: T. R. Marvin, 1859.

Collections of the Massachusetts Historical Society for the Year 1795. Vol. 4. 1795. Reprint, Boston: John H. Eastburn, 1835.

The Colonial Laws of New York from the Year 1664 to the Revolution. 5 vols. Albany: James B. Lyon, 1894.

Connolly, G. G., D. H. Krinsley, and L. A. Sirkin. "Late Pleistocene Erg in the Upper Hudson Valley, New York." *Geological Society of America Bulletin* 83 (1972): 1537–42.

Cook, Noble David. *Born to Die: Disease and New World Conquest, 1492–1650.* New York: Cambridge University Press, 1998.

Costa, David J. "The Dialectology of Southern New England Algonquian." In *Papers of the 38th Algonquian Conference,* edited by H. C. [Christoph] Wolfart, 81–127. Winnipeg: University of Manitoba, 2007.

Crockett, Walter Hill. *Vermont: The Green Mountain State.* 4 vols. New York: Century History, 1921.

Cronon, William. *Changes in the Land: Indians, Colonists, and the Ecology of New England.* New York: Hill and Wang, 1983.

Dally-Starna, Corinna, and William A. Starna, trans. and eds. *Gideon's People: Being a Chronicle of an American Indian Community in Colonial Connecticut and the Moravian Missionaries Who Served There.* 2 vols. Lincoln: University of Nebraska Press, 2009.

———. "Picturing Pachgatgoch: An Eighteenth-Century American Indian Community in Western Connecticut." *Northeast Anthropology* 67 (2004): 1–22.

Danckaerts, Jasper. *Journal of Jasper Danckaerts, 1679–1680.* Edited by Bartlett Burleigh James and J. Franklin Jameson. New York: Charles Scribners' Sons, 1913.

Day, Gordon M. "The Eastern Boundary of Iroquoia: Abenaki Evidence." *Man in the Northeast* 1 (1971): 7–13.

———. "English-Indian Contacts in New England." *Ethnohistory* 9, no. 1 (1962): 24–40.

———. "The Identity of the Sokokis." *Ethnohistory* 12, no. 3 (1965): 237–49.

———. "The Indian as an Ecological Factor in the Northeastern Forest." *Ecology* 34, no. 2 (1953): 329–46.

———. *In Search of New England's Native Past: Selected Essays by Gordon M. Day.* Edited by Michael K. Foster and William Cowan. Amherst: University of Massachusetts Press, 1998.

———. "Missisquoi: A New Look at an Old Village." *Man in the Northeast* 6 (1973): 51–57.

———. *The* Mots loups *of Father Mathevet.* Publications in Ethnology 8, National Museum of Canada. Ottawa: National Museum of Man, 1975.

———. "Oral Tradition as Complement." *Ethnohistory* 19, no. 2 (1972): 99–108.

———. "The Ouragie War." In *Extending the Rafters: Interdisciplinary Approaches to Iroquoian Studies,* edited by Michael K. Foster, Jack Campisi, and Marianne Mithun, 35–50. Albany: State University of New York Press, 1984.

———. "Western Abenaki." In Trigger, *Handbook of North American Indians,* vol. 15, *Northeast,* 148–59.

Day, Gordon M., and Bruce G. Trigger. "Algonquin." In Trigger, *Handbook of North American Indians*, vol. 15, *Northeast*, 792–97.

De Laet, Johannes [Johan]. "Extracts from the New World; or, A Description of the West Indies." *Collections of the New-York Historical Society*, 2d ser., 1 (1841): 281–316.

Delâge, Denys, *Bitter Feast: Amerindians and Europeans in Northeastern North America, 1600–64*. Translated by Jane Brierley. Vancouver: University of British Columbia Press, 1993.

Dennis, Matthew. *Cultivating a Landscape of Peace: Iroquois-European Encounters in Seventeenth-Century America*. Ithaca: Cornell University Press, 1993.

Desrosiers, Léo-Paul. *Iroquoisie, 1534–1645*. Vol. 1. Montreal: Études de l'Institut d'Histoire de l'Amérique française, 1947.

Dineen, Robert, Paul Huey, and Edgar M. Reilly Jr. *Geology and Land Uses in the Pine Bush, Albany County, New York*. New York State Museum and Science Service Circular 47. Albany: University of the State of New York, State Education Dept., 1975.

Dobyns, Henry F. *Their Number Become Thinned: Native American Population Dynamics in Eastern North America*. Knoxville: University of Tennessee Press, 1983.

Dorson, Richard M. "Comic Indian Anecdotes." *Southern Folklore Quarterly* 10 (1946): 113–28.

Douglas, Mary. "The Myth of Primitive Religion." *Commonweal* 93, no. 2 (1970): 41–44.

Drake, James D. *King Philip's War: Civil War in New England, 1675–1676*. Amherst: University of Massachusetts Press, 1999.

Dunn, Shirley W. "Adapting a Culture: The Mohican Experience at Shekomeko." In *The Continuance: An Algonquian Peoples Seminar; Selected Research Papers—2000*, edited by Shirley W. Dunn, 85–102. Mohican Seminar 1; New York State Museum Bulletin 501. Albany: University of the State of New York, State Education Dept., 2004.

———. *The Mohicans and Their Land, 1609–1730*. Fleischmanns NY: Purple Mountain Press, 1994.

———. *The Mohican World, 1680–1750*. Fleischmanns NY: Purple Mountain Press, 2000.

Eekhof, Albert, *Bastiaen Jansz. Krol, krankenbezoeker, kommies en kommandeur van Nieuw-Nederland (1595–1645). Nieuwe gegevens voor de kennis der estiging van ons kerkelijk en koloniaal gezag in Noord-Amerika*. 's-Gravenhage: M. Nijhoff, 1910.

Elliott, Dolores, "Otsiningo, an Example of an Eighteenth Century Settlement Pattern." In Funk and Hayes, *Current Perspectives in Northeastern Archaeology*, 93–105.

Elting, James J., and William A. Starna. "A Possible Case of Pre-Columbian Treponematosis from New York State." *American Journal of Physical Anthropology* 63, no. 3 (1984): 267–73.

Engelbrecht, William. *Iroquoia: The Development of a Native World.* Syracuse: Syracuse University Press, 2003.

Fenton, William N. *The Great Law and the Longhouse: A Political History of the Iroquois Confederacy.* Norman: University of Oklahoma Press, 1998.

———. "The Journal of James Emlen Kept on a Trip to Canandaigua, New York." *Ethnohistory* 12, no. 4 (1965): 279–342.

———. "Northern Iroquoian Culture Patterns." In Trigger, *Handbook of North American Indians*, vol. 15, *Northeast*, 296–321.

Fenton, William N., and Elizabeth L. Moore, eds. and trans. *Customs of the American Indians Compared with the Customs of Primitive Times by Father Joseph François Lafitau.* 2 vols. Toronto: Champlain Society, 1974, 1977.

Fenton, William N., and Elisabeth Tooker. "Mohawk." In Trigger, *Handbook of North American Indians*, vol. 15, *Northeast*, 466–80.

Fogelson, Raymond D. "History of the Study of Native North Americans." In *Native American Religions: North America*, edited by Lawrence E. Sullivan, 147–54. New York: Macmillan, 1989.

Foster-Clement Collection. Historical Society of Pennsylvania, Philadelphia.

Frazier, Patrick. *The Mohicans of Stockbridge.* Lincoln: University of Nebraska Press, 1992.

Funk, Robert E. *Archaeological Investigations in the Upper Susquehanna Valley, New York State*, with contributions by Robert J. Dineen et al. 2 vols. Buffalo NY: Persimmon Press, 1993.

———. *Recent Contributions to Hudson Valley Prehistory.* New York State Museum Memoir 22. Albany: University of the State of New York, State Education Dept., 1976.

Funk, Robert E., and Charles F. Hayes III, eds. *Current Perspectives in Northeastern Archaeology: Essays in Honor of William A. Ritchie.* Researches and Transactions of New York State Archaeological Association 17, no. 1. Rochester: New York State Archaeological Association, 1977.

Geherin, Christopher, "New Guinea: Racial Identity and Inclusion in the Stockbridge and Brothertown Indian Communities in New York." *New York History* 90, no. 3 (2009): 141–66.

Gehring, Charles T. "Encountering Native Americans in Unexpected Places: Slictenhorst and the Mohawks." In *The Challenges of Native American Studies: Essays in Celebration of the Twenty-Fifth American Indian Workshop*, edited by Barbara Saunders and Lea Zuyderhoudt, 281–88. Ithaca: Cornell University Press, 2004.

———, trans. and ed. *Fort Orange Court Minutes, 1652–1660.* Syracuse: Syracuse University Press, 1990.

Gehring, Charles T., and Robert S. Grumet. "Observations of the Indians from Jasper Danckaert's Journal, 1679–1680." *William and Mary Quarterly* 44, no. 1 (1987): 104–20.

Gehring, Charles T., and William A. Starna. "Dutch and Indians in the Hudson Valley: The Early Period." *Hudson Valley Regional Review* 9, no. 2 (1992): 1–25.

Gillette, Charles E., and Robert E. Funk. "Europeans Come to the Upper Susquehanna." In Funk, *Archaeological Investigations*, vol. 1, 85–91.

Goddard, Ives. "Delaware." In Trigger, *Handbook of North American Indians*, vol. 15, *Northeast*, 213–39.

———. "Eastern Algonquian Languages." In Trigger, *Handbook of North American Indians*, vol. 15, *Northeast*, 70–77.

———. "The Ethnohistorical Implications of Early Delaware Linguistic Materials." *Man in the Northeast* 1 (1976): 14–26.

———. "Linguistic Variation in a Small Speech Community: The Personal Dialects of Moraviantown Delaware." *Anthropological Linguistics* 52, no. 1 (2010): 1–48.

———. "Notes on Mahican: Dialects, Sources, Phonemes, Enclitics, and Analogies." In *Papers of the 39th Algonquian Conference*, edited by Karl S. Hele and Regna Darnell, 246–315. London ON: University of Western Ontario, 2008.

———. "Pidgin Delaware." In *Contact Languages: A Wider Perspective*, edited by Sarah G. Thomason, 43–98. Creole Language Library 17. Amsterdam: John Benjamins, 1997.

———. Review of *Indian Names in Connecticut*, by James Hammond Trumbull. *International Journal of American Linguistics* 43, no. 2 (1977): 157–59.

———. Review of *Riding on the Frontier's Crest: Mahican Indian Culture and Culture Change*, by Ted J. Brasser. *Ethnohistory* 22, no. 2 (1975): 185–87.

Gookin, Daniel. *Historical Collections of the Indians in New England. Of Their Several Nations, Numbers, Customs, Manners, Religion and Government, Before the English Planted There.* Boston: Apollo Press, 1792.

Gramly, Michael R. "Deerskins and Hunting Territories: Competition for a Scarce Resource of the Northeastern Woodlands." *American Antiquity* 42, no. 4 (1977): 601–5.

Grayson, Donald K. "The Riverhaven No. 2 Vertebrate Fauna: Comments on Methods in Faunal Analysis and on Aspects of Subsistence Potential of Prehistoric New York." *Man in the Northeast* 8 (1974): 23–39.

Grotius, Hugo. *De Iure Praedae Commentarius: Commentary on the Law of Prize and Booty.* Translated by Gwladys L. Williams, with collaboration of Walter H. Zeydel. London: Wildy, 1950. Reprint, New York: Oceana, 1964.

—. *The Freedom of the Seas or the Right Which Belongs to the Dutch to Take Part in the East Indian Trade. . . .* New York: Oxford University Press, 1916.

Grumet, Robert S. *Historic Contact: Indian People and Colonists in Today's Northeastern United States in the Sixteenth through Eighteenth Centuries.* Norman: University of Oklahoma Press, 1995.

—. *The Munsee Indians: A History.* Norman: University of Oklahoma Press, 2009.

—. *Native American Place Names in New York City.* New York: Museum of the City of New York, 1981.

—. "The Nimhams of the Colonial Hudson Valley, 1667–1783." *Hudson Valley Regional Review* 9, no. 2 (1992): 80–99.

—. "The Selling of Lenapehoking." In *Proceedings of the 1992 People to People Conference: Selected Papers*, edited by Charles F. Hayes III, 19–24. Research Records 23. Rochester N Y: Rochester Museum and Science Center, 1994.

Haefeli, Evan. "On First Contact and Apotheosis: Manitou and Men in North America." *Ethnohistory* 54, no. 3 (2007): 407–43.

Hamell, George R. "Trading in Metaphors: The Magic of Beads." In *Proceedings of the 1982 Glass Trade Bead Conference*, edited by Charles F. Hayes III, 5–28. Research Records 16. Rochester N Y: Rochester Museum and Science Center, 1983.

Hamilton, J. Taylor, and Kenneth G. Hamilton. *History of the Moravian Church: The Renewed Unitas Fratrum, 1722–1957.* Bethlehem PA: Moravian Church in America, 1967.

Hammond, Luna M. *History of Madison County, State of New York.* Syracuse: Truair, Smith, 1872.

Handlin, Oscar, and Irving Mark, eds. "Chief Daniel Nimham *v.* Roger Morris, Beverly Robinson, and Philip Philipse—An Indian Land Case in Colonial New York, 1765–1767." *Ethnohistory* 11, no. 3 (1964): 193–246.

Hanna, Charles A. *The Wilderness Trail; or, The Ventures and Adventures of the Pennsylvania Traders. . . .* 2 vols. New York: G. P. Putnam's Sons, 1911.

Hart, John P., and Christina B. Rieth, eds. *Northeast Subsistence-Settlement Change, A D 700–1300.* New York State Museum Bulletin 496. Albany: New York State Museum/New York State Education Dept., 2002.

Hart, Simon. *The Prehistory of the New Netherland Company: Amsterdam Notarial Records of the First Dutch Voyages to the Hudson.* Amsterdam: City of Amsterdam Press, 1959.

Hauptman, Laurence M. "The Dispersal of the River Indians: Frontier Expansion and Indian Dispossession in the Hudson Valley." In *Neighbors and Intruders: An Ethnohistorical Exploration of the Indians of Hudson's River*, edited by Laurence M. Hauptman and Jack Campisi, 242–60. Canadian

Ethnology Service Paper no. 39. Ottawa: National Museums of Canada, 1978.

———. "Refugee Havens: The Iroquois Villages of the Eighteenth Century." In *American Indian Environments: Ecological Issues in Native American History*, edited by Christopher Vecsey and Robert W. Venables, 128–39. Syracuse: Syracuse University Press, 1980.

Hauptman, Laurence M., and James D. Wherry, eds.. *The Pequots in Southern New England: The Fall and Rise of an American Indian Nation*. Norman: University of Oklahoma Press, 1990.

Havard, Gilles, *The Great Peace of Montreal of 1701: French-Native Diplomacy in the Seventeenth Century*. Translated by Phyllis Aronoff and Howard Scott. Montreal: McGill-Queen's University Press, 2001.

Heckewelder, John [Gottlieb Ernestus]. *History, Manners, and Customs of the Indian Nations Who Once Inhabited Pennsylvania and the Neighbouring States*. 1819. Rev. ed., edited by William C. Reichel. Memoirs of the Historical Society of Pennsylvania 12. Philadelphia: Historical Society of Pennsylvania, 1876.

———. "Indian Tradition of the First Arrival of the Dutch, at Manhattan Island, Now New York." *Collections of the New-York Historical Society*, 2d ser., 1 (1841): [69]-74.

———. *A Narrative of the Mission of the United Brethren among the Delaware and Mohegan Indians from Its Commencement in the Year 1740 to the Close of the Year 1880*. 1820. Reprint, New York: Arno Press, 1971.

Henige, David P. *Numbers from Nowhere: The American Indian Contact Population Debate*. Norman: University of Oklahoma Press, 1998.

Herrick, James W. *Iroquois Medical Botany*. Syracuse: Syracuse University Press, 1995.

Hodge, Frederick Webb, ed. *Handbook of American Indians North of Mexico*. 2 vols. Bureau of American Ethnology Bulletin 30, in 2 parts. Washington DC: U.S. Government Printing Office, 1907, 1910.

Hopkins, Samuel, *Historical Memoirs, Relating to the Housatunnuk Indians; or, An Account of the Methods Used, and Pains Taken, for the Propagation of the Gospel among that Heathenish Tribe, and the Success Thereof, under the Ministry of the Reverend Mr. John Sergeant*. . . . Boston: S. Kneeland, 1753.

Hough, Franklin B. [ed.] *Proceedings of the Commissioners of Indian Affairs*. . . . 2 vols. Albany NY: Joel Munsell, 1861.

Howat, John K. *American Paradise: The World of the Hudson River School*. New York: Metropolitan Museum of Art, 1987.

Huey, Paul R. "The Mahicans, the Dutch, and the Schodack Islands in the 17th and 18th Centuries." *Northeast Historical Archaeology* 21–22 (1994): 96–118.

Huey, Paul R., and Adam T. Luscier. "Some Early Rensselaerswijck Farms: A Documentary and Archeological Review." *de Halve Maen* 77, no. 4 (2004): 63–73.

Hunt, George T. *The Wars of the Iroquois*. Madison: University of Wisconsin Press, 1940.

Innis, Harold A. *The Fur Trade in Canada: An Introduction to Canadian Economic History*. Rev. ed. Toronto: University of Toronto Press, 1956.

Jacobs, Jaap. *New Netherland: A Dutch Colony in Seventeenth-Century America*. Leiden: Brill, 2005.

Jaenen, Cornelius. "Amerindian Views of French Culture in the Seventeenth Century." *Canadian Historical Review* 55, no. 3 (1974): 261–91.

Jameson, J. Franklin, ed. *Narratives of New Netherland, 1609–1664*. New York: Charles Scribners' Sons, 1909.

Jeffries, James B. "Denying Religion: Native Americans and French Missionaries in New France." In *Indigenous Symbols and Practices in the Catholic Church: Visual Culture, Missionization and Appropriation*, edited by Kathleen J. Martin, 55–74. Farnham, Surrey UK: Ashgate, 2010.

Jennings, Francis. *The Ambiguous Iroquois Empire: The Covenant Chain Confederation of Indian Tribes with English Colonies from Its Beginnings to the Lancaster Treaty of 1744*. New York: W. W. Norton, 1984.

———. *Empire of Fortune: Crowns, Colonies and Tribes in the Seven Years War in America*. New York: W. W. Norton, 1988.

———. *The Invasion of America: Indians, Colonialism, and the Cant of Conquest*. New York: W. W. Norton, 1975.

———. "Susquehannock." In Trigger, *Handbook of North American Indians*, vol. 15, *Northeast*, 362–67.

Johnson, Joseph. *To Do Good to My Indian Brethren: The Writings of Joseph Johnson, 1751–1776*. Edited by Laura J. Murray. Amherst: University of Massachusetts Press, 1998.

Johnson, William, Sir. *Papers of Sir William Johnson*. 14 vols. Edited by James Sullivan et al. Albany: University of the State of New York, 1921–1962.

Jones, Electa F. *Stockbridge, Past and Present; or, Records of an Old Mission Station*. Springfield MA: Samuel Bowles, 1854.

Journal of the Assembly of the State of New York, at Their Thirty-Second Session . . . 1808. Albany NY: Solomon Southwick, 1809.

Journal of the Senate of the State of New York. New York: S. Louden, 1785.

Kappler, Charles J., comp. and ed. *Indian Affairs: Laws and Treaties*. 7 vols. Washington DC: U.S. Government Printing Office, 1904.

Kent, Barry C., *Susquehanna's Indians*. Anthropological Series 6. Harrisburg: Pennsylvania Historical and Museum Commission, 1989.

Kirkland, Samuel. *The Journals of Samuel Kirkland: 18th Century Missionary to the Iroquois, Gov't Agent, Father of Hamilton College.* Edited by Walter Pilkington. Clinton NY: Hamilton College, 1980.

Lapore, Jill. *The Name of War: King Philip's War and the Origins of American Identity.* New York: Knopf, 1998.

Lavin, Lucianne, Marina E. Mozzi, J. William Bouchard, and Karen Hartgen. "The Goldkrest Site: An Undisturbed, Multi-Component Woodland Site in the Heart of Mahikan Territory." *Journal of Middle Atlantic Archaeology* 12 (1996): 113–29.

Laws of the State of New York Passed at the Sessions of the Legislature . . . Eighteenth and Nineteenth Sessions. Vol. 3. Albany NY: Weed, Parsons, 1887.

The Law Papers: Correspondence and Documents during Jonathan Law's Governorship of the Colony of Connecticut, 1741–1750. Vol. 1, *October 1741 — July 1745.* Collections of the Connecticut Historical Society 11. Hartford: Connecticut Historical Society, 1907.

Leach, Douglas Edward. *Flintlock and Tomahawk: New England in King Philip's War.* New York: W. W. Norton, 1958.

Le Clercq, Chrestien. *Premier Établissement de la Foy dans la Nouvelle-France.* 2 vols. Paris: Auroy, 1691.

Leder, Lawrence H., ed. *The Livingston Indian Records, 1666–1723.* Gettysburg: Pennsylvania Historical Association, 1956.

Lehman, J. David. "The End of the Iroquois Mystique: The Oneida Land Cession Treaties of the 1780s." *William and Mary Quarterly* 47, no. 4 (1990): 523–47.

Lenig, Donald. "Of Dutchmen, Beaver Hats and Iroquois." In Funk and Hayes, *Current Perspectives in Northeastern Archaeology,* 71–84.

Levinton, Jeffrey S., and John R. Waldman, eds., *The Hudson River Estuary.* New York: Cambridge University Press, 2006.

Limburg, Karin E., Kathryn A. Hattala, Andrew W. Kahnle, and John R. Waldman. "Fisheries of the Hudson Valley Estuary." In *The Hudson Valley Estuary,* edited by Jeffrey S. Levinton and John R. Waldman, 189–204. New York: Cambridge University Press, 2006.

Loskiel, George Henry. *History of the Mission to the United Brethren Among the Indians of North America.* Translated by C. I. La Trobe. London: Brethren's Society for the Furtherance of the Gospel, 1794.

Love, W. DeLoss. *Samson Occom and the Christian Indians of New England.* Boston: Pilgrim Press, 1899.

Malinowski, Bronislaw. *Argonauts of the Western Pacific.* New York: E. P. Dutton, 1922.

Mancall, Peter C. *Valley of Opportunity: Economic Culture along the Upper Susquehanna, 1700–1800.* Ithaca: Cornell University Press, 1991.

Mandell, Daniel R. *King Philip's War: Colonial Expansion, Native Resistance, and the End of Indian Sovereignty.* Baltimore: Johns Hopkins University Press, 2010.

Manley, Henry S. *The Treaty of Fort Stanwix, 1784.* Rome: Rome Sentinel, 1932.

Marr, John S., and John T. Cathey. "New Hypothesis for Cause of Epidemic among Native Americans, New England, 1616–1619." *Emerging Infectious Diseases* 16, no. 2 (2010): 281–86.

McVaugh, Rogers. *Flora of the Columbia County Area, New York.* New York State Museum Bulletin 360 and 360A. Albany: University of the State of New York, 1958.

"Melyn Papers, 1640–1699." *Collections of the New-York Historical Society for the Year 1913,* 46 (1914): 97–138.

Miles, Lion G. "The Red Man Dispossessed: The Williams Family and the Alienation of Indian Land in Stockbridge, Massachusetts, 1738–1818." *New England Quarterly* 67, no. 1 (1994): 46–76.

Miller, Christopher L., and George R. Hamell. "A New Perspective on Indian-White Contact: Cultural Symbols and Colonial Trade." *Journal of American History* 73, no. 2 (1986): 311–28.

Miller, Robert J. "The Doctrine of Discovery in American Indian Law." *Idaho Law Review* 42, no. 1 (2005): 1–122.

Morse, Jedidiah. *A Report to the Secretary of War of the United States, on Indian Affairs. . . .* New Haven CT: Converse, 1822.

Morton, Thomas. *New English Canaan; or, New Canaan.* 1637. Reprint, New York: Arno Press, 1972.

Murray, Jean E. "The Early Fur Trade in New France and New Netherland." *Canadian Historical Review* 19 (1938): 365–77.

Nammack, Georgiana C. *Fraud, Politics, and the Dispossession of the Indians: The Iroquois Land Frontier in the Colonial Period.* Norman: University of Oklahoma Press, 1969.

[Neisser, Georg]. *A History of the Beginnings of Moravian Work in America, Being a Translation of Georg Neisser's manuscripts.* Translated by William N. Schwarze and Samuel H. Gapp. Bethlehem PA: Archives of the Moravian Church, 1955.

Newcomb, William W., Jr. *The Culture and Acculturation of the Delaware Indians.* Anthropological Papers, Museum of Anthropology 10. Ann Arbor: University of Michigan, 1956.

Newman, Marshall T. "Aboriginal New World Epidemiology and Medical Care, and the Impact of Old World Disease Imports." *American Journal of Physical Anthropology* 84 (1976): 407–19.

Newman, W. S., D. H. Thurber, H. S. Zeiss, A. Rokach, and L. Musich. "Late Quaternary Geology of the Hudson River Estuary: A Preliminary Report." *Transactions of the New York Academy of Sciences* 31 (1969): 548–70.

Niemczycki, Mary Ann Palmer. *The Origin and Development of the Seneca and Cayuga Tribes of New York State.* Research Records 17. Rochester NY: Rochester Museum and Science Center, 1984.

Nissenson, S. G. *The Patroon's Domain.* New York: Columbia University Press, 1937.

Noble, Allen G. "The Hay Barrack: Form and Function of a Relict Landscape Feature." *Journal of Cultural Geography* 5, no. 2 (1985): 107–16.

Norton, Thomas Elliot. *The Fur Trade in Colonial New York, 1686–1776.* Madison: University of Wisconsin Press, 1974.

Obbard, Martyn E. "Fur Grading and Pelt Identification." In *Wild Furbearer Management and Conservation in North America,* edited by Milan Novak, James A. Baker, Martyn E. Obbard, and Bruce Malloch. Toronto: Ontario Trappers Association, 1987.

Oberly, James W. *A Nation of Statesmen: The Political Culture of the Stockbridge-Munsee Mohicans, 1815–1972.* Norman: University of Oklahoma Press, 2005.

O'Callaghan, E. B. [Edmund Bailey], comp. *Calendar of NY Colonial Manuscripts, Indorsed Land Papers in the Office of the Secretary of State of New York, 1643–1803.* 1864. Revised reprint, Harrison NY: Harbor Hill Books, 1987.

———, ed., *The Documentary History of the State of New York.* Vol. 3, quarto ed. Albany NY: Weed, Parsons, 1850.

———. *History of New Netherland; or, New York under the Dutch.* 2 vols. New York: D. Appleton, 1846, 1848.

O'Callaghan, E. B., and Berthold Fernow, eds. *Documents Relative to the Colonial History of New York; Procured in Holland, England, and France by John R. Brodhead.* 15 vols. Albany: Weed, Parsons, 1853–87.

Occum, Samson. *The Collected Writings of Samson Occum, Mohegan: Leadership and Literature in Eighteenth-Century Native America.* Edited by Joanna Brooks. New York: Oxford University Press, 2006.

O'Toole, Judith. *Different Views of Hudson River School Painting.* New York: Columbia University Press, 2008.

Otto, Paul. *The Dutch-Munsee Encounter in America: The Struggle for Sovereignty in the Hudson Valley.* New York: Berghan Books, 2006.

Parker, Arthur C. *Iroquois Uses of Maize and Other Food Plants.* New York State Museum Bulletin 144. Albany: University of the State of New York, 1910.

Pearson, Jonathan, trans., *Early Records of the City and County of Albany and Colony of Rensselaerswyck.* 4 vols. Vol. 1, Albany NY: J. Munsell, 1869. Vols. 2–4, revised and edited by A. J. F. van Laer. Albany: University of the State of New York, 1916–1919.

Peckham, Harriett C. Waite van Buren. *History of Cornelis Maessen van Buren Who Came from Holland to the New Netherlands. . . .* New York: Tobias A. Wright, 1913.

Pendergast, James F. "The Introduction of European Goods into the Native Community in the Sixteenth Century." In *Proceedings of the 1992 People to People Conference*, edited by Charles F. Hayes III, 7–18. Research Records 23. Rochester NY: Rochester Museum and Science Center, 1994.

Perrot, Nicholas. "Memoir on the Manners, Customs, and Religion of the Savages of North America." In *The Indian Tribes of the Upper Mississippi Valley and Region of the Great Lakes*, edited and translated by Emma H. Blair. 1911. Reprint, Lincoln: University of Nebraska Press, 1996.

Peterson, James B., John G. Crock, Ellen R. Cowie, Richard A. Boisvert, Joshua R. Toney, and Geoffrey Mandel. "St. Lawrence Iroquoians in Northern New England: Perdergast Was 'Right' and More." In *A Passion for the Past: Papers in Honour of James F. Pendergast*, edited by James V. Wright and Jean-Luc Pilon, 87–123. Mercury Series, Archaeology Paper 164. Gatineau QC: Canadian Museum of Civilization, 2004.

Pratt, Peter P. *Archaeology of the Oneida Iroquois*. Vol. 1. Occasional Publications in Northeastern Anthropology. George's Mill NH: Man in the Northeast, 1976.

Prucha, Francis Paul. *American Indian Treaties: The History of a Political Anomaly*. Berkeley: University of California Press, 1994.

Pulsipher, Jenny Hale. *Subjects unto the Same King: Indians, English, and the Contest for Authority in Colonial New England*. Philadelphia: University of Pennsylvania Press, 2005.

Purchas, Samuel. *Hakluytus Posthumus; or, Purchas His Pilgrimes*. 20 vols. Glasgow: James MacLehose and Sons, 1906.

Pynchon, John. *The Pynchon Papers*. Vol. 1. Edited by Carl Bridenbaugh; collected by Juliette Tomlinson. Boston: Colonial Society of Massachusetts, 1982.

Quinney, John W. "Interesting Speech of John W. Quinney, Chief of the Stockbridge Tribe of Indians." *Report and Collections of the State Historical Society of Wisconsin for the Years 1857 and 1858*, vol. 4 (1859): 313–20.

Reichel, William C. *A Memorial of the Dedication of Monuments Erected by the Moravian Historical Society, to Mark the Sites of Ancient Missionary Stations in New York and Connecticut*. Philadelphia: J. P. Lippincott, 1860.

————, ed., *Memorials of the Moravian Church*. Vol. 1. Philadelphia: J. P. Lippincott, 1870.

Report of Special Committee to Investigate the Indian Problem in the State of New York, Appointed by the Assembly of 1888. Albany NY: Troy Press, 1889.

Richter, Daniel K. *Before the Revolution: America's Ancient Pasts*. Cambridge MA: Belnap Press of Harvard University Press, 2011.

————. *Facing East from Indian Country: A Native History of Early America*. Cambridge MA: Harvard University Press, 2001.

————. *The Ordeal of the Longhouse: The Peoples of the Iroquois League in the Era of European Colonization*. Chapel Hill: University of North Carolina Press, 1992.

————. "War and Culture: The Iroquois Experience." *William and Mary Quarterly* 40, no. 4 (1983): 528–59.

Rife, Clarence White. "Land Tenure in New Netherland." In *Essays in Colonial History Presented to Charles McLean Andrews by His Students*. 1931. Reprint, Freeport NY: Books for Libraries Press, 1966.

Rink, Oliver A. *Holland on the Hudson: An Economic and Social History of Dutch New York*. Ithaca: Cornell University Press, 1986.

Ronda, James. "'We Are Well As We Are': An Indian Critique of Seventeenth-Century Christian Missions." *William and Mary Quarterly* 34, no. 1 (1977): 66–82.

Ronda, Jeanne, and James Ronda. "'As They Were Faithful': Chief Hendrick Aupaumut and the Struggle for Stockbridge Survival, 1757–1830." *American Indian Culture and Research Journal* 3, no. 3 (1979): 43–55.

Rudes, Blair A. "Indian Land Deeds as Evidence for Indian History in Western Connecticut." *Northeast Anthropology* 70 (2005): 19–48.

Ruttenber, Edward Manning. *History of the Indian Tribes of Hudson's River; Their Origin, Manners and Customs; Tribal and Sub-Tribal Organizations; Wars, Treaties, Etc., Etc.* 1872. Reprint, Port Washington NY: Kennikat Press, 1971.

Sahlins, Marshall. *Stone Age Economics*. Chicago: Aldine-Atherton, 1972.

————. *Tribesmen*. Englewood Cliffs NJ: Prentice-Hall, 1968.

Salisbury, Neal. "Indians and Colonists in Southern New England after the Pequot War: An Uneasy Balance." In Hauptman and Wherry, *Pequots in Southern New England*, 81–95.

————. *Manitou and Providence: Indians, Europeans, and the Makings of New England, 1500–1643*. New York: Oxford University Press, 1982.

————. "Toward the Covenant Chain: Iroquois and Southern New England Algonquians, 1637–1684." In *Beyond the Covenant Chain: The Iroquois and Their Neighbors in Indian North America, 1600–1800*, edited by Daniel K. Richter and James H. Merrell, 61–73. Syracuse: Syracuse University Press, 1987.

Salwen, Bert, "Indians of Southern New England and Long Island: Early Period." In Trigger, *Handbook of North American Indians*, vol. 15, *Northeast*, 160–76.

Savery, William. *A Journal of the Life, Travels, and Religious Labours of William Savery*. Compiled by Jonathan Evans. London: Charles Gilpin, 1844.

Schutt, Amy C. "Tribal Identity in the Moravian Mission on the Susquehanna." *Pennsylvania History* 66, no. 3 (1999): 378–98.

Scott, Kenneth, and Kenn Stryker-Rodda, eds. *New York Historical Manuscripts: Dutch. Council Minutes, 1638–1649*. Translated and annotated by Arnold J. F. Van Laer. 4 vols. Baltimore: Genealogical Publishing, 1974.

Shannon, Timothy J. *Indians and Colonists at the Crossroads of Empire: The Albany Congress of 1754*. Ithaca: Cornell University Press, 2000.

Shea, John Gilmary, trans., "Journal of Father Druillet[t]es." *Collections of the New-York Historical Society*, 2d ser., 3 (1857): 309–20.

Sherwood, J. M., ed., *Memoirs of Rev. David Brainerd, Missionary to the Indians of North America*. New York: Funk and Wagnalls, 1891.

Shorto, Russell. Foreword to *A Description of New Netherland*, by Adriaen van der Donck, edited by Charles T. Gehring and William A. Starna. Translated by Diederik Willem Goedhuys, ix–xvi. Lincoln: University of Nebraska Press, 2008.

Silverman, David J. "The Curse of God: The Idea and Its Origins among the Indians of New York's Revolutionary Frontier." *William and Mary Quarterly* 66, no. 3 (2009): 495–534.

———. "'Natural Inhabitants, Time Out of Mind': Sachem Rights and the Contest for Wampanoag Land in Colonial New England." *Northeast Anthropology* 70 (2005): 1–10.

———. *Red Brethren: The Brothertown and Stockbridge Indians and the Problem of Race in Early America*. Ithaca: Cornell University Press, 2010.

Simmons, William S., "Southern New England Shamanism: An Ethnographic Reconstruction." In *Papers of the Seventh Algonquian Conference*, edited by William Cowen, 217–56. Ottawa: Carleton University, 1976.

Smith, De Cost. *Martyrs of the Oblong and Little Nine*. Caldwell I D: Caxton, 1948.

Smith, Edward M. *Documentary History of Rhinebeck, in Dutchess County N Y*. . . . 1881. Reprint, Rhinebeck N Y: [A. C. M. Kelly], 1974.

Smith, George L. *Religion and Trade in New Netherland: Dutch Origins and American Development*. Ithaca: Cornell University Press, 1973.

Smith, James H. *History of Dutchess County, New York*. . . . Syracuse N Y: D. Mason, 1882.

Smith, J. Michael. "The Highland King Nimhammaw and the Native Proprietors of Land in Dutchess County N Y, 1712–1765." *Hudson Valley Regional Review* 17, no. 2 (2000): 69–108.

Smith, Richard. *A Tour of the Hudson, the Mohawk, the Susquehanna, and the Delaware in 1769, Being the Journal of Richard Smith of Burlington, New Jersey; edited, with a short history of pioneer settlements, by Francis W. Halsey*. 1906. Reprint, Fleischmanns N Y: Purple Mountain Press, 1989.

Snow, Dean R. *The Archaeology of New England*. New York: Academic Press, 1980.

———. "The Architecture of Iroquois Longhouses." *Northeast Anthropology* 53 (1997): 61–84.

———. "Eastern Abenaki." In Trigger, *Handbook of North American Indians*, vol. 15, *Northeast*, 137–47.

———. *The Iroquois*. Cambridge M A: Blackwell, 1994.

———. "Microchronology and Demographic Evidence Relating to the Size of Pre-Columbian North American Indian Populations." *Science* 268 (1995): 1601–4.

———. "Mohawk Demography and the Effects of Exogenous Epidemics on American Indian Populations." *Journal of Anthropological Archaeology* 15 (1996): 160–82.

———. *Mohawk Valley Archaeology: The Sites.* Occasional Papers in Anthropology, no. 23. Albany: Institute for Archaeological Studies, University at Albany, State University of New York, 1995.

———. "Setting Demographic Limits: The North American Case." In *Computing Archaeology for Understanding the Past C A A 2000: Computer Applications and Quantitative Methods in Archaeology.* Proceedings of the 28th Conference, Ljubljana, Slovenia, April 2000, edited by Zoran Stancic and Tatjana Veljanovski, 259–61. Oxford: Archeopress, 2001.

Snow, Dean R., and Kim M. Lanphear. "European Contact and Indian Depopulation in the Northeast: The Timing of the First Epidemics." *Ethnohistory* 35, no. 1 (1988): 15–33.

Spiess, Arthus E., and Bruce D. Spiess. "New England Pandemic of 1616–1622: Cause and Archaeological Implications." *Man in the Northeast* 34 (1987): 71–83.

Starna, William A. "Aboriginal Title and Traditional Iroquois Land Use: An Anthropological Perspective." In *Iroquois Land Claims*, edited by Christopher Vecsey and William A. Starna, 31–48. Syracuse: Syracuse University Press, 1988.

———. "American Indian Villages to Dutch Farms: The Settling of Settled Lands in the Hudson Valley." In *Dutch New York: The Roots of Hudson Valley Culture*, edited by Roger Panetta, 73–90. New York: Fordham University Press, 2009.

———. "Assessing American Indian-Dutch Studies: Missed and Missing Opportunities." *New York History* 84, no. 1 (2003): 5–31.

———. "The Biological Encounter: Disease and the Ideological Domain." *American Indian Quarterly* 16, no. 4 (1992): 511–19.

———. "A Checklist of Higher Edible Plants Native to the Upper Susquehanna Valley, New York State." In Funk, *Archaeological Investigations*, vol. 2, 21–36.

———. "The Pequots in the Early Seventeenth Century." In Hauptman and Wherry, *Pequots in Southern New England*, 33–47.

———. "The Repeal of Article 8: Law, Government, and Cultural Politics at Akwesasne." *American Indian Law Review* 18, no. 2 (1993): 297–311.

———. "Retrospecting the Origins of the League of the Iroquois." *Proceedings of the American Philosophical Society* 152, no. 3 (2008): 279–321.

———. "'The United States Will Protect You': The Iroquois, New York, and the 1790 Nonintercourse Act." *New York History* 83, no. 1 (2002): 5–33.

Starna, William A., and José António Brandão. "From the Mohawk-Mahican War to the Beaver Wars: Questioning the Pattern." *Ethnohistory* 51, no. 4 (2004): 725–50.

Starna, William A., and Robert E. Funk. "Floral and Faunal Resource Potential." In Funk, *Archaeological Investigations*, vol. 1, 51–63.

Starna, William A., George R. Hamell, and William L. Butts. "Northern Iroquoian Horticulture and Insect Infestation: A Cause for Village Removal." *Ethnohistory* 31, no. 3 (1987): 197–207.

Starna, William A., and John H. Relethford. "Deer Densities and Population Dynamics: A Cautionary Note." *American Antiquity* 50, no. 4 (1985): 825–32.

Stokes, I. N. Phelps, *The Iconography of Manhattan Island, 1498–1909: Compiled from Original Sources and Illustrated by Photo-Intaglio Reproductions of Important Maps, Plans, Views, and Documents in Public and Private Collections.* 6 vols. 1915–1928. Reprint, New York: Arno Press, 1967.

Strickland, William. *Journal of a Tour in the United States of America, 1794–95.* New York: New-York Historical Society, 1971.

Sturtevant, William C., "Two 1761 Wigwams at Niantic Connecticut." *American Antiquity* 40 (1975): 437–44.

Talcott, Joseph. *The Talcott Papers: Correspondence and Documents, 1737–1741.* Edited by Mary Kingsbury Talcott. Vol. 5. Hartford: Connecticut Historical Society, 1896.

Taylor, Alan. "Captain Hendrick Aupaumut: The Dilemmas of an Intercultural Broker." *Ethnohistory* 43, no. 3 (1996): 431–57.

———. *The Divided Ground: Indians, Settlers, and the Northern Borderlands of the American Revolution.* New York: Alfred A. Knopf, 2006.

Taylor, Francis R. *Life of William Savery of Philadelphia, 1750–1804.* Whitefish MT: Kessinger, 2009.

Thornton, Russell. *American Indian Holocaust and Survival: A Population History since 1492.* Norman: University of Oklahoma Press, 1987.

Thwaites, Reuben Gold. *Collections of the State Historical Society of Wisconsin.* Vol. 15. Madison: Democrat Printing, 1900.

———, ed. *The Jesuit Relations and Allied Documents: Travels and Explorations of the Jesuit Missionaries in New France, 1610–1791.* 73 vols. Cleveland: Burrows Brothers, 1896–1901.

Tompkins, Daniel D. *Public Papers of Daniel D. Tompkins, Governor of New York, 1807–1817.* Vol. 2, *Military.* Albany NY: J. B. Lyon, 1902.

Tooker, Elisabeth. *An Ethnography of the Huron Indians.* Bureau of American Ethnology Bulletin 190. Washington DC: Bureau of American Ethnology, 1964.

———. "The League of the Iroquois: Its History, Politics, and Ritual." In Trigger, *Handbook of North American Indians,* vol. 15, *Northeast,* 418–41.

Towns and Lands. 1st ser., 10 vols., 1629–1789. Connecticut State Archives, Hartford.

Trelease, Allen W. *Indian Affairs in Colonial New York: The Seventeenth Century*. Ithaca: Cornell University Press, 1960.

Trigger, Bruce G. *The Children of Aataentsic, A History of the Huron People to 1660*. 2 vols. Montreal: McGill-Queen's University Press, 1976.

———, ed. *Handbook of North American Indians*. Vol. 15, *Northeast*. Washington DC: Smithsonian Institution Press, 1978.

———. "The Mohawk-Mahican War (1624–1628): The Establishment of a Pattern." *Canadian Historical Review* 52 (1971): 276–86.

———. *Natives and Newcomers: Canada's "Heroic" Age Reconsidered*. Kingston: McGill-Queen's University Press, 1985.

Trumbull, Benjamin. *A Complete History of Connecticut, Civil and Ecclesiastical . . . to the Close of the Indian Wars*. 2 vols. New Haven CT: Maltby, Goldsmith and Samuel Wadsworth, 1818.

Trumball, James Hammond [vols. 1–3] and Charles J. Hoadley [vols. 4–15], eds. *The Public Records of the Colony of Connecticut, from April 1636 to October 1776 . . . transcribed and published (in accordance with a resolution of the General Assembly)*. 15 vols. Hartford: Lockwood and Brainard, 1850–90.

Ubelaker, Douglas H. "North American Indian Population Size, AD 1500 to 1985." *American Journal of Physical Anthropology* 77, no. 3 (1988): 289–94.

Van den Bogaert, Harmen Meyndertsz. *A Journey into Mohawk and Oneida Country, 1634–1635: The Journal of Harmen Meyndertsz van den Bogaert*. Translated and edited by Charles T. Gehring and William A. Starna. Syracuse: Syracuse University Press, 1988.

Van der Donck, Adriaen. *A Description of New Netherland, by Adriaen van der Donck*. Edited by Charles T. Gehring and William A. Starna. Translated by Diederik Willem Goedhuys. Lincoln: University of Nebraska Press, 2008.

Van Laer, A. J. F., trans. and ed. *Documents Relating to New Netherland 1624–1626 in the Henry E. Huntington Library*. San Marino: Henry E. Huntington Library and Art Gallery, 1924.

———. *Minutes of the Court of Albany, Rensselaerswyck and Schenectady, 1775–1680*. 3 vols. Albany: University of the State of New York, 1928.

Van Rensselaer, Jeremias. *Correspondence of Jeremias van Rensselaer, 1651–1674*. Translated and edited by A. J. F. Van Laer. Albany: University of the State of New York, 1932.

Van Rensselaer, Kiliaen. *Van Rensselaer Bowier Manuscripts: Being the Letters of Kiliaen van Rensselaer, 1630–1643, and Other Documents Relating to the Colony of Rensselaerswyck*. Translated and edited by A. J. F. van Laer. Albany: University of the State of New York, 1908.

Vecsey, Christopher, and William A. Starna, eds., *Iroquois Land Claims*. Syracuse: Syracuse University Press, 1988.

Venables, Robert W., "A Chronology of Brotherton History to 1850." In *The History and Archaeology of the Montauk*, 2d ed., vol. 3, edited by Gaynell Stone, 515–32. Stony Brook: Suffolk County Archaeological Association, 1993.

Venema, Janny. *Beverwijck: A Dutch Village on the American Frontier, 1652–1664*. Albany: State University of New York Press, 2003.

———, *Kiliaen van Rensselaer (1586–1643): Designing a New World*. Albany: State University of New York Press, 2011.

Versteg, Dingman, trans. *Kingston Papers*, edited by Peter R. Christoph, Kenneth Scott, and Kenn Stryker-Rodda. 2 vols. Baltimore: Genealogical Publishing, 1976.

Votes and Proceedings of the Twenty-Seventh General Assembly of the State of New Jersey. Trenton: Sherbun and Mershon, 1802.

Wallace, Paul A. W. *Conrad Weiser, 1696–1760, Friend of Colonist and Mohawk*. Philadelphia: University of Pennsylvania Press, 1945.

Waterman, Kees-Jan, ed. and trans. *"To Do Justice to Him and Myself"*: *Evert Wendell's Account Book of the Fur Trade with Indians in Albany, New York, 1695–1726*. Philadelphia: American Philosophical Society, 2008.

Waugh, Frederick W. *Iroquois Food and Food Preparation*. Geological Survey Memoir 36, Anthropological Series 12. Ottawa: Government Printing Bureau, 1916.

Weslager, C. A. [Clinton Alfred]. *The Delaware Indians: A History*. New Brunswick NJ: Rutgers University Press, 1972.

Westmeier, Karl-Wilhelm. *The Evacuation of Shekomeko and the Early Moravian Missions to Native North America*. Lewiston NY: Edward Mellon Press, 1994.

Wheeler, Rachel. "Chief Hendrick Aupaumut: Christian-Mahican Prophet." *Journal of the Early Republic* 25, no. 2 (2005): 187–220.

———. *To Live upon Hope: Mohicans and Missionaries in the Eighteenth-Century Northeast*. Ithaca: Cornell University Press, 2008.

White, John. *America 1585: The Complete Drawings of John White*, by Paul Hulton. Chapel Hill: University of North Carolina Press, 1984.

White, Marian E., William E. Engelbrecht, and Elisabeth Tooker. "Cayuga." In Trigger, *Handbook of North American Indians*, vol. 15, *Northeast*, 500–504.

Williams, James Homer. "Great Doggs and Mischievous Cattle: Domesticated Animals and Indian-European Relations in New Netherland and New York." *New York History* 76 (1995): 245–64.

Williams, Robert A., Jr. *The American Indian in Western Legal Thought: The Discourses of Conquest*. New York: Oxford University Press, 1990.

Winthrop, John. *Winthrop's Journal, "History of New England," 1630–1649.* Edited by James K. Hosmer. 2 vols. New York: Charles Scribner's Sons, 1908.

Wojciechowski, Franz Laurens. *Ethnohistory of the Paugussett Tribes: An Exercise in Research Methodology.* Amsterdam: DeKiva, 1992.

Wonderley, Anthony. "Brothertown, New York, 1785–1796." *New York History* 81, no. 4 (2000): 456–92.

Wood, William. *New England's Prospect.* 1634. Publications of the Prince Society 1. Boston: John Wilson and Son, 1865.

Wright, Harry Andrew, ed., *Indian Deeds of Hamden County: Being Copies of All Land Transfers . . . Together with Notes and Translations of Indian Place Names.* Springfield M A, 1905.

Zeisberger, David. *The Diary of David Zeisberger, A Moravian Missionary among the Indians of Ohio.* Edited and translated by Eugene F. Bliss. 2 vols. Cincinnati: Robert Clarke, 1885.

INDEX

tives and, 194–97, 198, 213–14; Treaty
   of Canandaigua and, 205–7
language, Mahican, 74–76, 104–5, 181
Leach, Douglas, 148
leaders and governing: Mahican, 65–
   68, 182–83, 187–89, 237n37; Mahican
   Confederacy and, 149–54; New Stock-
   bridge, 215–19
le Fèbvre de la Barre, Joseph-Antoine,
   156
Lenig, Donald, 80, 82
"Lenni Lanapes," 100, 150
Letechgoth, 176
Line of Property, 200
Livingston, Robert, 165
Livingston Indian Records, 152
Lokermans, Jacob, 106
Long Island Indians, 138, 215, 219
Louis, Colonel, 203–4
Loup B, 74
Louwrensen, Andries, 132
Lovelace, Francis, 146
Luycasse, Evert, 1

Macedonia Creek, 55
Machaknemeno, 136
Madison Lake, 210
Magdalen Island, 105
Mahican Channel, 89–90
Mahican Confederacy, 149–54
Mahicans: American Revolution and,
   197–200; assessing documentary and
   published record on, 59–63; and attempts to create "Indian perspective"
   on arrival of Europeans, 18–19, 228n1;
   boundaries with the Munsees, 19–20;
   campaigns against the Iroquois, 130–
   31; in Canada, 156–58; clans, 73; colonial
   period and, xi–xiv; Confederacy, 149–
   54; conversion to Christianity, 164, 168,
   176–77, 179–81; culture, xvi, 63–76, 152;
   demography, 43–45, 47; distinction between River Indians and, 154–55; education of, 184–85; employment by Europeans, 23–25; epidemics among, 45–48;
   Esopus Wars and, 131–38; farming by,
   63–65, 189–90; first impressions of Europeans, 25–29; food, 38–43, 63–65;

French and Indian War and, 192–97;
homeland boundaries, 99–106; hostility with Abenakis, 129–31; houses, 40–
41; at Kaunaumeek, 176–77; Kieft's War
and, 121–29; land transactions between
Dutch and, 106–18; language, 74–76,
104–5, 181; leaders and governing, 65–
68, 182–83, 187–89, 237n37; loss of land,
27–30; mapping by Europeans, 33–
36, 37, 101; meeting with Henry Hudson, 22–23; Northern Indians Wars
and, 138–49; objectives in writing history of, xi; other tribes confused with,
xiv–xv; peace with Mohawks, 160–61;
property rights, 106–18; relations with
the Mohawks after King Philip's War,
154–69; religious expression by, 68–72,
190–92, 238n52; resettlement of, 194–
97; settlements, 38–43, 170–79, 231n6;
at Shekomeko, 170–75; in Shekomeko, 170–79; social organization, 72–74;
at Stockbridge, 183–86; taxation of Mohawks, 89; trade with the Europeans,
21–22, 228n11; violence between Europeans and, 20, 90–91, 158–59, 161–62,
185; at Weataug, 105, 178–79, 180, 181; at
Wechquadnach, 172, 177–78, 181
Maikans, 94
Makuaes, 94
Manhattan Island, 4, 24, 46; mapping
   of, 33, 34, 37
Manitou, 70
maps, 33–36, 37, 39, 101
Marechkawiecks, 54
marriage among Mahicans, 72–73
Martens, Catelijntje, 1
Massachusetts Bay Colony, 124, 193
Mather, Increase, 148
Matouweskarine, 57
Megapolensis, Johannes, 9–10, 62
Melijn, Cornelis, 115
Menetto, 70
Menowniett, 180
Merrimack River Valley, 56
Metacom, 148
Metoxson, 177, 188–89
Miami Indians, 220

In The Iroquoians and Their World

Nation Iroquoise: A Seventeenth-Century Ethnography of the Iroquois
By José António Brandão

Your Fyre Shall Burn No More: Iroquois Policy toward
New France and Its Native Allies to 1701
By José António Brandão

Gideon's People, Volumes 1 and 2: Being a Chronicle of an American
Indian Community in Colonial Connecticut and the
Moravian Missionaries Who Served There
Translated and edited by Corinna Dally-Starna and William A. Starna

Iroquois Journey: An Anthropologist Remembers
By William N. Fenton
Edited and introduced by Jack Campisi and William A. Starna

William Fenton: Selected Writings
By William N. Fenton
Edited and introduced by William A. Starna and Jack Campisi

Oneida Lives: Long-Lost Voices of the Wisconsin Oneidas
Edited by Herbert S. Lewis
With the assistance of L. Gordon McLester III

The Texture of Contact: European and Indian Settler Communities
on the Frontiers of Iroquoia, 1667–1783
By David L. Preston

Kahnawà:ke: Factionalism, Traditionalism, and Nationalism
in a Mohawk Community
By Gerald R. Reid

From Homeland to New Land: A History of the Mahican Indians, 1600–1830
By William A. Starna

A Description of New Netherland
By Adriaen van der Donck
Edited by Charles T. Gehring and William A. Starna

To order or obtain more information on these or other University of Nebraska
Press titles, visit www.nebraskapress.unl.edu.